Word 2003

FOR

DUMMIES®

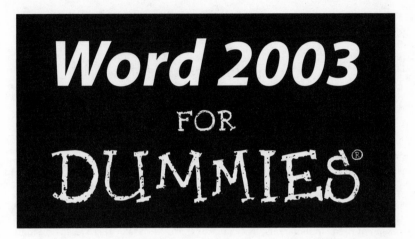

Word 2003 FOR DUMMIES®

by Dan Gookin

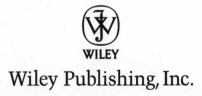

WILEY

Wiley Publishing, Inc.

Word 2003 For Dummies®

Published by
Wiley Publishing, Inc.
111 River Street
Hoboken, NJ 07030

www.wiley.com

Copyright © 2003 by Wiley Publishing, Inc., Indianapolis, Indiana

Published by Wiley Publishing, Inc., Indianapolis, Indiana

Published simultaneously in Canada

No part of this publication may be reproduced, stored in a retrieval system or transmitted in any form or by any means, electronic, mechanical, photocopying, recording, scanning or otherwise, except as permitted under Sections 107 or 108 of the 1976 United States Copyright Act, without either the prior written permission of the Publisher, or authorization through payment of the appropriate per-copy fee to the Copyright Clearance Center, 222 Rosewood Drive, Danvers, MA 01923, (978) 750-8400, fax (978) 646-8700. Requests to the Publisher for permission should be addressed to the Legal Department, Wiley Publishing, Inc., 10475 Crosspoint Blvd., Indianapolis, IN 46256, (317) 572-3447, fax (317) 572-4447, e-mail: permcoordinator@wiley.com.

Trademarks: Wiley, the Wiley Publishing logo, For Dummies, the Dummies Man logo, A Reference for the Rest of Us!, The Dummies Way, Dummies Daily, The Fun and Easy Way, Dummies.com, and related trade dress are trademarks or registered trademarks of John Wiley & Sons, Inc. and/or its affiliates. All other trademarks are the property of their respective owners. Wiley Publishing, Inc., is not associated with any product or vendor mentioned in this book.

For general information on our other products and services or to obtain technical support, please contact our Customer Care Department within the U.S. at 800-762-2974, outside the U.S. at 317-572-3993, or fax 317-572-4002.

Wiley also publishes its books in a variety of electronic formats. Some content that appears in print may not be available in electronic books.

Library of Congress Control Number: 2003101906

ISBN: 0-7645-3982-5

Manufactured in the United States of America

10 9 8 7 6 5 4 3 2 1

1O/RX/QZ/QT/IN

WILEY is a trademark of Wiley Publishing, Inc.

About the Author

Dan Gookin has been writing about technology for 20 years. He's contributed articles to numerous high-tech magazines and written over 90 books on personal computing technology, many of them accurate.

Dan combines his love of writing with his interest in technology to create books that are informative, entertaining, and yet not boring. Having sold more than 14 million titles translated into over 30 languages, Dan can attest that his method of crafting computer tomes does seem to work.

Perhaps his most famous title is the original *DOS For Dummies*, published in 1991. It became the world's fastest-selling computer book, at one time moving more copies per week than the New York Times #1 bestseller (though as a reference, it could not be listed on the NYT Bestseller list). From that book spawned the entire line of *For Dummies* books, which remains a publishing phenomena to this day.

Dan's most recent titles include *PCs For Dummies, 9th Edition; Buying a Computer For Dummies, 2004 Edition; Troubleshooting Your PC For Dummies; Dan Gookin's Naked Windows® XP;* and *Dan Gookin's Naked Office.* He also publishes a free weekly computer newsletter, the "Weekly Wambooli Salad," full of tips, how-tos, and computer news. He also maintains the vast and helpful Web page, www.wambooli.com.

Dan holds a degree in Communications/Visual Arts from the University of California, San Diego. Presently he lives in the Pacific Northwest, where he enjoys spending time with his four boys in the gentle woods of Idaho.

Publisher's Acknowledgments

We're proud of this book; please send us your comments through our online registration form located at www.dummies.com/register/.

Some of the people who helped bring this book to market include the following:

Acquisitions, Editorial, and Media Development

Project Editor: Paul Levesque

Acquisitions Editor: Greg Croy

Copy Editor: Kim Darosett

Technical Editor: Herb Tyson

Editorial Managers: Leah Cameron, Kevin Kirschner

Editorial Assistant: Amanda Foxworth

Cartoons: Rich Tennant (www.the5thwave.com)

Production

Project Coordinator: Regina Snyder

Layout and Graphics: Seth Conley, Joyce Haughey, Barry Offringa, Shae Lynn Wilson, Melanee Wolven

Proofreaders: David Faust, John Greenough, Carl Pierce, TECHBOOKS Production Services

Indexer: TECHBOOKS Production Services

Special Help: Virginia Sanders

Publishing and Editorial for Technology Dummies

Richard Swadley, Vice President and Executive Group Publisher

Andy Cummings, Vice President and Publisher

Mary C. Corder, Editorial Director

Publishing for Consumer Dummies

Diane Graves Steele, Vice President and Publisher

Joyce Pepple, Acquisitions Director

Composition Services

Gerry Fahey, Vice President of Production Services

Debbie Stailey, Director of Composition Services

Contents at a Glance

Table of Contents

Introduction

Welcome to *Word 2003 For Dummies,* the book that explodes the myths and renders sane the madness of Microsoft's latest and greatest word processor, for the year 2003 and beyond.

Word is impressive and often imposing. More than just a word processor, Word is capable of putting down on the page just about anything. Do you need to know all that stuff?

No! You probably don't even *want* to know everything that Word can do. You just want to know the basics, or some handy tricks, or read about some insight into the program so that you can hurry back to your work — and hopefully not be terrified in the process. If that's you, you've found your book.

This book informs and entertains. It has a serious attitude problem. After all, you don't need to *love* Word to use Word. It's a tool. While some mechanics may love their Snap-on™ tools, they just tools. So instead of hype, be prepared to read some informative, down-to-earth explanations — in English — of how to get the job done with Microsoft Word. You take your work seriously, but you definitely don't need to take Word seriously.

About This Book

I don't intend for you to read this book from cover to cover. It's not a novel, and if it were, I'd kill off all the characters at the end, so there would be no chance for a sequel (let alone a trilogy) and then no one would want to publish it anyway.

No, this book is a reference. Each chapter covers a specific topic or task that Word does. Within a chapter, you find self-contained sections, each of which describes how to perform a specific task or get something done. Sample sections you encounter in this book include

- ✔ Saving your stuff
- ✔ Cutting and pasting a block
- ✔ Quickly finding your place
- ✔ Aligning paragraphs

> ✔ Cobbling a table together quickly
>
> ✔ Opening a document for repair
>
> ✔ Using a document template

There are no keys to memorize, no secret codes, no tricks, no videos to sleep by, and no wall charts. Instead, each section explains a topic as though it's the first thing you read in this book. Nothing is assumed, and everything is cross-referenced. Technical terms and topics, when they come up, are neatly shoved to the side, where you can easily avoid reading them. The idea here isn't for you to learn anything. This book's philosophy is to help you look it up, figure it out, and get back to work.

How to Use This Book

This book is a doing book. It's about getting things done in Word and the only assumption made is that you know what you want to do or at least you have a general or even vague idea. That's fine in this book; nothing is assumed so you'll never be utterly confused.

Word uses the mouse and menus to get things done, which is what you would expect from Windows. Yet there are times when various *key combinations,* several keys you may press together or in sequence, are required.

This is a keyboard shortcut:

   Ctrl+Shift+P

This shortcut means that you should press and hold Ctrl and Shift together, press the P key, and then release all three keys.

Menu commands are listed like this:

   File⇨Open

This command means that you open the File menu (with the mouse or the keyboard — it's your choice) and then choose the Open command. You may see underlined letters on your menus; these letters represent "hot keys" used in Windows. You can press the Alt+F key combination to access the F in File and then the O (or Alt+O) to access the O in Open.

Note that in Windows, you may have to press the Alt key first (by itself) to activate the menu hot keys. Then you can use the hot keys to access menu and dialog box commands.

If I describe a message or something you see onscreen, it looks like this:

```
Cannot find hard drive, save elsewhere?
```

If you need further help operating your computer or a good general reference, I can recommend my book *PCs For Dummies,* published by Wiley Publishing, Inc. The book contains lots of useful information to supplement what you'll find in this book.

What You're Not to Read

Special technical sections dot this book like lemon pepper on Aunt Winnie's fried chicken. They offer annoyingly endless and technical explanations, descriptions of advanced topics, or alternative commands that you really don't need to know about. Each one of them is flagged with a special icon or enclosed in an electrified, barbed wire and poison ivy box (an idea I stole from the Terwilliker Piano Method books). Reading this stuff is optional.

Foolish Assumptions

Here are my assumptions about you. You use a computer. You use Windows, specifically Windows 2000 or Windows XP (Professional or Home). The Word 2003 product does not run on any other version of Windows (at least as this book goes to press). There are no specific issues between Word and Windows as far as this book is concerned.

Your word processor is Microsoft Word 2003, which may have come with your computer, or you may have purchased it separately either by itself or as part of the Microsoft Office 2003 suite of applications. Whatever. I refer to the program as "Word" throughout this book.

The program covered here is *not* Microsoft Works. That is a separate program sold by Microsoft; this book does not cover Works at all.

I do not assume that you have Microsoft Office installed. This book does not cover using Office or any of the other Office applications.

Finally, this book assumes that you're running Word with the personalized menu system switched off. To confirm this, follow these steps inside the Word 2003 program:

1. **Choose Tools➪Customize from the Menu bar.**

   This causes the Customize dialog box to appear.

2. **Click the mouse on the Options tab in the Customize dialog box.**

3. **Click to put a check mark by the item that reads, "Always show full menus."**

4. **Click the OK button.**

By marking this setting, Word displays the full menus every time you access a menu command. Otherwise, you may not see all the commands on the menus, which can be frustrating.

How This Book Is Organized

This book contains six major parts, each of which is divided into several chapters. The chapters themselves have been sliced into smaller, modular sections. You can pick up the book and read any section without necessarily knowing what has already been covered in the rest of the book. Start anywhere.

Here is a breakdown of the parts and what you can find in them:

Part I: Hello, Word!

This part covers basic word processing, from entering text to saving a document, search and replace, spell-checking, working with blocks, and printing.

Part II: Letting Word Do the Formatting Work

This part deals with formatting, from the smallest iota of text to formatting commands that span an entire document and more.

Part III: Sprucing Up Your Document

Beyond formatting, this part of the book covers additional things you can do with Word to make your document really stand out. Covered here are many of the intermediate-level features most users never bother with in Word.

Part IV: Land of the Fun and Strange

This part covers some general and miscellaneous topics, items that others might consider to be too borderline bizarre to be found in a "beginners" book on Word.

Part V: Creating Lotsa Stuff in Word

This part presents a sample of Word's potential. Each chapter outlines a special project you can do in Word by showing you step-by-step how to put things together.

Part VI: The Part of Tens

How about "The Ten Commandments of Word"? Or consider "Ten Truly Bizarre Things." Or the handy "Ten Things Worth Remembering." This section is a gold mine of tens.

What's Not Here

This book can be only so big. The book's author, on the other hand, can grow to immense size! To keep them both in check, I've created a companion Web page. This site covers issues that may arise after the book goes to press. It's not to contain anything "missing" from the book; no, you have everything you need right in your eager, ready-to-type hands. The Web page is just to keep things up-to-date. That way, I can offer you supplemental information after the book goes to press.

If you have Internet access and a Web browser, you can visit this book's Web page at

```
www.wambooli.com/help/word
```

Additionally, I publish a free weekly newsletter that often contains tips, Q&A, shortcuts, and various lessons expanding the basic word processing knowledge presented here. Read more about my Weekly Wambooli Salad newsletter on this Web page:

```
www.wambooli.com/newsletter/weekly
```

Icons Used in This Book

This icon flags useful, helpful tips or shortcuts.

This icon marks a friendly reminder to do something.

This icon marks a friendly reminder *not* to do something.

This icon alerts you to overly nerdy information and technical discussions of the topic at hand. The information is optional reading, but it may enhance your reputation at cocktail parties if you repeat it.

Where to Go from Here

Start reading! Observe the table of contents and find something that interests you. Or look up your puzzle in the index.

If you're new to Word, start off with Chapter 1.

If you're an old hand at Word, consider checking out Part V for some inspiration.

Is Word broken? Fix it by checking out Chapter 29.

Read! Write! Produce!

By the way, I am available on the Internet if you need me. My e-mail address is dgookin@wambooli.com.

I reply to all my e-mail, so drop a note if you feel like saying, "Hi," or have a question about Word or this book. And don't forget to stop by the book's Web page, mentioned earlier in this Introduction.

Enjoy the book. And enjoy Word. Or at least tolerate it.

Part I
Hello, Word!

The 5th Wave   By Rich Tennant

"I appreciate that your computer has 256 colors.
I just don't think that they all had to be used
in one book report."

In this part . . .

Back in the cave man days, our ancestors Og and Gronk sat around and dreamt of the day when they could have a proper computer with efficient word processing software available for them to express their thoughts. Alas, there was nothing there but rocks. So, as Og carefully began to carve his thoughts into the cave wall with a rock, Gronk let loose a tremendous prehistoric belch and the cave collapsed.

Don't let your word processing attempts be so easily thwarted! Sure, we've come a long way from carving rocks and drawing on cave walls. The Ancient Egyptians gave us paper. The Phoenicians developed the alphabet. Gutenberg developed movable type. And the typewriter allowed those of us with utterly illegible handwriting to actually practice the art of writing without making the reader's eyes cross.

And now we have the word processor. It's so commonplace that people forget about Egyptian papyrus and Gutenberg and that old typewriter. Words fling out magically and can be erased, moved, searched, saved, and printed with just a few deft flicks of the wrist. Don't let a prehistoric Gronk stand in the way of your word processing wishes. Cut lose and enjoy these several chapters that cover the bare basic beginnings of your word processing odyssey.

Chapter 1

The Big Picture

It was the best of times, it was the worst of times.

Don't we all dream of becoming a famous novelist someday? Or how about writing that award-winning screenplay? Then there's the less flashy: the reports, the memos, the notes jotted down, or that list of chores. It's all words, mind you. From the note to the teacher to the first paragraph in this century's first Great American Novel, it's just words.

Perhaps it was the most mediocre of times?

The software best designed to work with words, prophetic or mundane, is a word processor such as Microsoft's Word.

Then again, let history frame the times. I've got a credit card, and by gum, I'm going to use it!

This chapter is your introduction to Microsoft Word. It provides the groundwork for you to use and understand how Word fits into your computing life, plus it may show you a few fancy things you might not expect. All the better to hurry you on your merry way toward writing whatever great things your brain is eager to produce.

The Good, Best, and Worst Ways to Start Word

How do I start thee, Word? Let me count the ways. . . .

Anyone using a computer suspects that there is probably a better, faster, or more serious way to get things done. There are so many Who knows when someone will amble up to you and giggle at how you start your word processor. "You do *that*?" they'll snicker. Oh, no. What now?

Don't fret! There are more ways to start a program on your computer than there are ways intoxicated monkeys could wreck an antique store. What's certain, however, is that there is no point wasting time showing you everything. Instead, how about if I just illustrate the typical, better, and best ways of starting Word? (The worst ways can be found in another book by some other author.)

First, some basic steps you need to take no matter what:

1. **Ensure that your computer is on and toasty.**

   Any computer that's on is, in fact, toasty. The only way to make it toastier is to actually insert bread, which I don't recommend.

2. **Prepare yourself physically.**

   Make sure you're seated, with a nice, upright, firm posture. They tell me that your wrists should be even with your elbows and that you shouldn't have to tilt your head forward. Shoulders relaxed.

   Crack your knuckles. Are your fingers ready to dance on the keyboard? Good!

3. **Prepare yourself mentally.**

   Close your eyes. Unwind. Breathe in, breath out. Think of calm, blue waters. Prepare to let your thoughts flow into the computer. Remember, you are the master. Mutter that over and over: *I am the master. . . .*

If you need help starting your computer, refer to my book *PCs For Dummies* for quick and accurate turning-on-the-computer instructions.

You can stop muttering "I am the master" now.

A humble, yet unimaginative way to start Word

Without fail, the place to start any program in Windows is at the fabled Start button. It may not be the coolest way to start a program, but it's consistent and reliable — good things to have in a computer. Obey these steps:

1. Click the Start button.

Use your computer mouse to click the Start button, which is often found on the left side of the taskbar, at the bottom of the screen.

Clicking the Start button displays the Start menu.

2. Choose All Programs⇨Microsoft Word, or it could be as long as All Programs⇨Microsoft Office⇨Microsoft Office Word 2003

The menu may just read "Programs" instead of "All Programs."

Look at Figure 1-1. Note that the menu item may say Word or Microsoft Word or even Microsoft Word 2003.

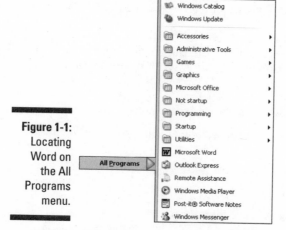

Figure 1-1:
Locating
Word on
the All
Programs
menu.

Watch in amazement as your computer whizzes and whirs. Before too long, Word appears on the computer's monitor, trying to be as friendly, inviting, and fun as the cockpit of a jet fighter.

Don't let Word's appearance overwhelm you! I discuss what you're looking at in the section, "Word on the Screen," later in this chapter.

Automatically starting Word every ding-dong time you start Windows

To get your computer to start Word whenever you start Windows, locate the Microsoft Word item on the All Programs menu (from the Start menu). Use your mouse to drag that menu item up and into the Startup submenu, which automatically opens to accept Word as a new entry. This shuffles the Word menu item into the Startup folder, from which it will automatically run every time you begin your Windows session.

If you make a mistake, press Ctrl+Z (the "undo" key) and try again. Or if this maneuver seems beyond your skills, have your computer expert or guru manage the task for you.

My favorite way to start Word

Microsoft
Word

My favorite way to run Word is by opening a shortcut icon pasted to the desktop or by clicking a button on the Quick Launch bar. Both ways are more direct than using the silly Start menu, and the Quick Launch bar method is the fastest because you need to click the button only once to start Word.

Whether you're pasting a Word shortcut icon to the desktop or to the Quick Launch bar, the first step is the same: to create the Word shortcut icon. This can be a little technical, so put on your Paying Attention cap as you follow these steps:

1. **Locate the Start menu's Microsoft Word menu item.**

   Don't start Word now! Just point the mouse at the Microsoft Word menu item, shown in Figure 1-1.

2. **Right-click the Microsoft Word menu item.**

   A pop-up menu appears.

3. **Choose Send To⇨Desktop (Create Shortcut).**

   There. You've just created a Word shortcut icon on the desktop. That was too cinchy! To prove it:

4. **Click the mouse on the desktop.**

   The desktop is the background you see when you use Windows. Clicking the desktop hides the Start menu.

5. Locate the Microsoft Word shortcut icon.

It looks like the figure shown in the margin at the start of this section; the blue W in a square icon, with "Microsoft Word" displayed beneath. That's your shortcut to Word.

You can now use the shortcut icon to start Word without having to mess with the Start menu.

If you'd rather have Word on the Quick Launch bar, drag and drop the shortcut icon down there: Use your mouse to drag the Word icon to the Quick Launch bar, and then release the mouse button to "drop" the icon, as shown in Figure 1-2. (You may need to resize the Quick Launch bar to see the Word icon; refer to *PCs For Dummies* for more information on the Quick Launch bar.) Now, Word is only one quick click away from in-your-face word processing.

Word shortcut icon on the desktop

Figure 1-2:
Putting
Word on
the Quick
Launch bar.

Drag the Word icon here.

Starting Word by opening a document

anti-gravity
mirror.doc

You use Word to create documents. These are like paper documents, but on the computer they're stored as *files*. These files appear as happy little graphical icons on the screen. Any time you spy a Word document icon, you can double-click it with the mouse to start up Word and open that document for editing. Here's how such a thing might happen:

1. Open the My Documents folder.

My Documents

The My Documents folder is where Word, as well as other applications, stores the stuff you create. You can find this folder on the desktop or possibly in the main Start menu: Point the mouse at the folder and click twice to open it.

2. Locate a Word document.

Word documents appear as a document icon with a blue *W* to one side, as shown in the margin at the start of this section.

3. Double-click the Word document icon.

This opens the document, starts Word, and loads the document for editing, reading, modifying, perusing, cussing, mangling, and potentially fouling up beyond all recognition.

You can open any Word document by following these steps. The document can be on the desktop, in the My Documents folder, or in any other folder or any location where a Word document icon can lurk.

- The document name appears below the icon. You can use the name to determine the document's contents — providing that the document was properly named when it was saved to disk. More on that later.

- If you have one document you open consistently, consider putting a shortcut to that document on the desktop for quick access: Right-click the document's icon and choose Send To➪Desktop (Create Shortcut).

- You can see a list of the recent documents you've worked on by choosing the My Recent Documents menu from the main Start menu: Click the Start button and then look for the My Recent Documents list. (Some versions of Windows may merely say *Document.*) Choose your document from that list to open it.

- Some Word documents will appear with .doc at the end of the name. This is the filename extension, and displaying that .doc part of the filename is optional. Depending on how you've configured Windows, you may or may not see the .doc part of the name.

Word on the Screen

Right after starting Word, I prefer to maximize. That doesn't mean that I sit down and stuff myself with pizza. No, maximizing is a Windows trick you can pull to increase the amount of screen real estate Word uses.

To run Word in full-screen mode, click the Maximize button (the middle one) in the upper-right corner of the window. This button maximizes Word to fill the entire screen. If Word is already maximized, two overlapping boxes appear on the button; you don't need to click anything in that case.

Now that you can see Word long and tall on the screen, follow along with this text and Figure 1-3 to locate the many fresh and exciting items on the typical blank Word screen.

Figure 1-3:
Word in all
its basic,
naked glory.

Gizmos and gadgets

Word's goal is to help you write. Well, perhaps not *write* in the sense that
Charles Dickens or Jane Austen writes. No, it's actually the processing of
words that Word does best. That's why the largest portion of the Word screen
is for composing text (refer to Figure 1-3).

Surrounding the text-composing area are various bells, whistles, switches,
and doodads that would be interesting only if they were edible. And the good
news is that with Word, all that stuff is totally customizable by you (better
know what it all means before you go changing everything):

✔ **The title bar,** which lists the document's title, or merely `Document 1`
  until you give the document a title by saving it to disk.

✔ **The menu bar,** which contains a full list of Word's various and sundry
  commands.

- ✔ **The Standard and Formatting toolbars,** which are on top of each other in Figure 1-3, although they occasionally (and annoyingly) appear on the same row. (You can rearrange them at your whim.)
- ✔ **The ruler,** which helps with setting margins and tabs.
- ✔ **The task pane,** which lists commands or options relevant to whatever you're doing in Word.

Below the writing area are two items:

- ✔ **The View buttons,** located to the left of the horizontal scroll bar, control how your document is displayed.
- ✔ **The status bar** dishes up lots of trivia about your document, some of which is interesting.

What each of these various buttons, bars, and menus does — and whether it's important — is covered elsewhere in this book. Right now, you just need to know the names of things so that you don't get lost later.

- ✔ Most of this stuff is customizable. And not only can you change and rearrange Word's options to suit you, you can make most of the stuff you see on the screen go away so that you see only the blank part where you write.
- ✔ Typically most folks don't change anything. Alas.
- ✔ The status bar is not a yuppie hangout. It contains cubbyholes in which random and often cryptic information is displayed. This book explains when the information is useful to you.
- ✔ Figure 1-3 shows Word in Print Layout view. If it looks different on your screen, choose View⟿Print Layout from the menu. (Some people prefer to use Word in Normal view.)

- ✔ If you want the Standard and Formatting toolbars to appear on separate rows, click the down-pointing arrow at the end of either toolbar. That displays a drop-down menu, from which you can choose the command Show Buttons on Two Rows. That fixes things.
- ✔ The task pane may not show up until it's needed or until you use specific commands in Word. Choose View⟿Task Pane to show or hide the task pane.
- ✔ The Windows taskbar, located at the bottom of the screen, is a part of Windows itself and not Word. However, as you open documents in Word, buttons representing those documents appear on the Windows taskbar.
- ✔ Notice the mouse pointer in Figure 1-3? It's the *insertion* pointer, shaped like an I-beam. That's the way the mouse pointer appears when it's sliding over your document in Word. The I-beam means "I beam the insertion pointer to this spot when you click the mouse."

✔ The lines next to (or beneath) the insertion pointer are part of Word's click-and-type feature. Using click-and-type is covered in Chapter 18, in the section that discusses automatic formatting as it happens.

✔ You can use the mouse to see what some of the little buttons and things with pictures on them do in Word. Just hover the mouse pointer over the button, and — voilà! — it's like Folgers Instant Information Crystals.

✔ If you don't actually see the Standard or Formatting toolbars or the ruler, or you want to change the way the Word screen looks *right now,* hop on over to Chapter 28 on modifying Word's appearance.

The blank place where you write

After Word starts, you're faced with the electronic equivalent of The Blank Page, the same concept that induced mind-numbing writer's block in generations of writers. It makes you wonder if ancient Egyptian scribes ever experienced "papyrus block."

The key to writing in Word is to look for the blinking *toothpick cursor* — a blinking bar in your text that shows you where your typing will appear on the screen:

Choose View⇨Normal from the menu.

In Normal view, more of the screen is devoted to writing text. However, in this view, a horizontal line appears on the screen, just below the blinking toothpick cursor. That's that the *End-of-Text marker.* Consider it the steel beam that supports your text, keeping it from harm's way, in the evil nothingness that exists below your text:

Choose View⇨Print Layout from the menu.

In Print Layout view, the End-of-Text marker disappears. Unlike in Normal view, the focus here is how the words look on the page. Personally, I prefer to write in Normal view and then switch to Print Layout for formatting and editing.

✔ Writing (or typing, depending on how good you are) is covered in the next chapter. That would be Chapter 2.

✔ Any weird stuff you see onscreen (a ¶, for example) is a Word secret symbol. Chapter 2 tells you why you may want to view those secret symbols and how to hide them if they annoy you.

✔ The *cursor* shows the exact spot where text appears. The cursor is also called an insertion pointer because traditional computer cursors are underlines that slide under what you type. I prefer the term *toothpick cursor* because *insertion pointer* is just too medically geometric for my tastes. Characters you type appear immediately to the left of where the toothpick cursor is flashing, and then the cursor moves forward and waits for the next character.

Word's Feeble Attempts to Help You

There are many ways to get help from Word, most of which are covered in Chapter 2. For now, on the screen, you may see two places to get help.

First, there's the Ask a Question box, which is located on the right end of the menu bar, as shown in Figure 1-4. You click the mouse in that space, and then type a question or keyword. Be cryptic when you type; pretend that you're a robot. So instead of typing in "Tell me how to format this paragraph?" type in "formatting paragraphs." Press the Enter key. Word displays helpful information in the task pane.

Right here

Figure 1-4:
The Ask a
Question
box.

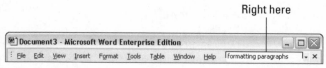

Second, and more interesting than the Ask a Question box, is the Office Assistant.

If the Office Assistant isn't visible on the screen, choose Help⇨Show the Office Assistant from the menu. What appears is a helpful character, normally an animated paper clip with bulging eyes, but you can change the character to something else if you like (I tell you how in Chapter 2). The paperclip Office Assistant, officially known as Clippit, is shown in Figure 1-5.

Figure 1-5:
The paper
clip.

The Office Assistant is there to help you. Most of the time, however, it just sits there watching while you type or getting bored while you rummage for a thought.

Here are my Office Assistant musings:

✔ You can move the Office Assistant around by dragging it with the mouse. I put my assistant down in the lower-right corner of the screen, where he won't get into any trouble.

✔ Right-click the Office Assistant to see a list of its menu options. My favorite menu item is Animate, which makes the Office Assistant do something interesting.

✔ You can choose from among a host of Office Assistants: Right-click the Office Assistant and choose the Choose Assistant item from the pop-up menu. My favorite assistant is the dog, though I'm also fond of Merlin.

✔ If you detest the Office Assistant, right-click on his nose and choose the Hide menu option. Hey, the screen is crowded enough!

✔ The Office Assistant hides when you switch from Word to other applications.

✔ Using the Office Assistant to get help is covered in Chapter 2.

A Look at Your Keyboard

The shortest distance between your brain and a Word document is down your arms and through your fingers onto the computer keyboard. You'll use the keyboard not only for typing text, but also for editing your text and using various commands that spiff up what you write.

Figure 1-6 shows the typical PC keyboard used during the turn of the century (the turn from the 20th to the 21st century, not from the 19th to the 20th century, when "keyboard" typically implied a piano.)

Notice how the keyboard is divided into separate areas, each of which has a special function? In Word, you use the keys in these groups either alone or in combination with other keys:

✔ **Function keys:** These keys are located along the top row of the keyboard, labeled F1 through F12. You can use them alone or in cahoots with the Ctrl, Alt, and Shift keys.

✔ **Typewriter keys:** These are the standard alphanumeric keys you find on any typewriter: A through Z, 1 through 0, plus symbols and other exotic characters.

- **Cursor keys:** These arrow keys move the toothpick cursor around the screen. Also lumped in are the Home, End, PgUp (or Page Up), PgDn (or Page Down), Insert, and Delete keys. Oh, and the big plus and minus keys on the number pad are counted as well.

- **Mon key:** A derogatory term for a primate or ape.

- **Numeric keypad:** These keys toggle (meaning that they can't make up their minds) between cursor keys and number keys. The split personality is evident on each key cap, which displays two symbols. The Num Lock key and its corresponding light are on if the numeric keypad (1, 2, 3) is active. If the cursor keys (arrows, Home) are active, Num Lock is off.

- **Shift keys:** These keys don't do anything by themselves. Instead, the Shift, Ctrl, and Alt keys work in combination with other keys.

Figure 1-6:
Famous
attractions
on the
typical PC
keyboard.

Here are some individual keys worth noting:

- **Enter:** Marked with the word *Enter* and sometimes a cryptic, curved arrow-thing: ↵. You use the Enter key to end a paragraph of text.

- **Esc:** The "escape" key doesn't really do anything in Word; however, in a dialog box pressing the Esc key is the same as clicking the Cancel button with the mouse.

- **Spacebar:** The only key with no symbol; inserts spaces between the words.

- **Tab:** Inserts the tab "character," which shoves the next text you type over to the next tab stop. An interesting and potentially frustrating for-matting key (but nicely covered in Chapter 13).

- **Backspace:** Your backing-up-and-erasing key. Very handy.

- **Delete:** Also labeled Del and works like Backspace but doesn't back up to erase. More on that in Chapter 4.

Depressing the keys

When I tell you to "depress the Enter key," you should look at your keyboard, stare the Enter key squarely in the eye, and say aloud, "You, you funny-looking key. You're worthless. All the other keys hate you. My right pinky hates you. You're despised! You should leave the keyboard right now and hide in shame, you worthless key, you!" There, now the Enter key is quite depressed.

Seriously, you don't "depress" any key on your keyboard. You press keys. Press them down, and then release them. Any swift tapping motion will do. And the better keyboards pleasingly click for you, making your typing as noisy as it would be on an old manual Olympia.

Typing key combinations

Aside from regular typing, you need to use various key combinations to tell Word how to carry out certain commands. For example:

Ctrl+P

Say, "control pee." That's the Control+P key combination. Or, if you can palm a basketball in one hand, you can try:

Ctrl+Shift+F12

That's "control shift F twelve." Both keyboard shortcuts open the Print dialog box — which isn't really important right now. What is important is what these key combinations tell you to do, namely: Press and hold the Ctrl key while you press P and then release both keys; or press and hold the Ctrl and Shift keys and then press the F12 key. Release all three keys.

Always press and hold the first key (or keys) and then press the last key: Press and release.

- ✔ This key combination method works just like pressing Shift+F to get a capital F. It's the same thing, but with the odd Ctrl (Control) and Alt (Alternate) keys.

- ✔ Yeah, you have to really reach to get some of those key combinations.

- ✔ You don't need to press hard. If you're having trouble working a keyboard shortcut, pressing harder doesn't make the computer think, "Oh, Lordy, she's pressing really hard now. I think she means it. Wake up, wake up!" A light touch is all that's required.

✔ Remember to release the keys: With Ctrl+P, for example, press and hold the Ctrl key, press P, and then release both keys. If you don't know which one to release first, release the second key and then the Shift key (Shift, Ctrl, Alt) last.

 ✔ Click the Cancel or Close button if you accidentally open the Print dialog box; you can also press the Esc key on the keyboard. See Chapter 9 for more information on canceling printing.

Quitting Word When You're All Done

Knowing when to leave is the height of proper etiquette. I typically excuse myself from a party before people start breaking things or setting fire to the furniture. And sometimes it pays to not even show up. But Word cares not for social graces. When the writing is done, or you're done writing, it's time to quit Word:

1. **Choose File⇨Exit from the menu.**

   This is the standard way to quit any Windows program.

2. **Save any files, if Word prompts you to do so.**

   Word always warns you before it leaves; if you have any unsaved documents, you're prompted to save them to disk. You see a warning displayed on the screen. If the Office Assistant is visible, it explains the warning in a cartoon bubble, as shown in Figure 1-7.

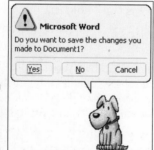

Figure 1-7:
Arf! Arf!
Arf!

Click Yes to save your file. You may be asked to give the file a name if you haven't yet done so. (Chapter 2 tells you how to do this.)

If the slop you typed isn't worth saving, click No.

You can click Cancel to "quit" the Exit command and return to Word for more word processing delight.

If you elect to quit, Word leaves the screen, and you return to the Windows desktop, where you can busy yourself with yet another game of FreeCell.

Do not reset or turn off your computer to quit Word! Doing so can potentially scramble files on your computer's hard disk. Computers are troublesome enough by themselves. No point in your contributing to that madness by doing something sloppy.

How to quit what you're doing without quitting Word

The File⇨Exit command quits any and all Word documents you may be working on. If you merely want to quit a single document and leave others open, or perhaps you merely want to quit what you're working on and start something new, use the File⇨Close command instead.

The File⇨Close command closes the document window, making it vanish from the screen. The "white space" in the window disappears. But note that Word does not quit; its toolbars and such are still visible, giving you more options on what to do next.

- ✔ Why close a document? Because you're done working on it! Maybe you want to work on something else or quit Word after closing. The choices are yours, and I explain them in the next chapter.

- ✔ Closing a document in Word is similar to ripping a sheet of paper out of your typewriter — but without the satisfying *SSHHHHHTHWP!* sound it makes.

- ✔ There is no need to close a document, really. In fact, I work on a document over a period of days and keep it open (and my PC on) the entire time. Doesn't hurt a thing. (I do save it to disk, which *is* important.)

- ✔ If you try to close a document before it has been saved, Word displays a warning dialog box. Click the Yes button to save your document. If you want to continue editing, click the Cancel button and get back to work.

- ✔ If you're working on several documents at once, closing one makes another one appear onscreen in place of the document you just closed.

Starting a new document

One of the things you can do after closing a document is to start work on a new one. To do this, choose File⇨New, which summons the New Document task pane. From there, click the Blank document item, and you're ready to start work on something new.

✔ You can also start up a new document quickly by clicking the New Document button on the Standard toolbar.

✔ Another thing you can do is to open a document previously saved to disk. You do this with the File⇨Open command, which I introduce in the next chapter.

✔ You don't have to quit Word when you just want to start working on a new document.

Chapter 2

How Most Folks Use Word

*W*hen it comes to using Word, most people barely scratch the surface of what it can do. It's not a bad thing; it's just that few people dive into the program or are as lucky as you are and have a book to unveil all the secrets. But normally, people use Word like this:

Imagine these two warriors in full outer space garb, climbing into the cockpit of this fantastic, futuristic spacecraft. They flip buttons, check dials, and punch in codes. They say things like, "Quantum fusion grid, on-line!" and "Check!" and "Enabling anti-gravity proton field" and "Roger." The ground rumbles, and the incredible machine vibrates with turbines whining and lights blinking. And then: "Engage!" The warriors throttle forward, and the machine lurches 30 feet ahead in a thunderous roar. But then the warriors turn everything off and get out.

That's how most people use Word.

This chapter gives you the basic steps to take as you use Word every day. In fact, if this book were a pamphlet, this chapter would be it. (The rest of the book just offers more details and highly useful information, as well as justification for the hefty cover price.)

Overview (For the Impatient)

The Word word processing process goes like this:

1. **Start a new document in Word.**
2. **Type.**
3. **Format.**
4. **Save.**
5. **Preview.**
6. **Print.**
7. **Close.**

Everyone follows these steps in one way or another. A good Word user repeats Steps 2, 3, and 4, sometimes varying the order. (Most of the time, you're typing in Word. Toward the end of the process, you should start formatting, though many people format as they type.)

If you saved a document earlier and want to work on it again, replace Step 1 with "Open a document on disk." (See Chapter 8 for more information on the Open command.)

Steps 5 and 6 are necessary only when you're done and plan on printing your work. (Chapter 9 discusses Preview and Print.)

The rest of this chapter elaborates on these steps.

Starting a New Document

When Word starts, it presents you with a blank document, suitable for typing. Your next step, logically, is to type: la-di-da.

If you need to start a new document while you're already editing something in Word (such as when you're writing a letter to a friend and realize that you forgot to type up that urgent business letter), do this:

1. **Choose File⇨New from the menu.**

   The New Document task pane appears on the left, giving you a smattering of options for creating a new something or other. What you want is a new document.

2. **Click to choose Blank Document.**

   The task pane goes away, and you get your blank page, ready for typing.

A quicker way to do this is to click the New button on the toolbar. That opens a blank page for typing a new document without having to mess with the annoying task pane and its confusing options.

> ✔ Yes, Word lets you work with more than one document at a time. This is all explained and exploited in Chapter 10.

> ✔ Another way to start your work is to open a document on disk (see Chapter 8 for more information). After the document is open, it appears in a window just like any other document you've created. Work away!

Typing (Or Hunting and Pecking)

Forget all the gizmos and fancy features! Most of your time in Word is spent typing.

> *Clackity-clack-clack-clack.*

Go ahead, type away; let your fingers dance upon the keycaps! What you type appears onscreen, letter for letter — even derogatory stuff about the computer. (Your PC doesn't care, but that doesn't mean that Word lacks feelings.)

New text is inserted right in front of the blinking toothpick cursor. For example, you can type this line:

```
Belching at the table is acceptable.
```

To change this sentence, move the toothpick cursor to just before the *A* in *acceptable*. Use the keyboard's left-arrow key to move the toothpick cursor back. (Do not use Backspace.) With the toothpick cursor blinking before the A, type the following:

```
un
```

The new text is inserted as you type, with any existing text being pushed off to the right (even to the next line), happily making room.

The whole sentence should now read:

```
Belching at the table is unacceptable.
```

> ✔ Every character key you press on the keyboard produces a character onscreen. This fact holds true for all letter, number, and symbol keys. The other keys, mostly gray on your keyboard, do strange and wonderful things, which the rest of this book tries hard to explain.

- If you're a former typewriter user, you're probably pushing 40! Man, you're old! Seriously, don't use the L or I key for a number one or the O (oh) key for a zero in a word processor. This is wrong. Please type **1** for the number one and **0** for the number zero.

- Don't be afraid to use your keyboard! Word always offers ample warning before anything serious happens. A handy Undo feature recovers anything you accidentally delete; see Chapter 4.

- The Shift key produces capital letters, just like on a typewriter (if you've ever used one).

- The Caps Lock key works like the Shift Lock key on a typewriter. After you press that key, the Caps Lock light on your keyboard comes on, and everything you type is in ALL CAPS.

- Sorry for all the typewriter analogies.

- The number keys on the right side of the keyboard are on the numeric keypad. To use those keys, you must press the Num Lock key, and you see the Num Luck light on the keyboard turn on. When the Num Lock light is off, the number keys serve as duplicate cursor-control, or arrow, keys.

- In some cultures, belching is perfectly acceptable at the table. In fact, it's considered rude *not* to belch.

When to press that Enter key

Press the Enter key only when you reach the end of a paragraph.

Read that again. It's an admonishment:

Press the Enter key only when you reach the end of a paragraph!

"Do I need to learn to type?"

No one needs to learn to type to use a word processor, but you'll do yourself a favor if you learn. My advice is to get a computer program that teaches you to type. I can recommend the Mavis Beacon Teaches Typing program, even though I don't get any money from her. I just like the name Mavis, I suppose.

Knowing how to type makes a painful experience like Word a wee bit more enjoyable.

Unlike plain typing, word processing is about words and *paragraphs,* not lines of text. It's important that you tell the word processor where the paragraph ends. The line of text? That's not a problem: When your typing reaches the right margin on a page, the word processor automatically *wraps* the text down to the next line. So the only time you need to press the Enter key is at the end of a paragraph.

For example, type the following text. Just type it all and don't bother pressing the Enter key, nope, not at all:

```
We sat silent but eager as we watched Grandma carefully
unwrap the present. She gingerly peeled back the tape and
unfolded the wrapper as she always did; a child of the Great
Depression she would save the festive paper and use it again
later. Then she beamed with delight as she beheld her first
digital camera. We exploded in applause! Bill had already set
it up, so we all posed and smiled broadly as Grandma put the
camera up to her face and quickly clicked off a photograph of
her own nose.
```

Notice how the text wraps? The last part of the text on the end of one line moves down to the start of the next line. It's automatic! There's no "ding!" — nor is there any need to press Enter at the end of the line. Press Enter only at the end of a paragraph.

✔ The wrapping of text from one line to the next is called *word wrap.*

✔ Some people end a paragraph with two presses of the Enter key; others use only one press. If it's extra space you want between paragraphs, you should use Word's paragraph formatting commands, as I describe in Chapter 12 of this book.

✔ Double-spacing your lines is *also* done with a paragraph-formatting command. Do not press Enter if you want double spacing! See Chapter 12 for more information.

✔ If you want to indent the next paragraph, press the Tab key after pressing Enter.

✔ If you press the Enter key in the middle of an existing paragraph, Word splits the paragraph in two, making two new paragraphs. The text above the toothpick cursor becomes its own paragraph, and the text following the toothpick cursor becomes the next paragraph.

✔ You can delete the Enter character by using the Backspace or Delete keys. Removing the Enter character joins two paragraphs.

The lure of the soft return

Another way to end a paragraph — but not really end it — is to use the Shift+Enter key combination, also called a *soft return* or *line break*. This allows you to end one line of text and start a new line, but without creating a new paragraph. Type this line:

```
Serving the Hendersons
```

Now press Shift+Enter. A new line starts. Continue typing:

```
(Not a cookbook)
```

Now press the Enter key to end the paragraph.

All of the text you typed is one paragraph, yet it appears on two lines. That's the essence of a soft return or line break. Mostly they're used in titles, headings, or tables, though you may find a purpose for them if you're creating forms, Web pages, or other documents where such formatting is necessary.

✔ No, you probably won't use soft returns as much as you use real returns (also called *hard* returns, coincidentally).

✔ See Chapter 20 for moron tables — I mean *more on* tables.

When to whack the spacebar

You use the spacebar to insert spaces between words or sentences. Withoutityourtextwouldbehardtoread.

In Word, as in all typing you do on a computer, you put only one space between sentences. (If you're a touch-typist, this habit is tough to break, but it's possible.)

The only peeve I have about the spacebar is that too often folks use spaces to line up columns of information or to indent. This is terribly wrong, and, as those folks discover, the output on paper looks tawdry. Yes, cheap and tawdry.

Rather than use the spacebar to indent or line up text, use the Tab key. The Tab key is the best way to organize information on the screen. Unlike the spacebar, the Tab key indents text to an exact position so that when you print, everything lines up nice and neatly. (See Chapter 13 for more Tabby information.)

- ✔ Use that spacebar to put a single space between words and sentences.

- ✔ One space between sentences is all you need. Whenever you feel like using more than one space, such as arranging text in columns or lining things up, use a Tab instead (see Chapter 13).

- ✔ I hear that typing teachers still tell students to put two spaces between sentences. Well, guess what? They're wrong!

- ✔ The Romans couldn't put spaces between words carved on buildings because the Chiselers Union didn't know how to charge for it.

Things to notice whilst you type

Lots of interesting things go on while you type, some of which may puzzle you, others of which may annoy you, and a few that may cause you undue consternation.

The status bar

The first thing to notice while you type is the status bar at the bottom of the screen. The information there tells you something about your document and where you're typing in it. Figure 2-1 explains everything, although the only items I refer to are the Page (current page you're editing), and the total pages in the document (the last number in item C in Figure 2-1).

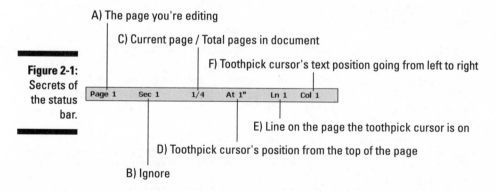

A) The page you're editing

C) Current page / Total pages in document

F) Toothpick cursor's text position going from left to right

Figure 2-1: Secrets of the status bar.

Page 1   Sec 1   1/4   At 1"   Ln 1   Col 1

E) Line on the page the toothpick cursor is on

D) Toothpick cursor's position from the top of the page

B) Ignore

Life between pages

Word likes to show you where one page ends and another begins. This is a good thing to know because most of what you create ends up on a sheet of paper — or maybe two sheets, but you wanted only one. In that case, you can always use the status bar (refer to Figure 2-1) to see how many pages you have or which page you're on. But Word has visual methods as well.

Word uses two visual clues to show you where a new page happens, depending on which *view* you're using to see your document.

If you choose View⇨Print Layout (the way Word naturally looks), the break between pages shows up on the screen in a virtual manner. Figure 2-2 shows the details. The pages are white, and the space between them is gray.

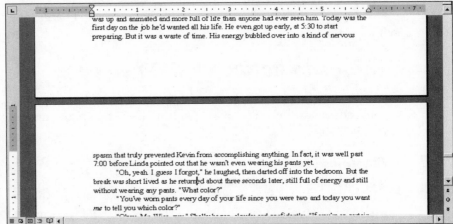

Figure 2-2:
A page
break in
Print Layout
view.

If you choose View⇨Normal, which is how I use Word, the break between pages shows up as a line of ants marching across the screen. *Don't spray 'em with bug killer!*

That thing (shown above) is a Normal view page break. The text you see above the ants, er, dots, is on the preceding page; text below the dots is on the next page.

✔ You cannot delete this type of page break. You can change where it happens, but if your text is too long for the page, Word automatically places it on the next page.

✔ A row of dots close together — very friendly ants — marks a hard page break. The words `Page Break` even appear right in the middle of the line. This on-purpose page break is covered in Chapter 14.

Spots between words!

There is no cause for alarm if you see spots — or dots — onscreen when you press the spacebar or Enter key — like this:

`This·can·be·very·annoying.¶`

> # Ridding your document of that final, blank page
>
> One common problem many Word users have is that Word tells them their document is one page longer than it should be, and that final page is blank. To remove that trailing blank page, do this: Press Ctrl+End, which moves the toothpick cursor all the way to the very bottom of your document, onto that last page. Then, carefully, keep pressing the Backspace key until that final blank page is gone. That will do it!

What's happening is that Word is showing you the *nonprinting characters*. Word uses various symbols to represent things you normally wouldn't see: spaces, tabs, and the Enter key.

Why bother? By displaying the nonprinting characters, you can easily find things that may be screwing up your text formatting but otherwise would be hard to see. For example, two tabs in a row may suddenly jerk your text around as you're editing. The only way to know that there are two tabs in a row would be to view the nonprinting characters.

✔ To turn the nonprinting characters off, press the Ctrl+Shift+8 key combination. (Press it again to turn them on, if you're curious.) Use the 8 on the keyboard, not on the numeric keypad.

✔ You can also click the Show/Hide button on the Standard toolbar to display or hide the nonprinting characters.

✔ The symbols show up onscreen but — fortunately — not in a printed document.

Underline squiggly wigglies

Adding underline to your text in Word is cinchy; Chapter 11 tells you all about it. Yet, there are times when Word may do some underlining by itself, with red, green, and purple underlines of zigzag and dotted styles. What Word is doing is alerting you to certain special things about that underlined text.

Spelling errors in Word are underlined with a red zigzag. That's Word's annoying real-time spell checker in action. It's saying, "Hmmm! I'm not sure about the spelling of this red underlined word!"

Grammatical errors in Word are underlined with a green zigzag. Word is telling you that some English-language sin has been committed. (Relax, it's usually wrong.)

The dotted purple underline is used in Word as a *smart tag*. That flags a potential contact person, date, or place that you may want to share with Microsoft Office and the Outlook program.

Generally speaking, ignore all squiggly lines until you move into the editing phase for your document. (Well, unless you become obsessive, but that tends to slow down the writing process.)

✔ Refer to Chapter 7 for more information on fixing spelling and grammar errors in Word — and for turning the zigzag line feature off, if you're so inclined.

✔ Chapter 34 explains all you need to know about Smart Tags, including how to turn them off.

Watch the Office Assistant!

As you type, the Office Assistant does various interesting things, which you may find amusing. In fact, if you wait too long while reading or composing your thoughts, you may notice the Office Assistant going to sleep (see the dog in the margin). That's a good clue that you should stop staring off into space and get back to work!

"Oops! I made a boo-boo!"

If you make a mistake, press the Backspace key to back up and erase. This key is named Backspace on your keyboard, or it may have a long, left-pointing arrow on it: ←.

Pressing and holding down the Backspace key puts you in Rapid Consumption mode — a whole lotta characters to the left of the blinking toothpick cursor are erased — until you release the Backspace key.

The Delete key also gobbles characters, though it deletes the character to the *right* of the blinking toothpick cursor.

For even larger boo-boos *(booboous maximus),* Word has an Undo key. It doesn't erase text, but it helps you yank back text you accidentally erase. See Chapter 4 for more Undo information.

Formatting Your Document

Formatting is what makes your document look professional and not like it came from an abused typewriter at the public library. You can format several things in your document:

✔ Characters

✔ Paragraphs

✔ Tabs

✔ The entire document

✔ Pages

✔ Columns

✔ Headers and footers

Your primary duty in word processing is to get down the text. After that, you typically go back and format, changing the text style or adjusting the margins. This is all covered in Part II of this book.

✔ Word can format your document for you. I describe how in Chapter 18.

✔ Most folks format text as they type, adding italics or bold or whatever. You can also format paragraphs as you write, although some major formatting chores are best done *after* you write your text. (Examples of both techniques are shown in Part II.)

✔ Word also lets you format your document by adding drawings, pictures, lines, tables, columns, or other elements that can really make things look snazzy. Parts III and V cover those topics.

Getting Help

You can get help for just about anything by pressing the F1 key. This key presents the Microsoft Word Help task pane, which you can use for help. You can either type in a phrase or question to search for an answer or click a Table of Contents link to view Word's enormous and confusing online manual. Pick your torture!

You can also venture out to Microsoft.com on the Internet and look for on-line assistance or training. But you have this book, and it should help you with most of the general chores; no point in wasting time (and money) trying to pinch that information out of Microsoft.

Another way to get help is to use the Office Assistant (if it's visible). Clicking the mouse on the Office Assistant displays a cartoon bubble over his head, asking, "What would you like to do?" Type in your question, as shown in Figure 2-3. Press the Enter key, and the dog answers your question:

Bark! Woof! Woof! Woooooooff!

Figure 2-3:
The Office
Assistant is
ready to
help.

Seriously, the Office Assistant goes out and tries to find help, the results of which appear in the task pane in a few connecting-to-the-Internet moments. You can then click to choose an item to read and, gods willing, it will actually be helpful.

Save Your Stuff!

The computer is dumb. The computer is forgetful. And it loses things. To help the computer remember, you must tell it to save your stuff. Everything you create in Word should be saved to disk, stored there as a document.

 To save a document to disk, choose the File⇨Save command (or press Alt+F, S). (You can also click the Save button, which looks like a wee li'l disk, on the Standard toolbar.)

If you're saving your document for the first time, the Save As dialog box appears, as shown in Figure 2-4.

Figure 2-4:
The Save As
dialog box.

Type a name for your document in the File Name area. The name The Forest is shown in Figure 2-4. If you make a mistake typing, use the Backspace key to back up and erase.

Click the Save button to save your document.

- Chapter 8 offers more details about saving your document.

- The filename is how you recognize the file later, when you want to edit or print it again. It's important to think up and use a good, descriptive filename.

- The fastest way to save a file is to use the keyboard. The Save File key combination is Ctrl+S. Press and hold the Ctrl (Control) key and press the S key. If you can pick up a basketball with one hand, you can also use the Shift+F12 key combo.

- When you save a document, watch the status bar — it temporarily displays a message telling you that Word is saving your document (or fast saving, for our Frequent Fliers).

- You can generally name a file anything, however Word (or the Office Assistant) tells you when you enter a forbidden filename. Click OK and try again.

- After the document is saved to disk, you see its name displayed on the window's title bar. That name is your clue that your document has been saved to disk.

- If you're not in a clever mood, you may decide to name your file with the name of a file already on disk. This decision is a boo-boo because the newer file overwrites the other file with the same name already on disk. For example, if you decide to save your new letter by using the LETTER filename and LETTER already exists on disk, the new file overwrites the old one. There is no way to get the original back, so use another, more clever name instead. You're warned with this message:

The file *filename* already exists.

Click Cancel or choose the option to save the file to disk with a different name. Start over.

Getting It Down on Paper (Printing)

The great authors didn't worry about printing. Shakespeare never had to save his document or use Print Preview. Poe wrote *The Raven* on paper, so "printing" was what he did as he wrote. And Mark Twain, who wrote *The Adventures of Tom Sawyer* on that newfangled typewriter, well, he was pretty high tech. And you?

Printing is the result of your word processing labors. Hercules? He had to retrieve some gal's girdle. You? You have to print your document. Everything looks nice and tidy on paper — almost professional.

First, preview your printing

To see what your document will look like without wasting valuable paper, use the Print Preview command. Choose File➪Print Preview or click the handy Print Preview button on the toolbar.

Figure 2-5 shows you what Print Preview mode looks like. Your document is shown exactly as it will print, including any pictures, headers, or footers or other items that may not show up properly when you're editing.

Okay. It looks good. Click the Close Preview button to return to your document for editing or printing.

Time to print

To print your document in Word — the document you see onscreen, all of it — do the following:

1. **Make sure that your printer is on and ready to print.**

   See Chapter 9 for additional information about preparing the printer if you need to.

2. **Choose the File➪Print command.**

   The Print dialog box opens. This is a busy place where printing and related activities happen.

3. **Click the OK button.**

   The document comes out of your printer.

   ✔ You can also summon the Print dialog box by pressing Alt+F, P, or Ctrl+P. This method is more desirable if you have long fingers or do needlepoint or if the mouse is off eating the cheese again.

   ✔ Notice that saving comes before printing. It doesn't have to, but I'm a stickler for saving, saving, saving your document.

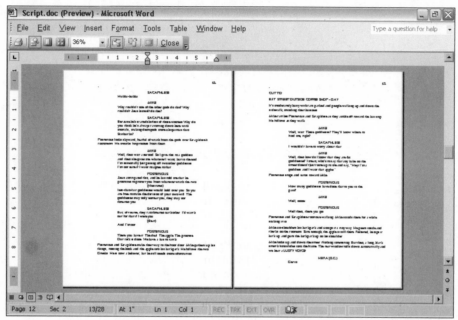

Figure 2-5:
Print
Preview
mode.

Close 'Er Up

To close a document when you're done, choose the File➪Close command (Ctrl+W). This step closes the document window and makes it vanish from the screen. Zzzipp! (You have to say "Zzzipp!" when you do this; Word is strangely mute on the point.) This step is covered succinctly in Chapter 1; for all the details, see the section about how to quit what you're doing without quitting Word.

✔ Why close a document? Because you're done working on it! Maybe you want to work on something else or quit Word after closing. The choices are yours.

✔ If you try to close a document before it has been saved, Word displays a warning dialog box. Click the Yes button to save your document. If you want to continue editing, click the Cancel button and get back to work.

✔ If you're working on only one document and you close it, Word looks like it has vacated the premises: Toolbars and menus dim, as do scroll bars and other screen debris. Don't panic; you've just closed a document, and Word has little else to do. Word sits patiently and waits for your next command.

✔ If you're done with Word, quit. Otherwise, you can start working on another document. Refer to "Starting a New Document," earlier in this chapter.

Chapter 3

Basic Movement

• •

In This Chapter

▶ Moving the toothpick cursor

▶ Using key combinations to move up, down, to the top, to the bottom — you get the idea

▶ Using the Go To command

▶ Bookmarking memorable bits o' text

▶ Using the secret scroll bar buttons

• •

Once upon a midnight dreary, while I pondered, weak and weary, blaring from the TV bleary comes another infomercial leery.

Writing means rewriting, which means that there will be times when you're just perusing your document, up and down. If you need a mental image, picture a typewriter with only one long sheet of paper — like a scroll. To reread your document, you would have to rewind or "scroll" it back through the platen until you found the part you wanted. Ugh. What a chore!

Fortunately, Word has some basic toothpick cursor movement commands that let you scroll, read, or edit through your document much easier than cranking a knob. It's all about movement! Exercise! Be active! Avoid late night TV!

Moving around Your Document

When you scribble on a pad of paper, it's hard to lose your place. And in the old typewriter days, a page of paper was only so big. But with Word, your documents can be downright humongous. Unfortunately, only a small part of that humongousness appears on your computer screen at a time. To get from one place to another, you need to do more than just press the arrow keys. You need to find out about Word's navigation keys and other special commands you can use to get around in your document.

Going hither, thither, and yon (basic arrow keys)

The most common way to move about in your document is to press the arrow keys, which are also called the *cursor-control keys* because they control the toothpick cursor onscreen. These keys can be used alone or with other keys on your keyboard to zippity-zap the toothpick cursor all over your document.

If you use the arrow keys on the numeric keypad, make sure that the Num Lock light is off. Do this by pressing the Num Lock key. If you don't do this, you see numbers in your text rather than the toothpick cursor dancing all over — like444this.

The four basic arrow keys move the toothpick cursor up, down, right, and left:

Key	What It Does
↑	Moves the cursor up to the preceding line of text
↓	Moves the cursor down to the next line of text
→	Moves the cursor right to the next character
←	Moves the cursor left to the preceding character

If you press and hold the Ctrl (Control) key and then press an arrow key, you enter afterburner mode. The supercharged toothpick cursor jumps in desperately quick leaps in all four directions:

Press These Keys	To Do This
Ctrl+↑	Moves the cursor up to the start of the previous paragraph
Ctrl+↓	Moves the cursor down to the start of the next paragraph
Ctrl+→	Moves the cursor right to the start (first letter) of the next word
Ctrl+←	Moves the cursor left to the start (first letter) of the previous word

Use the Ctrl key with the arrow key in the same way that you use the Shift key with the *s* key to get a capital *S:* Press and hold the Ctrl key and then press an arrow key. Release both keys. You don't have to press hard.

✔ You cannot move the toothpick cursor beyond the limits of your document: You cannot scroll "higher" than the first line or "lower" than the last line of a document, nor can you attempt to place the cursor in the nether regions between pages by clicking your mouse.

✔ If you like, you can direct Word to beep at you when you try to move the cursor beyond the limits of a document: Choose Tools⇨Options from the menu. Click the General tab in the Options dialog box, and put a check mark by the item Provide Feedback with Sound. Click OK, and follow the directions on the screen. When it's all set up, Word cacophonously beeps when you attempt to force the toothpick cursor off the page.

✔ Moving the cursor does not erase characters; using the Backspace and Delete keys erases characters (among other things discussed in Chapter 4).

✔ The word *yon* was used in English as another form of the word *there.* Here is here, there is there, and yon is like *there,* but farther off. It's short for *yonder.*

Making that toothpick cursor skedaddle (moving by great leaps and bounds)

Not all your fingers are the same length. Look at them right now! See how some are shorter and some are longer? The short ones are probably that way because you press the arrow keys on your keyboard in an improper manner. For shame. There are better ways to jump around a document.

Instead of woodpeckering your keyboard, try using some of the arrow key (and non-arrow key) combinations in the following sections to really make that toothpick cursor fly around your document.

Paging Mr. PgUp and Mr. PgDn!

PgUp is keyboard language for Page Up. And PgDn is keyboard language for Page Down. Your keyboard has both sets of keys: keyboard language PgUp and PgDn on the numeric keypad, and Page Up and Page Down on the cursor area (to the left of the keypad). Isn't that nice?

One would think, logically, that the Page Up set of keys moves a document up one page and that the Page Down set of keys moves a document down. 'Tain't so, though. Rather than slide your document around a page at a time, these keys move things one *screen* at a time:

PgUp The PgUp key moves the toothpick cursor up one screen. Or, if you're at the tippy-top of your document, this key moves you to the top of the screen.

PgDn Moves the cursor down one screen or to the end of the document, if you happen to be there, or to the end of the document if you happen to be less than a screen away.

As with the regular cursor movement keys (arrow keys), you can combine Mr. PgUp and Mr. PgDn with the Ctrl key for some interesting leaps and bounds:

Ctrl+PgUp With the Ctrl key pressed, the PgUp key actually does move to the top of the page in your document. You'll have to view the status bar (near the bottom of the window) to confirm this. Press Ctrl+PgUp again to move to the top of the previous page.

Ctrl+PgDn When combined with the Ctrl key, the PgDn key moves the toothpick cursor to the top of the next page.

Note that you can change the function of the Ctrl+PgUp and Ctrl+PgDn keys. Normally they do leap around by full pages. I describe how to change this later in this chapter.

Finally, here are two more key combinations that are just this side of pressing all the keys on the keyboard at once:

Ctrl+Alt+PgUp Moves the cursor to the top of the current screen.

Ctrl+Alt+PgDn Moves the cursor to the bottom of the current screen.

Personally, I've never used those keys because it's just easier to click the mouse wherever I want to put the toothpick cursor.

There is no logic in the computer industry.

Beginnings and endings

Up/down, top/bottom, begin/end — sometimes you just need to get right there. These are the keys that do it — and they're named surprisingly well:

Key or Combination	Where It Puts Your Cursor
End	This key sends the toothpick cursor to the end of a line of text.
Home	This key sends the toothpick cursor to the start of a line of text.
Ctrl+End	This key combination whisks the toothpick cursor to the very, very end of your document.
Ctrl+Home	This key combination takes you to the tippy-top of your document. Zoom!

Ctrl+End is an easy key combination to mistakenly press. It throws you — literally — to the end of your document. If you do this and feel that you have boo-booed, press Shift+F5, the Go Back keyboard shortcut, to return from whence you came (that is, back to your previous edit). Also see "Going Back," later in this chapter.

Using the mouse to move yerself around

The mouse provides a quick and easy way to move the toothpick cursor: First, spy a new location for the cursor onscreen. Then move the mouse pointer to where you want the cursor to be and click. The cursor relocates there instantly. It's point and click.

You can also use your mouse to manipulate the vertical scroll bar (to the right of the document window). The scroll bar is a standard Windows toy, working in Word like it does in all of Windows. The only bonus you get here is that if you drag the elevator button with the mouse, you see a pop-up balloon telling you approximately which page you're dragging to in your document, as shown in Figure 3-1. You might even see the current part heading or chapter title as you drag the elevator button.

Figure 3-1:
Vital page-numbering information.

Page: 8

Finally, if your PC sports one of the new "wheel" mice, such as the Microsoft IntelliMouse, you can scroll through your document using the center wheel button:

Roll the wheel up or down to scroll your document up or down. (You use the Mouse icon in the Windows Control Panel to set the number of lines the document scrolls.)

Click the wheel to exert super-mousian control over the vertical scroll bar to quickly scroll your document up and down.

Press the wheel like a button and drag the mouse to smoothly scroll up and down or "pan" your document from left to right.

Oh, I just love those mouse toys!

✔ Watch out when you're using the vertical scroll bar to move around your document! Scrolling the screen does not make the cursor flippity-jibbit all over. You must *click the mouse* in the text to actually move the cursor to a given spot. So, for example, you may scroll to view page 5, but the toothpick cursor is still a-blinkin' on page 3. When you start to type, the new text appears on page 3 where the toothpick cursor is, not on page 5 where you're looking.

✔ You must click the mouse to move the cursor to that spot. If you don't click the mouse, you're just messing with the computer's mind.

Going Here or There with the Go To Command

Go To, as in the Shakespearean "Getteth thee outta hereth," enables you to go directly to just about wherever in the document you want to be. The Go To command lets you find a specific page number, line, or what-have-you in your document.

To use the Go To command, choose Edit➪Go To, and the Go To tab in the Find and Replace dialog box appeareth before thine eyes (see Figure 3-2).

You can go to lots of places, as the confusing items in the Go To What list in Figure 3-2 demonstrate. Usually, though, you want to go to a specific page number.

Type a page number into the Enter Page Number box.

Figure 3-2:
Tell 'em
where to
go on the
Go To tab.

Find and Replace	? ✕
Find	Replace	Go To

Go to what:
- Page
- Section
- Line
- Bookmark
- Comment
- Footnote
- Endnote

Enter page number:

Enter + and – to move relative to the current location. Example: +4 will move forward four items.

Previous | Next | Close

For example, type **14** in the box and press Enter, and you go to page 14. That's supposing you have a page 14 to go to.

- You can also press the F5 key to open the Go To tab in the Find and Replace dialog box.

- Heck, you can also press the Ctrl+G keyboard shortcut. (Makes more sense than F5, anyway.)

- If you click twice on the page number on the status bar (muttering "Change, you idiot — change, change," while you do this helps), the Go To dialog box appears like a genie out of a lamp.

- To be even more specific in your Go To commands, see "Don't Dog-Ear Your Monitor! Use the Bookmark Command," just ahead in this chapter.

Going Back

They say that once you commit, there's no going back. That is, unless you're running for office or using Word. If you go anywhere you don't want to be, press Shift+F5, and Word carries you back to where you started.

The Shift+F5 keyboard shortcut works only in Word; you can't use this command in real life.

Pressing Shift+F5 returns you to where you were before; pressing it again takes you back to where you were before that. This keyboard shortcut works about three times before it starts repeating itself. Repeating itself. Repeating itself.

Don't Dog-Ear Your Monitor! Use the Bookmark Command

As the scatterbrained type, I often find myself working on several parts of a document at once. Maybe you do that, too. Or perhaps you're reading what you wrote and need to remember a specific spot to come back to. Whatever the reason, often it's necessary to, well, put a bookmark in your document. That's tough to do without bending the corner of your monitor, which I doubt would work anyway.

Welcome to Word's Bookmark command.

Setting a bookmark

To mark your place in your document, set a bookmark. Follow these steps:

1. Put the toothpick cursor where you want to place a bookmark.

2. **Choose the Insert⇨Bookmark command (or, if you have three hands, try Ctrl+Shift+F5).**

   The Bookmark dialog box opens, as shown in Figure 3-3.

Figure 3-3:
The
Bookmark
dialog box.

3. **Type a name for the bookmark.**

   Be clever! The name reminds you of where you are in your document. So if you're creating a term paper, memorable flags for various parts of your document (and their original sources) would be proper.

   Bookmark names cannot contain spaces. However, you can use underlines to separate words, as shown in Figure 3-3.

4. **Press Enter or click the Add button.**

Finding a bookmark and moving to that spot in your document

To return to a bookmark, use the Go To command, as covered in "Going Here or There with the Go To Command," earlier in this chapter. These steps keep you from turning the page and losing your train of thought:

1. **Press the F5 key.**

   The Find and Replace dialog box splats across your screen.

2. **Highlight Bookmark on the Go To What list.**

   Bookmark is the fourth item down.

The Enter Page Number box changes to read Enter Bookmark Name. Your most recent bookmark appears in that space.

If you don't see your bookmark, click the down arrow, and you see a long list of bookmarks in your document. Click the one you want.

3. Click the Go To button.

You're there!

4. Click the Close button to get rid of the Find and Replace dialog box and return to editing your document.

Using Secret Scroll Bar Buttons to Navigate

Lurking at the bottom of the vertical scroll bar are three buttons, as shown in the margin. These are the *browse* buttons, which allow you to scroll through your document in leaps and bounds of various sizes.

 The top button is the *Browse Up* button.

 The bottom button is the *Browse Down* button.

 And the center button is the *What The Heck Am I Browsing For?* button.

When you click the center button, a pop-up palette of things to browse for appears, as shown in Figure 3-4. Pointing the mouse at any one of the items displays text that explains the item in the bottom part of the palette.

Figure 3-4:
Various
things to
browse for.

✔ Choosing an item from the palette controls how the browse buttons work.

✔ The Ctrl+PgUp key combination is linked to the Browse Up button.

✔ The Ctrl+PgDn key combination is linked to the Browse Down button.

How the secret scroll buttons work

 Unless you've chosen another item from the browsing palette (refer to Figure 3-4), the Browse buttons (and Ctrl+PgUp, Ctrl+PgDn) leap through your document by full pages.

Whenever an option other than Page is chosen, the Browse buttons change color. So when the buttons are black, you know you're browsing by page. But if they turn blue, then the Browse buttons are searching for something else. (Alas, the browsing palette doesn't tell you which option is currently chosen.)

 A handier item to choose is to browse by edits. If you select the Browse by Edits button from the palette, then you can use the Browse Up or Browse Down buttons to leap through your document and review the three most recent places where you've edited text. This comes in very handy for when you screw things up.

Using the buttons with the Find command

The Browse buttons are also related to the Find command (covered in Chapter 5). When you choose the Find option, clicking the Browse Up or Browse Down button locates the last item you've searched for.

For example, you use the Find command to locate some bit of text. After that, you can choose the Find button from the browsing palette (refer to Figure 3-4) and use the Browse arrows to continue searching for that text without having to resummon the Search dialog box. Very handy.

Chapter 4

Basic Editing

. . . .

In This Chapter

▶ Using Insert and Overtype modes

▶ Deleting text with Backspace and Delete

▶ Deleting lines, sentences, and paragraphs

▶ Undoing your mistakes

▶ Using the Redo (un-undo) command

. . . .

*E*diting. It sounds so neat and tidy, doesn't it? It's a helping word. To edit is to help, "Here, let me edit this for you. I'm just going to touch it up a tad. Nip and tuck. Hone your points. Focus your thoughts." That's the way I'd like to think of editing. But the truth is far more ugly. Yes, editing is about destruction.

To edit is to cut. To whack. To destroy. To lay down swaths of burnt text, the stubble and stumps of excess words and mangled thoughts too gross and graceless for the printed page. That's the legacy of editing. And it's the subject of this chapter.

Word processing is more than just typing and moving the cursor around. It's playing with the text. Retyping. Deleting. Undoing. These are the basic editing tasks you find in the text that follows (which I typed, retyped, overtyped, deleted, and undid many times over).

To Insert or to Overtype: That Is the Question

Betcha didn't know that Word is usually in Insert mode. That means that any new text you type is inserted just before the blinking toothpick cursor. The new stuff pushes any existing text to the right and down as you type. This is Insert mode.

Insert mode's evil twin is Overtype mode. In Overtype mode, all the text you type overwrites the existing text onscreen, replacing it as you go.

To switch to Overtype mode, press the Insert key on your keyboard. Either the key labeled Insert or the Ins key on the numeric keypad (with Num Lock off) does the trick.

When you're in Overtype mode, the three letters OVR are highlighted on the status bar. In fact, you can double-click those letters to switch between Insert and Overtype modes.

Honestly, there is no reason to type in Overtype mode. Insert mode is fine by itself; you can use the various commands in this chapter to delete text at your whim.

✔ In Overtype mode, new text gobbles up text already on the screen. If you see this weirdness happen, double-click the OVR thing on the status bar to stop it, and then use the Ctrl+Z (Undo) keyboard shortcut to yank back any deleted text.

✔ So the answer to this section's title is that Insert mode is the answer.

Deleting Stuff

I knew a writer who was utterly afraid to delete *anything*. Rather than toss out the random paragraph or two, he'd merely copy the paragraphs as *blocks* and move them to the end of the document for "safekeeping." Yeah. And if he eventually becomes the next Bill Shakespeare, posterity will have all those discarded blocks of text to marvel over. Aren't we lucky?

Sad but true, deleting text is a part of the editing process, just like writing. Everyone edits, and everyone deletes text. In fact, I'm fond of saying that you can probably delete the opening paragraph of any first draft you do. If that's your urge, or if even deleting small stuff is in order, this part of the book is the right place to come.

✔ It's said that Isaac Asimov never did second drafts of anything. That's not to say that he didn't go back and self edit — just that he was probably much better at writing than most folks I know.

✔ Marking and moving blocks is covered in Chapter 6.

Your basic delete keys: Backspace and Delete

You can use two keys on the keyboard to delete single characters of text:

✔ **Backspace key:** Deletes the character to the left of the toothpick cursor.

✔ **Delete key:** Deletes the character to the right of the toothpick cursor.

```
We were happy with Bob manning the bar|becue, as long as the
fire department was just down the street.
```

In the preceding line, the toothpick cursor is "flashing" (okay, it *would* be flashing on a computer screen) between the *r* and the *b* in *barbecue*. Pressing the Backspace key deletes the *r;* pressing the Delete key deletes the *b*.

✔ After deleting a character, any text to the right or below the character shuffles over to fill the void.

✔ If you're in Overtype mode, the Backspace key still pulls the rest of the text to the right.

✔ Backspace doesn't work like the Backspace key on a typewriter. The difference is that when you press Backspace in Word, the cursor backs up and *erases*. (The Word equivalent of the typewriter's Backspace key is the left-arrow key.)

✔ Special types of text in Word cannot easily be deleted using either the Backspace or Delete keys. An example is an updating text field, which is special text that always shows, say, today's date. Such text appears shaded in a light gray color when you try to delete it. That's Word reminding you of the text's specialness. You need to press the Delete or Backspace key once again to delete such text.

✔ You can press and hold Backspace or Delete to continuously "machine-gun-delete" characters. Release the key to halt such wanton destruction.

Deleting a word

Word has two commands that gobble up an entire word:

✔ Ctrl+Backspace deletes the word in front (to the left) of the cursor.

✔ Ctrl+Delete deletes the word behind (to the right) of the cursor.

To delete a word by using Ctrl+Backspace, position the cursor at the last letter of the word. Press Ctrl+Backspace, and the word is gone! The cursor then sits at the end of the preceding word or the beginning of the line (if you deleted the first word in a paragraph).

To delete a word by using Ctrl+Delete, position the cursor at the first letter of the word. Press Ctrl+Delete, and the word is gone. The cursor then sits at the beginning of the next word or the end of the line (if you deleted the last word in a paragraph).

Unfortunately, if you're in the middle of the word, commands delete only from that middle point to the start or end of the word. Therefore, I bestow the following trick:

To delete a word, the whole word, and nothing but the word, point the mouse at the offending critter and double-click the mouse button. This action selects the entire word, highlighting it on the screen. Press the Delete key to zap the word away.

After deleting the text, Word neatly wraps up the remaining text, snuggling it together in a grammatically proper way.

No mere pencil eraser can match Ctrl+Delete or Ctrl+Backspace for sheer speed and terror!

Deleting lines, sentences, and paragraphs

In Word, there is a difference between a line of text, a sentence, and a paragraph. Heed these definitions:

- ✔ A **line of text** is merely a line across the page (not really a grammatical thing at all). The Ln indicator on the status bar tells you which *line* of text you're on, as measured from the top of the page. For example, right now Word tells me that I'm editing line 23. Whatever.

- ✔ A **sentence** is a sentence. You know: Start with a capital letter and end with a period, question mark, or exclamation point. You probably learned this concept in grammar school, which is why they call it *grammar* school anyway.

- ✔ A **paragraph** is a bunch of text ending with a press of the Enter key. So a paragraph can be one line of text, a sentence, or several sentences.

And just who cares? Well, all this stuff comes into play when you want to delete various bits of text. There are different ways to delete lines, sentences, and paragraphs.

Deleting a line of text

Word has no single command for deleting a line of text from the keyboard. But with the mouse, deleting a line is only a matter of a click and a key press. Follow these steps:

1. **Move the mouse into the left margin of your document.**

   The cursor changes into an arrow pointing northeast rather than northwest.

2. **Point the mouse pointer arrow at the line of text you want to obliterate.**

3. **Click the mouse.**

   The line of text is highlighted, or selected.

4. **Press the Delete key to send that line into the void.**

When the mouse cursor is pointing northeast, you can drag it down the left margin and select as many lines of text as you care to. All the lines can then be deleted with one stroke of the Delete key.

Also see Chapter 6, where I talk about marking text as a block and then blowing it to the hereafter.

Deleting a sentence

Making a sentence go bye-bye is cinchy. Well, you could just press the Delete key once for each character in the sentence. But, as with everything in a computer, there's always a better, easier way:

1. **Point the mouse at the offending sentence.**

2. **Press and hold the Ctrl key and click the mouse.**

   The sentence is selected.

3. **Press the Delete key.**

   Oomph! It's gone.

Deleting a paragraph

The fastest way to delete a full paragraph:

1. **Point the mouse at the paragraph.**

2. **Click the mouse button three times.**

   There's no place like home. There's no place like home. There's no place like home.

3. **Press the Delete key.**

Three clicks may be too much for you. If so, then move the mouse over to the left of the offending paragraph so that it changes into the northeasterly pointing mouse. Click the mouse twice, and it selects the entire paragraph (as opposed to clicking once to select merely a line of text). Then you can whack the paragraph by pressing the Delete key.

Deleting odd shapes with blocks

Word can delete characters, words, and lines with nifty, specific commands. To delete anything else, you have to mark it as a block of text and then delete the block.

Refer to Chapter 6 for more information on marking a block of text. After any block is marked in your document, pressing the Delete key removes it. Oh, and Backspace can delete the block as well. (If only getting rid of warts were so easy. . . .)

Erase Your Mistakes with Undo Haste

Now mark me how I will undo myself.

—*Richard II, William Shakespeare*

There is no need to be afraid of doing anything in Word. Anything! That's because Word has a handy Undo command. The Undo command remembers the last several things you added or deleted and quite easily unravels any mistakes you made. Furthermore, there's a Redo command, which is essentially Undo-Undo, though that's a double negative, and it pains my brain to think about it.

The blessed Undo command

To undelete any text you just accidentally zapped, do any of the following:

- ✔ Press Ctrl+Z.
- ✔ Choose Edit➪Undo with the mouse.
- ✔ Click the Undo tool on the toolbar.

 These are the three ways to use the Undo command. (I prefer the Ctrl+Z key combination myself.)

- ✔ Unlike other programs, using the Undo command in Word twice doesn't undo your last undo. For example, pressing Ctrl+Z may replace text you just deleted. If you press Ctrl+Z again, it does not re-delete the text (undoing the undo).
- ✔ The Undo item on the Edit menu changes to pertain to whatever needs undoing: Undo Bold, Undo Typing, Undo Boo-boo, and so on.

✔ If you click the down arrow by the Undo button, you see a drop-down list of the last several things you've done in Word. You can select the whole group of them (by dragging the mouse through the list) to undo all your previous actions in one swift swath.

✔ There are sporadic times when Undo will not work. Before this happens, Word warns you. For example, you may see a message such as, "There is not enough memory to undo this operation, Continue?" Proceed at your own risk.

✔ The Undo command won't work if there is nothing to undo, or if something just cannot be undone. For example, you cannot undo a save-to-disk operation.

✔ To undo an Undo, choose Redo. See the section "Redo, or take two" a couple of sections from now.

Redo, or take two

If you undo something and — whoops! — you didn't mean to, you must use the Redo command to set things back. To undelete any text you just accidentally zapped, do any of the following:

✔ Press Ctrl+Y.

✔ Choose Edit⇨Redo with the mouse.

✔ Click the Redo tool on the toolbar (if available).

How does this work? Well, pretend that after one particularly heavy lunch you return to the office for some vigorous typing. Alas, sleep eventually overcomes you, and your head slams into the keyboard where your eyebrows type random things. After you snap awake — and check to ensure that no one witnessed such an embarrassing episode — you decide to undo the typing your eyebrows just did: Ctrl+Z, Ctrl+Z, Ctrl+Z.

But — whoops! — you pressed one Ctrl+Z too many times. In that case, use the Edit⇨Redo command (or Ctrl+Y) to yank back the stuff you just undid.

And what if there's nothing to redo? Then the Redo command becomes the Repeat command, which is covered in the section about taking advantage of the Repeat key, in Chapter 10.

✔ Honestly, no one uses the Redo command that much. If you do, you find that it can be very frustrating because it tends to redo things you really wanted undone in the first place. (You'll understand this if you ever use Redo several times in a row.)

✔ Refer to Chapter 10, the section "Taking Advantage of the Repeat Key," for another fun thing the Redo command can do. Or redo.

✔ The Redo button on the toolbar may not be visible. I implore you to rearrange your toolbars, which I cover in Chapter 28.

✔ Like the Undo command, the Redo command has a button on the Standard toolbar. Next to the button is a down arrow, which you can click to review the last few things you just undid. Or redid. Or katydid. Oy.

Chapter 5

Search for This, Replace It with That

● ●

In This Chapter

▶ Finding text in your document

▶ Using various options of the Find command

▶ Finding text above or below the toothpick cursor

▶ Finding text that cannot be typed at the keyboard

▶ Finding formatting codes in your document

▶ Using the Replace command

● ●

Wouldn't it be swell if anything you lost could easily be found? Car keys. Wallet. Your old sneakers. That girl named Cynthia at summer camp. Or your entire recollection of where you spent your 23rd birthday during that tequila-soaked Mexican holiday. Yes, it would be swell if you could find all those missing bits of anything as easily as Word's Find command can locate lost or wandering bits of text.

Thanks to Word's Find command, Little Bo Peep can locate her sheep, New Age hippies can find the lost continent of Atlantis, and even mean old Mr. Potter from *It's a Wonderful Life* could find his heart. Not only that, when you combine Find with the Replace command, alchemists could handily turn lead into gold. It may not be as lucrative as they imagined, but it's possible. This chapter has all the details.

Text, O Text! Wherefore Art Thou?

Word can quickly locate any tidbit of text anywhere in your document, from a bombastic oratory to the tiniest iota of plot. The command used to find text is called, surprisingly enough, the Find command. It dwells on the Edit menu. Follow these steps to use the Find command and locate text lurking in your document:

1. **Think of some text you want to find.**

   For example, *sheep.*

2. **Choose the Edit⇨Find command.**

   You see the Find and Replace dialog box, shown in Figure 5-1. Notice that this dialog box is also used by the Replace and Go To commands, as indicated by the tabs. They're all similar things, but for now you want to find text, so the Find tab is up front. Good.

Figure 5-1:
The Find and Replace dialog box.

3. **Type the text you want to find.**

   Enter the text in the Find What box — for example, **sheep.** Type it exactly as you want to find it.

   If you're not sure whether the text is typed in uppercase or lowercase letters, use lowercase.

4. **Click the Find Next button to start the search.**

   Or you can just press Enter.

If any text is found, it's highlighted onscreen. The Find and Replace dialog box does not go away until you click the Cancel button or press the Escape key. (The dialog box remains so that you can keep searching for more text, if you're so inclined.)

- ✔ The quick shortcut key for finding text is to press Ctrl+F (the F stands for Find in this case).

- ✔ Type exactly the text you want to find. It can be one word, multiple words, or a complete sentence you want to find. (Do not end the text with a period unless you want to find the period also.)

- ✔ If the text isn't found, a dialog box (or the Office Assistant, if he's visible) lets you know that Word has searched the entire document, high and low, and the text was not found. Oh, well: Close the Find and Replace dialog box.

✔ If the text isn't found and you're *certain* that it's in there, check your spelling. If that's okay, try searching for a single word instead of two or more words or a sentence.

✔ If you're working on more than one document at a time, be aware that Word finds text only in the current document (the one you see on the screen). To find text in another document, click that document's button on the taskbar and try again.

✔ Refer to Chapter 27 for information on searching for text in multiple documents.

✔ To find an additional occurrence of the text, click the Find Next button.

✔ You can also use the Browse Up or Browse Down buttons to find the next occurrence of text — even if the Find and Replace dialog box is no longer visible on the screen. So, if you've already searched for and found *sheep,* clicking the Browse Down button finds even more *sheep.*

✔ You can also use Ctrl+PgUp or Ctrl+PgDn to find the previous or next occurrence of the text. O! These options are abundant!

✔ Your Office Assistant may grow a light bulb over its head after you close the Find and Replace dialog box. Clicking the light bulb displays additional information about the Find command, most of which is summarized in the preceding bullets.

Re-searching

Word remembers the last bit of text you searched for. It appears selected (highlighted) the next time you summon the Find and Replace dialog box. That's handy if you want to find the same bit of text again — or you can edit that text, modifying it slightly, to find something else.

If you cast your eyes to the right side of the Find What box, you see a drop-down arrow gizmo, as shown in Figure 5-2. Clicking that gizmo displays a scrolling list of text you've previously searched for. To re-search for a bit of text you've already searched for, click the drop-down arrow and click the text you want to find again. Click the Find Next button, and you're off on your way.

Figure 5-2:
Re-
searching
for some-
thing you
previously
looked for.

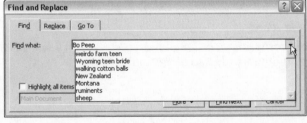

Finding more stuff

The basic finders-keepers dialog box (refer to Figure 5-1) is okay for quickly finding tidbits of text. But sometimes you may want to find more detailed stuff, or stuff you can't readily type from the keyboard (like a new paragraph's Enter keystroke). Or, you may want to find text that specifically matches *Poobah* rather than plain old *poobah*. In those cases, you need to use the more robust Find and Replace dialog box.

To activate more options in the Find and Replace dialog box, press Ctrl+F. Click the More button. The Find and Replace dialog box gets taller, with a bunch of options and doodads at the bottom, as illustrated in Figure 5-3.

Figure 5-3:
The more
detailed
Find and
Replace
dialog box.

The following sections tell you why you may want to mess with some of those doodads.

Finding an exact bit of text

There is a difference between *Bob* and *bob*. One is a name, and the other is a a haircut. To use the Find command to find one and not the other, select the Match Case option under Search Options. That way, *Bob* matches only words that start with an uppercase *B* and have lowercase *ob* in them.

Finding a whole word

The Find Whole Words Only option allows you to look for words such as *right* and *set* without finding words like *alright* and *upset*.

Finding text that you know only a small part of (using wildcards)

Here's a can-o-worms for you. It's possible to use wildcards to find words you know only a part of, or a group of words with similar letters. This trick is a highly technical thing, so I advise you not to drive or operate heavy machinery when reading the following.

The two basic wildcard characters are ? and *, where ? represents any single letter and * represents a group of letters. So, suppose that you type the following line in the Find What box:

```
?up
```

If you select the Use Wildcards option (in the More part of the Find and Replace dialog box), Word searches for any three-letter word that starts with any old letter but must end with *up: cup, pup,* and *sup,* for example.

The asterisk finds a group of characters, so the following wildcard locates any word starting with *W* and ending with *S* (there are lots of them):

```
w*s
```

You can use a bunch of other wildcard characters to find text in a number of interesting and strange ways. For example:

```
adverti[sz]e
```

This bracket-and-wildcard nonsense actually finds the word *advertise* or *advertize* depending on how you prefer to spell it.

Word has many more variations of wildcards available, although * and ? are the most popular and should get you by. To see the rest of the wildcards available, click the question mark button in the upper-right corner of the Find and Replace dialog box and then select the Use Wildcards option.

Finding text that sounds like something else

The Sounds Like option allows you to search for homonyms, or words that sound the same as the search word. You know: their and there, or deer and dear, or hear and here. How this is useful, I'll never know.

Oh! This is not a rhyming search command. If you try to use it to find everything that rhymes with *Doris,* for example, it doesn't find *Boris, chorus, pylorus,* or anything of the like.

Finding variations of a word

"No, no, no! Superman doesn't walk anywhere! He flies! Change this!" So off you go into Word, searching for every variation of the word *walk: walking, walked,* and so on. Word can do it. Just type **walk** into the Find What box and select the Find All Word Forms option.

Searching up, down, left, and right

Janus was the Roman god of beginnings and endings. He had two faces looking in two directions, ideal for watching a tennis match or for finding stuff you've lost. The Find command is like Janus in that it looks for stuff all over your document — unless you tell it to look one way or the other, by selecting a direction from the Search drop-down list in the More part of the Find and Replace dialog box:

- ✔ **All.** When this option is chosen, Find searches the entire document, from the toothpick cursor's location down to the end of the document, back up to the beginning, and then back to the toothpick cursor's location.

- ✔ **Down.** Find searches from the toothpick cursor's location to the end of your document, and then it stops.

- ✔ **Up.** Find searches from the toothpick cursor's location to the start of your document, backwards. Then it stops.

As soon as you reach the end of your document, Word (or the Office Assistant) asks whether you want to search again from the beginning. You do, so you click Yes. Eventually, the Find command stops looking when it returns to where the toothpick cursor was when you first cast the Find command spell.

I was just kidding about searching left and right in this section's title. Left is actually "up," or before the toothpick cursor; right is "down," or after the toothpick cursor. And starboard is right, and port is left, if you happen to be using Word on a laptop somewhere in the ocean.

Finding stuff you just can't type in

No, this isn't a censorship issue. Some characters you just can't properly type in the Find and Replace dialog box — unprintable, unmentionable stuff. No, not Victoria's Secret types of things. I'm talking about characters you can't rightly type. For example, try finding a Tab character: You can't! Press the Tab key in the Find and Replace dialog box, and — whoops! — nothing happens. That result is because Tab and a few other keys are special, and you must force-feed them to the Find and Replace dialog box.

To find a special, unprintable character, click the More button to see the expanded Find and Replace dialog box (refer to Figure 5-3), and then click the Special button. Up pops a list of various characters Word can search for but that you would have a dickens of a time typing, as shown in Figure 5-4.

Choose one of the items from the list to search for that special character. When you do, a special, funky shorthand representation for that character (such as ^t for Tab) appears in the Find What box. Click the Find Next button to find that character.

Here are some of the most useful special characters available when you click the Special button in the Find and Replace dialog box:

- **Any Character, Any Digit, and Any Letter** are special characters that represent, well, just about anything. These buttons are used as wildcards for matching lots of stuff.

- **Caret Character** allows you to search for a caret (^) symbol, which is a special character. If you just type the caret symbol itself (^), Word thinks that you're trying to type another special character.

Paragraph Mark
Tab Character
Any Character
Any Digit
Any Letter
Caret Character
§ Section Character
¶ Paragraph Character
Column Break
Em Dash
En Dash
Endnote Mark
Field
Footnote Mark
Graphic
Manual Line Break
Manual Page Break
Nonbreaking Hyphen
Nonbreaking Space
Optional Hyphen
Section Break
White Space

Figure 5-4:
Items to search for that you can't type.

 ✔ **Paragraph Mark** (¶) is a special character that's the same as the Enter character — what you press to end a paragraph.

 ✔ **Tab Character** is the character that moves the cursor to the next tab mark.

 ✔ **White Space** is any blank character: a space or a tab, for example.

Yes, you can mix and match the special characters with other text you want to find. If you want to find a Tab character followed by *Hunter,* you use the Special button to insert the tab character (^t on the screen), and then you type **Hunter** using your fingers. It looks like this:

```
^tHunter
```

You don't have to use the Special pop-up menu, as long as you can remember the special characters. I do this all the time; because I know that ^p is the shortcut for the Enter key, I can just type it in and not have to bother with clicking the More button in the Find dialog box. Here's a handy shortcut list of the common special characters, in case you want to memorize them:

Paragraph mark	^p
Tab character	^t
Any character	^?
Any digit	^#
Any letter	^$
Caret character	^^
Manual line break	^l
Manual page break	^m
White space	^w

If you actually want to search for the paragraph character, ¶, then choose Paragraph Character. Otherwise, the Paragraph Mark item looks for those places where you've pressed the Enter key.

Finding formatting

The final and most insane thing the Find command can do for you is to find formatting codes laced throughout your document. For example, if you want to find only those instances of the word *lie* in boldface type, you can do that.

To find formatting stuff in a document, use the More part of the Find and Replace dialog box (refer to Figure 5-3). Click the Format button to see a pop-up list of formatting options in Word, as shown in Figure 5-5.

Figure 5-5:
Various
formatting
options to
search for.

Font...
Paragraph...
Tabs...
Language...
Frame...
Style...
Highlight

Each one of the menu items displays one of Word's formatting dialog boxes. Within those dialog boxes, you can select the formatting attributes to search for. You use the Font dialog box to select specific font formats to search for, and use the Style dialog box to search for text formatting using a specific style, for example. (Again, it helps if you know how Word uses these dialog boxes to format your text.)

Suppose that you want to find the bold-faced *lie* in your document. Follow these steps:

1. **Summon the Find and Replace dialog box.**

   Pressing Ctrl+F is the only sane way to do this step.

   Optionally, delete any previously searched-for text in the Find What text box. (The last text you searched for always hangs around, just in case you forget what you last found.)

2. **Type lie in the Find What box.**

   You're trying to find the word *lie,* but you want to also find that word formatted with bold text. You need to give *more* information:

3. **Click the More button to display the bottom part of the Find and Replace dialog box.**

   This step isn't necessary if the bottom part is already showing. (And we all know how embarrassing that can be.)

4. **If the No Formatting button is available, then click it.**

   This button is used to clear any previous formatting attributes you may have searched for. If the button can be clicked, click it to clear out those attributes and start over a-fresh.

5. **Click the Format button.**

6. **Choose Font from the list.**

   The Font dialog box appears, which is where you set or control various font attributes and such. Because the text you're searching for is bold, you need to apply the Bold formatting option in the Font dialog box.

7. **Choose Bold from the Font Style list.**

8. **Click OK.**

   The Font dialog box goes away, and you return to the Find and Replace dialog box.

   Notice the text just beneath the Find What box? It says `Format: Font: Bold`. That's telling you that Word is now geared up to find only bold text.

9. **Click the Find Next button to find your formatted text.**

   Word locates occurrences of the word *lie* that are formatted with bold type.

If you want to search for a format only, leave the Find What text box blank (refer to Step 2). That way you can search for text formatting attributes without caring what the text reads.

- ✔ You can use this technique to look for specific occurrences of a font, such as Courier or Times New Roman, by selecting the font from the selection list. Scroll through the font menu to see what you can choose.

- ✔ You can look for a particular size of type (24 point, for example) by selecting it from the Size list.

- ✔ You can also search for paragraph formatting by choosing Paragraph rather than Font from the Format pop-up list in the Find and Replace dialog box.

- ✔ The remaining options on the Format pop-up list are fairly obscure, although if you become fluent with Word, know that you can search for text formatting with those, well, whatever-they-ares.

- ✔ Many formatting searches require that you know a bit about how Word formats text, characters, and documents. I highly recommend that you familiarize yourself with the chapters in Part II of this book if you haven't yet done so.

- ✔ Word remembers your formatting options! When you go to search for non-formatted text, you need to click the No Formatting button. Doing so removes the formatting options and allows you to search for plain text again. After you forget this a few times, it really heats you up that Word cannot find your text. Do not forget to click the No Formatting button to return Word to normal text-finding mode!

Finding and Replacing

By itself, the Find command is really handy. But its true power lies in its ability to not only find text but also replace that text with something else. It's one of the word-processor features that helped put various typewriter companies out of business.

If you've mastered the Find command, your black belt in the Replace command is only a paragraph away. In fact, the only trouble you'll have with the Replace command is its shortcut key.

No, it's not R — the Ctrl+R shortcut command is used to right-align text in a paragraph. (Nice try, though.) Apparently, Microsoft thought that more folks out there would be desperate to right-align paragraphs than who would desire to search and replace.

Okay, just give up now. Every other word you can think of for *replace* (oust, relieve, substitute, zap) has a shortcut key of its own. So the shortcut key for the Replace command is . . . Ctrl+H!

Enough dallying. Suppose that you want to replace the word *pig* with *pork*. Both mean the same thing, but you don't eat pig, you eat pork — well, unless your religion forbids such things, in which case you eat chicken or one of the many delightful vegetarian dishes. Enough!

1. **Choose Edit⇨Replace.**

   Or, if you can remember what the Heck H stands for, type Ctrl+H. Honestly.

   The Replace part of the Find and Replace dialog box, shown in Figure 5-6, appears onscreen. This tab is another panel in the Find and Replace dialog box — which makes sense because finding is a big part of find and replace.

Figure 5-6:
The Replace
part of the
Find and
Replace
dialog box.

The Find and Replace dialog box also has a More button. If you see the More options, click the Less button to make your screen look like Figure 5-6. (Refer to the section "Finding more stuff," earlier in this chapter, for information on what those options mean; they all apply to finding and replacing.)

2. **In the Find What box, type the text you want to find.**

   This is the text you want to replace with something else.

   Press the Tab key when you're done typing.

3. **In the Replace With box, type the text you want to use to replace the original text.**

4. **Ask yourself, "Do I want a chance to change my mind before replacing each bit of found text?"**

   If so, click the Find Next button (taking this action is usually a good idea). If not, you can click the Replace All button; text is found and replaced automatically, giving you no chance to change your mind.

5. **If you click Find Next, Word pauses at each occurrence of the text.**

   The found text is highlighted onscreen just like in the regular Find task. When this highlighting happens, you can click the Replace button to replace it or click Find Next to skip it and find the next matching bit of text. Click the Cancel button or press the Escape key when you tire of this process.

   Word may find your text, such as *use,* in the middle of another word, such as *causes.* Oops! Click the More button and select the Find Whole Words Only option to prevent that from happening.

If there's nothing more to replace, Word (or the Office Assistant) lets you know. A summary of how many things were replaced is stated, which is for trivial purposes only. For example, the dog says:

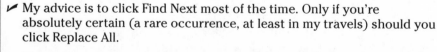

```
Word has completed its search of the document and has made 9
replacements.
```

Of course, the number of replacements depends on what you were searching for.

✔ If you don't type anything in the Replace With box . . . oops! Forgetting to type replacement text does not turn the Replace command into the Find command. No, Word just assumes that you want to find the text and replace it with *nothing.* Yup, that means deleting all the text that's found. This process can be a scary thing, so be sure to click Find Next. Otherwise, you may zap parts of your document and, boy, would you be bummed (until you used the Undo command).

✔ My advice is to click Find Next most of the time. Only if you're absolutely certain (a rare occurrence, at least in my travels) should you click Replace All.

✔ The Undo command restores your document to its preceding condition if you foul up the Replace operation.

✔ Having Ctrl+H be the shortcut key for the Replace command makes no sense to me. But diligent reader Robin R. has pointed out that the H key is right there with the F and G keys on the keyboard. It just so happens that Ctrl+F for Find, Ctrl+G for Go To, and Ctrl+H for Replace are the three commands represented in the Find and Replace dialog box. Clever.

Finding and Replacing Formatting

You can also use the Find and Replace dialog box to find and replace text formatting. This works similarly to the way the Find command can locate text formatting, but with the addition of a replacement format specified in the Replace With text box.

As an example, suppose you wanted all the text formatted with the Courier typeface to also be colored blue. To do that, first click the mouse in the Find What box, and then click the Format button and choose Font. In the Font dialog box, select Courier as the typeface.

Next, click the mouse in the Replace With box. Click the Format button and choose Font again. Because you're replacing Courier text with Courier-plus-blue text, choose both Courier from the font list and blue from the list of Font colors. Click OK to close the font dialog box.

Now the dialog box says that you're finding `Format: Font: Courier` and replacing it with `Format: Font: Courier, Font color: Blue`.

Finally, click the Find Next button to begin replacing text.

Needless to say, this is a tricky — nay, an "advanced" — aspect of using Word, so save your document before you try any formatting search and replacements.

Chapter 6

Working with Blocks of Text

*W*hat would writing be without blocks? No, I'm not talking about writer's block. That's the brain lock some people claim to have when they can't find the right word or when the opening paragraph of a chapter seems to elude them. It's a myth, in my opinion; writer's block is a catchy phrase and easier to blame than the fact your fingers just aren't doing what your brain wants.

In Word, though, a *block* is a piece of text. Word lets you rope off a chunk of text — words, sentences, paragraphs, or the whole document — and then do fun and interesting things with that block of text. This chapter is all about those blocky things. Hey! It's time to play with blocks, boys and girls!

Marking Blocks of Text

A seasoned and famous writer once told me to triple-space everything, to type on thick, 20-pound paper, and to keep scissors and rubber cement handy to help me rearrange and edit. After all, he boasted, cutting and pasting your text beats typing it over and over again. The writer was Jerry Pournelle, award-winning science fiction and technology writer, and his advice was true in 1978, but it's nuts today.

Word lets you do numerous things with blocks of text. And you don't have to worry about triple-spacing, typing on 20-pound paper, or even spending $1.29 for the industrial-size vat of rubber cement. Instead, you need to know how to mark the block. As usual, Word offers you several trillion ways to do this. I describe some of those methods here, each of which is well suited for marking different-size chunks of text.

A Shifty way to mark tiny bits of text

To quickly mark a small chunk of text — a word, line, or paragraph — you can use the Shift key in combination with any of the arrow keys (also known as cursor-movement keys). This technique is best suited to marking a small slab of text onscreen. Let Table 6-1 be your guide.

Table 6-1	Shifty Selection Wizardry
To Do This	*Press This*
Select a character at a time to the right of the toothpick cursor	Shift+→
Select a character at a time to the left of the toothpick cursor	Shift+←
Select a block of text from the toothpick cursor to the end of the line	Shift+End
Select a block of text from the toothpick cursor to the beginning of the line	Shift+Home
Select a block of text from the toothpick cursor to a line above	Shift+↑
Select a block of text from the toothpick cursor to a line below	Shift+↓

Some thoughts on using the Shift key to select text:

- ✔ Either Shift key works.

- ✔ Using the Shift key is handy for marking small bits of text. There are better ways, however, of marking blocks larger than a line or two.

- ✔ Refer to Chapter 3 for more information about cursor-movement keys.

- ✔ I use the left Shift key and then work the arrow keys on the right side of the keyboard. If you can train yourself to work that way also, you can get quite deft at these Shift+arrow-key selection methods.

✔ If you use the Shift key to mark to the end of a paragraph, note that the Enter keypress (marking the end of the paragraph) is also selected. That means if you delete or reformat the block, it may also change the formatting of the next paragraph. To avoid that, press Shift+← to back up and not select the Enter keypress at the end of the paragraph.

Marking a block with your mouse

Mickey may have been born to rule a kingdom, but your computer's mouse was born to select text. Seriously! Outside of fine-tuning graphics, computer mice are the darlings of the text-selecting world.

It's a drag to select text

To best select a block of text with your mouse, follow these rodent-like steps:

1. **Position the mouse pointer where you want the block to start.**

2. **Hold down the left mouse button and drag the mouse over your text.**

   As you drag, the text becomes highlighted, or selected, as shown in Figure 6-1. Drag the mouse from the beginning to the end of the text you want to mark as a block.

3. **Release the mouse — stop the dragging — to mark your block's end.**

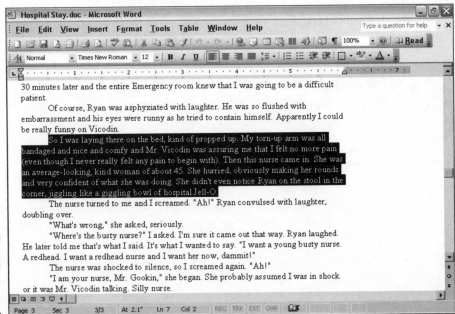

Figure 6-1:
A block of text is selected.

You can select a chunk of text of any size with a mouse. However, my advice is to select only as much text as you can see on the screen at one time. If you try to select text beyond what you see on the screen, you have to select and scroll — which can be unwieldy; the mouse scrolls the text up and down quickly, and, well, things get out of hand.

Quick-click mouse techniques to mark your text

Table 6-2 tells you how to put your roborodent to work selecting specific-size chunks of stuff.

Table 6-2	Mouse Selection Arcana
To Accomplish This	*Perform This Bit of Mouse Magic*
Select a word	Point at the word with your mouse and double-click.
Select a line	Move the mouse into the left margin beside the line you want to select. The mouse pointer changes to a northeasterly-pointing arrow. Click the mouse to select a line of text, or drag the mouse to select several lines.
Select a sentence	Point the mouse at the sentence and Ctrl+click; press the Ctrl key and click the mouse. The sentence is selected.
Select a paragraph	Point the mouse somewhere in the paragraph's midst and triple-click.

The old poke-and-point method of selecting

A final technique I use to select a block of text of any size with the mouse is what I call the poke-and-point technique:

1. **Start by positioning the toothpick cursor where you want the block to start — the anchor point.**

2. **Scroll through your document using the scroll bar.**

   You must use the scroll bar to scroll through your document. If you use the cursor-movement keys, you reposition the toothpick cursor, which isn't what you want.

3. **To mark the end of the block, press and hold the Shift key and click the mouse where you want the block to end.**

   The text from the toothpick cursor to wherever you clicked the mouse is selected as a block.

Would you rather select text by letter or by word?

When selecting text with the mouse, note that the mouse tends to grab your stuff a word at a time. If you'd rather have Word select text by characters instead of words (which is what I prefer), then follow these steps:

1. **Choose Tools⇨Options from the menu.**

2. **Click the Edit tab.**

3. **Remove the check mark by the item When Selecting, Automatically Select Entire Word.**

4. **Click OK.**

This method works well for selecting a chunk of text of any size, especially when you need to scroll the document to mark the block's end.

Using the miraculous F8 key to mark a block

Who in their right mind would assign the F8 key to mean "select text?" Probably the same gang of microbrew-swilling, Volvo-driving, stock-option-obsessed people at Microsoft who brought you the F12 key. Remember F12? Probably not, because it's too obscure to mention, but it's the Save As key command. Weird? Hey, you ain't seen weird yet.

If you can find room in your skull to remember the F8 key, you can put it to good use. F8 selects text in unique chunks, unavailable with other commands. What follows is a small sampling of what it does best.

Select a word. Pressing the F8 key twice selects a word. But, honestly, if you're going to point at the word to move the toothpick cursor there anyway, you may as well go ahead and double-click the word to select it.

Select a sentence. Position the toothpick cursor in a sentence and then press the F8 key three times to select the sentence.

Select a paragraph. Position the toothpick cursor in a paragraph and then press the F8 key four times to select the whole paragraph.

Select your document. Pressing the F8 key five times selects your entire document, but there's a better way to do that as well, which is covered in the section, "Marking the whole dang-doodle document," later in this document.

Oh! And pressing the F8 key only one time? Does that order you a new cup of coffee? Turn on WebTV? Activate Voice mode? Nope! Keep reading in the next section to learn the awful secret.

Dropping anchor with the F8 key

What the F8 key does is place Word into handy (but potentially annoying) Extended Selection mode. In this mode, the F8 key "drops anchor" on one end of a block. You can then use the cursor keys, the mouse, or even a letter key to continue marking the block. However — and this is most important — the entire time you're in Extended Selection mode, you cannot use Word for anything other than selecting a block.

Don't let this annoy you! Sure, it may confuse you at times, but using the F8 key in Extended Selection mode is the best way to select a chunk of text spanning more than one screen.

Heed these steps to use Extended Selection mode:

1. **Position the toothpick cursor at the start of the block of text you want to mark.**

2. **Press the F8 key.**

   The F8 key drops anchor, marking one end of the block.

   Notice the three letters EXT on the status bar? This is an important hint. You're now in Extended Selection mode, and the keys on your keyboard serve to select text, not to write anything. Beware!

3. **Select the block of text.**

   You can select the block of text by using the arrow keys or any of the cursor-navigation keys discussed in Chapter 3.

   You can also press a letter key to select text up to and including that letter. If you press N, you select all text up to and including the next *N* in your document. Nice. Nifty. Bitchen.

   Word highlights text from the point where you dropped anchor with F8 to wherever you move the toothpick cursor (refer to Figure 6-1). Text appears in white-on-black.

4. **After the block is marked, you're ready to do something with it.**

5. **Do something with the selected block of text.**

This is the annoying part. After you mark a block, you *must* perform some block command. See the status bar? The EXT is still highlighted. You're still marking a block! So unless you copy, cut, paste, spell check, or do something else, you're still in block-marking mode.

If you want to cancel the extended selection, press the Esc key. Or, you can double-click EXT on the status bar (which forces you to pay attention to EXT so that it doesn't frustrate you later).

✔ You can use the mouse and the F8 key to get really fancy. Position the cursor at either end of the block you want to mark and press the F8 key. Then position the mouse cursor at the other end of the block and press the left mouse button. Everything from there to there is marked.

✔ No matter how many times you press F8, be aware that it always drops anchor. If you press it twice or thrice (see the preceding section), F8 marks a chunk of text — but you're still in Extended Selection mode. Do something with the block or press Esc to cancel that mode.

✔ Get used to using the keyboard commands to block your text, and you will be much happier, believe me.

Selecting more than one chunk of text

It's possible, though not really practical, to select more than one bit of text as a block. For example, you can select a group of names from a document as a block, even though the names aren't all in the same place. Figure 6-2 shows this feature in action.

Figure 6-2:
Selecting
multiple
blocks.

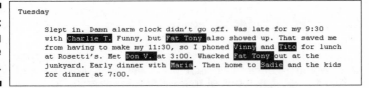

```
Tuesday

     Slept in. Damn alarm clock didn't go off. Was late for my 9:30
with Charlie T. Funny, but Fat Tony also showed up. That saved me
from having to make my 11:30, so I phoned Vinny and Tito for lunch
at Rosetti's. Met Don V. at 3:00. Whacked Fat Tony out at the
junkyard. Early dinner with Maria. Then home to Sadie and the kids
for dinner at 7:00.
```

To select multiple chunks of text in a single document, you need two tools: the mouse and the Ctrl key on your keyboard. Follow these steps:

1. **Initially select a block of text.**

   You can use any of the block-marking techniques covered earlier in this chapter.

2. **Press and hold the Ctrl key.**

   You can use either Ctrl key on your keyboard.

3. **Drag the mouse to select an additional block of text.**

   Keep repeating this step to select additional blocks of text.

Note that each block of text is separate. Only the text highlighted on the screen is contained in the block. The text between, which is unselected, is not part of the block. The secret is pressing and holding the Ctrl key while you drag with the mouse.

The text you select this way is still considered by Word as a single block; it's just that the text is culled from several locations in your document. If you cut the text, it all disappears from the various places you've selected. Pasting the text back into the document pastes each separate chunk as a paragraph of text.

Note that some block commands will not work when text is selected in this fashion.

Marking the whole dang-doodle document

To mark everything in your document as a block, choose Edit⇨Select All. The Windows key equivalent for the Select All command is Ctrl+A.

In Word, you can also use the obscure Ctrl+5 (the 5 on the numeric keypad) key combo or whack the F8 key five times.

Naaaa: Just press Ctrl+A to mark the whole thing.

Deselecting a Block

Now that you have a block marked, uh, what were you going to do with it? And how do you go back to Normal mode, getting rid of the highlighted block so that you can actually type something? Frustrated? Be no more!

Here are some handy ways to deselect that pesky block of highlighted text:

- ✔ **Press the ← key.** This action unhighlights the block and returns the toothpick cursor to the point where the block started, or to the top of your document if you selected the whole document. This technique works for stuff you've selected with the mouse or with the Shift key.

- ✔ **Click the mouse.** This method deselects the block and puts the tooth-pick cursor wherever you click. This method works for selections made with the mouse or with the Shift key.

- ✔ **Press the Esc key and then the ← key.** This method works when you're using the Extended Selection command (the F8 key or the EXT button on the status bar — remember?).

> ✔ **Don't forget the Shift+F5 command!** Pressing this key combo not only deselects the block (whether you selected it with the mouse, the Shift key, or the F8 key) but also returns you to the text you were editing before making the selection. Nifty!

Copying a Block

After a block is marked, you can copy it into another part of your document. The original block remains untouched by this operation. Follow these steps to copy a block of text from one place to another:

1. **Mark the block.**

   Detailed instructions about doing this task are offered in the first part of this chapter.

2. **Choose Edit⇨Copy.**

Word places a copy of the marked block in the Clipboard — a storage area for text or graphics that you cut or copy. To complete the copy operation, all you have to do is paste the block, which is covered in the section "Pasting a Block," later in this chapter.

> ✔ The shortcut key for copying in Word (and Windows) is Ctrl+C.
>
> ✔ You can also click the Copy tool on the toolbar to copy a selected block of text.
>
> ✔ If you accidentally press Ctrl+C twice to copy a block, you might see the Clipboard view pane. You can find more information on this topic in the section "Copying Multiple Blocks (Collect and Paste)," later in this chapter.
>
> ✔ Also refer to the section "Copying Multiple Blocks (Collect and Paste)" for more information about the Clipboard.

Moving a Block

To move a block of text, you cut and paste it. This is Microsoft terminology, not mine. Traditionally, word processors move blocks of text. Cutting and pasting is what kids do in school. But I digress.

Moving a block of text works like copying a block except that you use the Ctrl+X (or Edit⇨Cut) command rather than Ctrl+C. The selected block of text disappears. Well, actually, it goes into the Clipboard. But from there, you can paste it anywhere else in your document.

Don't be alarmed when the block disappears. Remember, this is a move operation; the original block will be put somewhere else (as covered in the next section).

- ✔ You can use the Cut tool on the toolbar to move a block of text.
- ✔ Additional information about marking a block is in the first two sections of this chapter.
- ✔ The Ctrl+Z Undo shortcut undoes a block move.
- ✔ After you cut and move a block, you can paste it into your document a second time. This subject is covered in the next section, "Pasting a Block."

Pasting a Block

After you've copied or cut a block of text, the next step is to paste that chunk of text. It doesn't matter whether the block was copied or cut; pasting works the same for both. Follow these steps:

1. **Move the cursor to the position where you want the block.**

   Don't worry if there isn't any room there! Word inserts the block into your text just as though you had typed it yourself.

2. **Choose Edit⇨Paste.**

   And there is the block again.

When you paste text in Word, the Paste Options icon appears near the end of the pasted text, as shown in the margin. Do not be alarmed. That button allows you to select formatting for the pasted block because occasionally the block may contain formatting that, well, looks very ugly after you paste in the text.

Using the Paste Options icon is utterly optional. In fact, you can continue typing or working in Word, and the icon instantly disappears. But if you want to adjust the pasted text's formatting, follow these steps:

1. **Point the mouse at the Paste Options icon.**

   The icon turns into a "button," with a downward-pointing triangle on one end. If you've been using Windows for any length of time, you'll recognize this as a drop-down menu gizmo.

2. **Click the downward-pointing triangle.**

   A menu appears, from which you can select various formatting options (see Figure 6-3).

Figure 6-3:
Various
Paste
command
formatting
options.

Here's a quick summary of the options available:

✔ **Keep Source Formatting:** The formatting is fine; don't do a thing.

✔ **Match Destination Formatting:** Reformat the pasted block so that it looks like the text it's been pasted into.

✔ **Keep Text Only:** Just paste in the text. No formatting.

✔ **Apply Style or Formatting:** Display the view pane with various text and styles and other stuff to junk up the screen.

Choose an option to match the formatting you want. I can recommend either the first or second choices. The last one is definitely opening the door to the land of the strange and ugly.

✔ You can also use the Ctrl+V shortcut to paste a block of text.

✔ Oh, and you can click the Paste tool to paste a copied or cut block of text. Decisions, decisions. . . .

✔ The Paste Options icon generally doesn't go away until you start typing new text or use some other text-editing command.

✔ If you tire of the Paste Options button, you can turn off that feature: Choose Tools➪Options and select the Edit tab. Remove the check mark next to the Show Paste Options Buttons item. Click OK.

✔ After you copy a block, you can paste it into your document a second time. That's because whenever a block of text is cut or copied, Word remembers it. You can yank that block into your document again at any time — sort of like pasting text again after it's already been pasted in. You use Ctrl+V, the Paste shortcut. Pasting text again simply pastes down a second copy of the block, spit-spot (as Mary Poppins would say).

✔ You can even paste the block into another document you're working on, or into another application. (This is a Windows trick, which most good books on Windows discuss.)

More than pasting, it's special pasting!

When Word pastes text into your document, it does so by pasting it in fully formatted and with all the bells and whistles. You can override this setting by choosing one of the options from the Paste Options icon. Or, you can just tell Word *how* to paste your text before you paste it, by using the Edit⇨Paste Special command.

The Paste Special command may not be readily visible on the Edit menu. To see it, click the down arrow at the bottom of the Edit menu. This action displays the full menu, complete with lots of options you'll probably never use. Among them, you'll find Paste Special.

Choosing the Paste Special command displays the Paste Special dialog box, which lists several options for pasting in the text: Document Object,

Formatting Text, Unformatting Text, Picture, and so on. Each of these items tells Word how to paste in the information. To discover what each option does, select it from the list and read the description in the Result area of the dialog box.

For example, when I want to paste in text from a Web page but don't want all that HTML-blah-blah formatting, I use the Paste Special command and choose the Unformatted Text option. I click OK, and the text is pasted into Word as plain text and not as some Web object.

By the way, this dialog box is how Word pastes in links to other Office applications, such as an Excel spreadsheet or information from Access. To link the pasted object, choose the Object item from the list.

Copying or Moving a Block with the Mouse

If you have to move a block only a short distance, you can use the mouse to drag-move or drag-copy the block. This feature is handy, but usually works best if you're moving or copying between two locations you can see right on the screen. Otherwise, you're scrolling your document with the mouse, which is like trying to grab an angry snake.

 To move any selected block of text with the mouse, just point and drag the block: Point the mouse cursor anywhere in the blocked text, and then drag the block to its new location. Notice how the mouse pointer changes, as shown in the margin. That means you're dragging and copying text.

 Copying a block with the mouse works just like moving the block, though you press the Ctrl key as you drag. When you do that, a plus sign appears in the mouse pointer (see the margin). That's your sign that the block is being copied and not just moved.

- ✔ The Paste Options icon appears after you've "dropped" the chunk of text. Refer to the preceding section for more information on the Paste Options icon.

- ✔ When you drag a block of text with the mouse, you're not copying it to the Clipboard. You cannot use the Paste (Ctrl+V) command to paste in the block again.

- ✔ A *linked copy* is created by dragging a selected block of text with the mouse and holding down *both* the Shift and Ctrl keys. When you release the mouse button, the copied block plops down into your document looking very ugly:

```
{LINK Word.Document.1 "Document2" "OLE_LINK2" \a \r}
```

Gadzooks! This advanced feature of Word (hence that techy guy in the margin) links the copied block to the original so that a change to one affects both. They made it ugly so that, like Medusa, you would avoid it and not want to look at it. Better save this trick for the advanced Word book I haven't written yet.

Copying and Moving with the F2 key

Another way to move or copy a block is to use the F2 key after you select the block. This can be very handy, but it works best if you're copying or cutting and pasting immediately. If you need to copy, work, and then paste later, use Ctrl+C and then Ctrl+V. Otherwise the F2 key works like this:

1. **Select a block of text.**

2. **Press the F2 key.**

   Notice how the status bar says, "Move to where?"

3. **Move to where you want to paste.**

   Use the cursor keys or scroll with the mouse. Wherever you move the toothpick cursor will be where the text is pasted.

4. **Press Enter to paste the text.**

   And the block is moved.

To copy a block instead of move, press Shift+F2 in Step 2.

If you select a chunk of text with the mouse before Step 4, the block you're pasting will replace that chunk of text.

Copying Multiple Blocks (Collect and Paste)

One of Word's nifty features is the ability to store more than one cut or copied block of text in the Clipboard at a time. So you can cut, cut, cut or copy, copy, copy and then pick and choose which of those blocks you want pasted back into your document. They call it "collect and paste," and I firmly believe that this is a handy and welcome feature — but one that also takes a bit of explaining.

The Clipboard can hold blocks of text large and small. But, normally, the Clipboard holds only one item at a time.

Looking at the Clipboard

You can view items copied or cut by peering into Word's special Clipboard. Here's how:

1. **Summon the task pane.**

   If the task pane isn't already visible (on the right side of the document area, as shown back in Figure 1-3), choose View⇨Task Pane.

2. **View the Clipboard task pane.**

   Click the downward-pointing triangle in the task pane. Choose Clipboard from the menu. The Clipboard task pane appears, as shown in Figure 6-4.

The scrolling list contains the last several items you've copied, not only from Word but from other programs as well.

Pasting items from the Clipboard is covered in the next section.

   ✔ The Clipboard can hold only 24 items. If any more than that are copied or cut, the older items in the list are "pushed off" to make room for the new ones. The current number of items is shown at the top of the task pane.

   ✔ Other programs in Microsoft Office (Excel and PowerPoint, for example) also share this collect-and-paste feature.

   ✔ You can close the task pane when you're done with collect and paste: Click the X in the upper-right corner of the task pane window.

Figure 6-4:
The
Clipboard
task pane.

Pasting from the Clipboard

To paste any collected text in the Clipboard, click that chunk of text with the mouse. The text is copied from the Clipboard to the toothpick cursor's location in your document.

To paste in everything in the Clipboard — all that stuff — click the Paste All button. Thwap! Everything is pasted into your document at once.

It's possible to pick and choose what you paste. For example, position the toothpick cursor and choose a specific item to paste. Then move the toothpick cursor and paste in something else. You can paste like this all day as long as the Clipboard task pane is visible.

After pasting, the Paste Options icon appears next to the pasted text. Refer to the section "Pasting a Block," earlier in this chapter, for what do to with that thing.

Cleansing the Clipboard

You're free to clean up Word's Clipboard whenever the Clipboard task pane is visible. To remove a single item, point the mouse at that item and click the downward-pointing triangle (refer to Figure 6-4). Choose Delete from the shortcut menu, and that one item is zapped from the Clipboard.

How to get rid of writer's block

I don't have writer's block. I don't even know what it is, though I can imagine. That's because I know the secret to getting rid of writer's block. Like all deep truths and wisdom, foolish people will scoff at this advice. They'll mock it. But the wise writer will understand the meaning and press on to write more and more stuff without ever sitting and drooling at the screen.

The secret to getting rid of writer's block? *Lower your standards.* If you can't get the words on the page, then you're shooting higher than your talent can reach.

Don't think it's for a lack of talent that you have writer's block; it's merely that you haven't yet learned to exploit your talent at the level it works best. Therefore, lower your standards. You'll find that you will not only be more prolific, but your stuff will read better as well.

Hey: It's all in your head, isn't it?

To whack all the items on the Clipboard, click the Clear All button at the top of the Clipboard task pane. I do this if I plan on collecting several items to be pasted at once elsewhere. For example, I click Clear All and then go out and copy, copy, copy. Then I move the toothpick cursor to where I want everything pasted and click the Paste All button, and I'm done.

Note that you cannot undo any clearing or deleting done in the Clipboard task pane. Be careful!

Other Things to Do with Your Blocks

There are hat blocks, engine blocks, building blocks, mental blocks, nerve blocks, down-blocks, and finally blocks of text. I don't know about the other things, but when you have a block of text, you can do any of a number of things to it. The command you use affects only the text within that block.

Aside from using the Copy, Cut, and Paste commands, you can do the following with a block of text in Word:

- ✔ Format the block (see Part II).
- ✔ Use the Replace command to find and replace only in the block of text (refer to Chapter 5).
- ✔ Print the block (see Chapter 9).
- ✔ Delete the block with the Delete or Backspace keys.

Chapter 7

How to Doing Your Speling and Grammer

Mark Twain put it best when he described spelling in the English language as "drunken." Specifically, Twain blamed the alphabet. And why not? Without the alphabet, we wouldn't have to spell. We'd use pictograms like the ancient Egyptians or Chinese. Ever see a Chinese spelling bee? It goes like this: The host says, "Spell 大." And the little girl says, "大" Then everyone claps.

Specifically I think vowels are the problem. But whatever you think, the solution is to use Word's automatic spell checker, which deftly slashes suspect expressions and quickly suggests potential replacements. Coupled with that is the grammar checker or "proofer" that flags common English language blunders and boo-boos that would make any seventh grade English teacher blanch.

This chapter covers Word's amazing spell checker, grammar proofer, plus a number of other interesting language tools and tidbits, some of which will even fool the experts into thinking you're a better writer than you really is.

Automatic spell-checking doesn't work!

In a few instances, automatic spell-checking doesn't seem to work. If that happens to you, try these things:

First, check to ensure that on-the-fly spell checking is activated. See the nearby section "Let's turn this on (or off)."

Second, go visit the Options dialog box: Choose Tools⇨Options. Click the Spelling & Grammar tab. If a check mark is by the Hide Spelling Errors in This Document item, click to remove it. Click OK.

Third, your document may be formatted by an older version of Word with "no proofing" language. To solve that problem, select your entire document by pressing Ctrl+A. Then choose Tools⇨Language⇨Set Language. In the Language dialog box, choose English (US) (for the United States). Also confirm that the check box is empty near the bottom, where it says, Do Not Check Spelling or Grammar. Click OK. This should reactivate the on-the-fly spell-checking.

Ewe Spell Grate

It's widely known that word processors come with the ability to flag incorrectly spelled or otherwise suspect words. Heck, even your e-mail program does that (and if not, you haven't upgraded to the latest version).

Today's computers are so fast that they can catch a misspelled word or awkward grammar the instant you type it. In some cases, the boo-boo is corrected automatically. Ta-da. In other cases, it's underlined with Word's wiggly pen — red ink for bad spelling or green ink for ugly grammar. Don't let this intrusion of linguistic propriety vex you! Instead, peruse the next few sections to learn the ways of Word's spell checker in depth.

Word's spell checker instantly tells you whether it recognizes a word. It does not, however, tell you whether the word is properly used. Just because a document contains no misspelled words doesn't mean that the document is perfect.

Let's turn this on (or off)

To ensure that Word automatically checks your typing, choose Tools⇨Options from the menu. Click the Spelling & Grammar tab, which is shown in Figure 7-1.

Look up top for the Check Spelling as You Type option. A check mark by that option means that Word's automatic spell-checking has been activated.

Figure 7-1:
Various
spelling and
grammar
options.

If you detest automatic spell checking, you can click in the box to remove the check mark. Word no longer annoys you with red wiggly-underline text, though you can still use the Tools⇨Spelling and Grammar command to check your document at any time.

Click OK to dismiss the Options dialog box.

The automatic spell checker in action

Word automatically checks everything you type as you type it. Make a boo-boo, and Word lets you know. The second you press the spacebar or type some punctuation character, Word examines what you typed and immediately flags it as wrong, wrong, wrong. It does this by underlining the word using a red zigzag pattern. See Figure 7-2 for a sampling.

Figure 7-2:
The word
tobbaco is
flagged as
misspelled.

"Don't touch it!"
      "What? Huh? Why not," Wayne asked, backing away from the body.
      "What did you jest shoot?" Red asked, plugging a large piece of tobacco chew inside his cheek.
      Wayne looked at the dead man. It was a hideous corpse, stinking with rotting flesh and a perverse moistness that made his gut wrench. "It's a freaking corpse, Red!"
      "Yup." Red rolled the tobbaco around in his mouth. Then he spit out a long, greasy streamer. "You shot a dead corpse, Wayne. It was dead when it was walking toward you, and it's dead now."
      "So?"
      "So if it could get up and walk before, why isn't it moving now?"
      Wayne hadn't thought of that. As he looked at the downed corpse again, he noticed it wasn't motionless like he thought. It was rousing like a drunk after a hangover. The thing was getting up. Slowly.

Un-adding words to the dictionary

Over time, you find yourself adding lots of words to the dictionary — words that you know are spelled correctly but that the dictionary doesn't recognize. You know: street names, cities, relatives, alien names, and stuff like that. Word stores those added words in what's called the Custom dictionary.

The Custom dictionary is not something you normally mess with, which is why I'm talking about it here, in a techy sidebar. But I do occasionally get e-mail from readers who desperately need to delete a word they accidentally added to the Custom dictionary. Oops. When that happens, you need to access the Custom dictionary to remove the improperly added word. Here's how:

1. **Choose Tools➪Options from the menu.**

2. **In the Options dialog box, click the Spelling & Grammar tab.**

3. **Click the Custom Dictionaries button.**

   This step displays a list of all custom dictionaries you may have. Most likely, only one is on the list, CUSTOM.DIC.

4. **Select the CUSTOM.DIC dictionary file and click the Modify button.**

   You see a scrolling list of words you've previously added to the Custom dictionary. You can delete any of those words by selecting the word and then clicking the Delete button.

   (You can also add words here by typing the word into the Word text box and then clicking the Add button.)

   When you're done, keep clicking the various OK buttons until all the dialog boxes have gone away and you're back to using Word.

My advice: Keep typing. Don't let the "red zigzag of a failed elementary education" tweak you. It's more important to get your thoughts up on the screen than to stop and fuss over inevitable typos. (Besides, I show you a trick in the next section to automatically correct your more common mistakes.)

When you're ready, go back and fix your spelling errors. I do this every two or three paragraphs:

1. **Find the misspelled word.**

   Look for the red underline.

2. **Right-click on the misspelled word.**

   This step pops up a shortcut menu, similar to the one shown in Figure 7-3.

3. **Choose from the list the word you intended to type.**

   In Figure 7-3, the word *tobacco* fits the bill. Click that word, and it's automatically inserted into your document, replacing the bogus word.

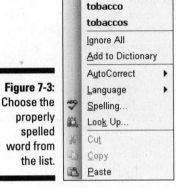

Figure 7-3:
Choose the
properly
spelled
word from
the list.

tobacco
tobaccos
Ignore All
Add to Dictionary
AutoCorrect ▶
Language ▶
Spelling...
Look Up...
Cut
Copy
Paste

If the word you intended to type isn't on the list, don't fret. Word isn't *that* smart. You may have to use a real dictionary or take another stab at spelling the word phonetically and correct it again.

A faster way to spell-check ("So now he tells me!")

One of the easiest ways to breeze through a document and check your spelling is to double-click the Spell icon on the status bar (near the bottom of Word's window). As you double-click, you're taken to the next spelling (or grammatical) error, and the pop-up window (Figure 7-3) is displayed to show your options.

What to do when the spell checker stupidly assumes a word is misspelled, but in fact it isn't

Word's spell checker only knows so many words. Occasionally it bumps into a word it doesn't know, such as your last name or perhaps your city. When such a word is encountered, and you're certain that it's spelled correctly, you have two options, both of which are found on the pop-up menu when you right-click the word (refer to Figure 7-3).

Ignore All. Select this item if the word is properly spelled and you don't want Word to keep flagging it as misspelled. For example, suppose the little boy really does say "pasgetty" instead of "spaghetti." In that case, you can ignore all the "pasgetty" words in your document.

Add to Dictionary. This item is used to add commonly used words to Word's dictionary. For example, my last name is Gookin, which Word thinks is a misspelling of the word *Goofing.* No, no, no. So I click the Add to Dictionary menu item to insert the word *Gookin* into Word's internal dictionary. I'll never have to spell check that work again.

- ✔ The Ignore All command ignores spelling mistakes for a certain word only in the document you're editing. If you want to ignore the word forevermore, choose the Add to Dictionary command to add the word to Word's this-is-spelled-okay list.

- ✔ If the word looks right but is red-wiggly-underlined anyway, it may be a repeated word. Those are flagged as misspelled by Word, so you can either choose to delete the repeated word or just ignore it.

The Joys of AutoCorrect

There are some words that you just cannot misspell in Word. Take the word *misspell,* as an example.

If you try to type in *mispell* (with only one *S*), Word automatically corrects what you've typed back in to the more proper *misspell.* It's miraculous! Either that, or it's just Word's AutoCorrect feature in action.

AutoCorrect keeps track of commonly misspelled words in its internal dictionary. Words such as *often, achieve, brief, receive,* and many others are commonly misspelled in English. They're common typos that AutoCorrect fixes for you without the need to click the mouse.

Finally, if that weren't enough, Word lets you add your own special list of words to the AutoCorrect repertoire. For example, if you often type *ecxuse* rather than *excuse,* you can tell — nay, *order* — Word to always AutoCorrect it for you. The following sections tell you how.

Activating AutoCorrect

Word's AutoCorrect feature only works when it's on. To ensure that it's on and working, follow these steps:

1. Choose Tools⇨AutoCorrect Options from the menu.

The AutoCorrect dialog box appears, as shown in Figure 7-4.

Figure 7-4:
The
AutoCorrect
dialog box.

2. **Ensure that there is a check mark by Replace Text as You Type.**

   That activates AutoCorrect. Likewise, removing the check mark disables AutoCorrect.

3. **Click OK.**

Now AutoCorrect is ready for action.

Using AutoCorrect

There's nothing to using AutoCorrect; it happens automatically. The only trick is how to add your own slate of words to AutoCorrect's list. That's easy.

To throw any misspelled word into the AutoCorrect bin, right-click on the word. Rather than choose the proper spelling from the menu, choose the AutoCorrect item. Up pops a submenu containing various corrections, as shown in Figure 7-5. Choose the properly spelled word from the submenu that appears. That word is then added to AutoCorrect's list, and as a special favor, Word corrects the word in your text as well.

If possible, try to add only lowercase words with AutoCorrect. For example, Figure 7-5 shows the word *Werd* being added; *Werd* will be corrected to *Word*. It would be better, however, to add the word *werd,* with no capital letters. That way, AutoCorrect fixes all variations of *werd,* upper- or lowercase.

Figure 7-5:
Auto-
Correcting
a werd.

Undoing AutoCorrect's correction

If AutoCorrect makes a change you don't like, you can undo it. Pressing the Ctrl+Z shortcut for the Undo command right after you see the automatically corrected text does the trick.

If you press the Backspace key instead of Ctrl+Z to undo an AutoCorrected word, a small, blue rectangle appears under the word. Point the mouse at that rectangle to see the AutoCorrect Options icon. Clicking the downward-pointing arrow on the icon displays some choices (see Figure 7-6) because Word is concerned about why you wanted to erase the AutoCorrection.

Figure 7-6:
Adjusting
an Auto-
Correction.

You can undo your undo by selecting the first menu item, Change Back to [whatever]. Whew.

Choosing the second item removes the word from AutoCorrect's repertoire, which is good if you don't like the correction.

The final option displays the AutoCorrect dialog box, shown in Figure 7-4. From there, you can make further adjustments, if needed. (These are covered later in this chapter.)

Click anywhere else in your document or press the Esc key to hide the pop-up AutoCorrect Options menu.

Other AutoCorrect tricks

Try typing the following line in Word:

```
Copyright (C) 2001 Sterling Worbletyme Inc.
```

When you type the (C), Word automatically converts it into the © copyright symbol. That's also a function of AutoCorrect in action.

Try this one too:

```
Look at the ugly picture of Paul-->
```

The —> turns into a right-pointing arrow.

And then there's the ever-popular:

```
I'm sorry about the cat. :-)
```

See how the :-) turns into a ☺.

If you don't like the change, then press Ctrl+Z to undo or use Backspace to fix the AutoCorrect option.

Then there's the joy of AutoText

Another Word trick that works like AutoCorrect is AutoText. Unlike AutoCorrect, which rewrites text you may misspell, AutoText *finishes* writing words you start to spell.

As an example, try to type the following line in Word:

```
Ladies and Gentlemen:
```

When you get to about the *i* in *Ladies,* a box of text appears above the tooth-pick cursor. It says `Ladies and Gentlemen: (Press ENTER to Insert).` That's AutoText in action. Press the Enter key to have Word complete the tidbit of text for you.

Word has a swarm of AutoText items, from the current date to your name to most common salutations and closings. Like AutoCorrect, you can add your own AutoText entries. Keep reading!

Reviewing your AutoCorrect and AutoText settings

You can check out the AutoCorrect and AutoText vocabularies, because either you're curious or you want to remove or add words or phrases. To do this, you must summon the AutoCorrect dialog box: Choose Tools⇨AutoCorrect Options, as described earlier in this chapter (refer to Figure 7-4).

You find the AutoCorrect settings under the AutoCorrect tab. The top part of the dialog box (refer to Figure 7-4) lists options for fixing common boo-boos and typos. The bottom part of the dialog box contains a scrolling list of AutoCorrect entries, plus a place for you to create your own AutoCorrect items.

The following sections assume that the AutoCorrect dialog box is open and ready for business.

Manually adding an AutoCorrect entry

On the AutoCorrect tab in the AutoCorrect dialog box, you can manually create your own entries by using the Replace and With boxes:

- ✔ Typos and misspellings go in the Replace box.
- ✔ The correct word goes into the With box. (Choose Plain Text to ensure that your formatting stays okay.)
- ✔ Click the Add button to add an entry.
- ✔ Click OK to close the AutoCorrect dialog box when you're done.

Being cruel with AutoCorrect is entirely possible. For example, inserting a meanie like *thier* for *their* would drive some people nuts. Remember, AutoCorrect is subtle. If you type looking at the keyboard rather than the screen, you never know what it's up to.

Removing unwanted AutoCorrect entries

To remove an item from AutoCorrect, locate it on the list. For example, AutoCorrect lists *hda* as a correction for *had,* but you're working on a project named HDA and you don't want it corrected to *had* every time you type it.

When you find the offending spelling on the list, position the mouse pointer over it and click to select it and then click the Delete button. The offender is gone.

Click OK to close the AutoCorrect dialog box when your destructive urges have been quenched.

Adding a new AutoText entry

To add a new AutoText entry (remember, that's where Word finishes the typing for you), click the AutoText tab in the AutoCorrect dialog box. This action displays information about AutoText, as shown in Figure 7-7.

AutoText has no Replace/With type of setup. Just type the word or phrase you want Word to finish typing for you, such as your address or name, into the Enter AutoText Entries Here box:

```
Sir Jeremiah Robert Eddington III, Esquire, Ret.
```

Clicking the Add button places that item in AutoText's bin. Now, whenever you type **Sir** in a document, AutoText takes over and displays the rest of the name. Press Enter to insert it.

Click the OK button to close the AutoCorrect dialog box.

Figure 7-7:
The
AutoText
dialog box.

> ✔ The quick way to get to the AutoText dialog box is to choose Insert⇨AutoText⇨AutoText from the menu.
>
> ✔ Any selected text in your document automatically appears in the AutoCorrect/AutoText dialog box. That's a nifty way to put long, detailed information into the dialog box without having to retype it: Just select the text you want to add to AutoText, summon the AutoCorrect or AutoText dialog box, and click Add; the selected text is added.

✔ Be certain that if you do not want selected text in your document to appear in the AutoText entry that no text is selected.

✔ AutoText entries are classified by the text style they're formatted in. If you want to place an AutoText entry into a specific category (or menu), then format that text with a style. The name of the style will be the name of the category the AutoText entry appears under.

Removing an AutoText entry

You don't need a midget clairvoyant to rid your AutoText house of unwanted spirits. Instead, just choose the item you don't want, highlighting it on the list, and click the Delete button.

Click OK to close the AutoCorrect dialog box when you're done cleaning house.

Grammar Be Good

If spelling is drunken, grammar is a hallucination. Oh, I could rant on this for hours. Suffice it to say, no matter what the grammarians think, English is not Latin. It can't be. Latin usually has one, very proper way to say something. English has many ways and many words with which to express the same thought. That's why English is so poetic. That's why so-called English grammar has so many exceptions it's silly to make any rules.

Regardless of what I think, Word does come with a grammar checker, and it does, at times, underline suspicious words or phrases in an angry green zigzag. That's your clue that you've somehow offended Word's sense of grammatical justice. Figure 7-8 shows an example. Right-clicking on the green-underlined text displays a pop-up menu, similar to the spell checker's menu.

That is the broom I rode into town on.

| I rode into town on that broom |
| Ignore Once |
| Grammar... |
| About This Sentence |
| Look Up... |
| Cut |
| Copy |
| Paste |

Figure 7-8: An evil preposition lurks at the end of this sentence!

The pop-up menu either lists some alternatives, such as the one offered in Figure 7-8, or simply tells you that the sentence is too long or a fragment and offers no suggestions or poor grades for your efforts. Just choose a correct sentence, and Word replaces the foul sentence in your document, or try again until you please the Grammar Gods.

- ✔ If you select About This Sentence from the pop-up menu, the Office Assistant dog explains which part of the English Language Book of Rules you offended.

- ✔ Sometimes the grammar checker seems to be wrong. But don't give up! Always check your entire sentence for a potential error. For example, it may suggest *had* in place of *have*. Chances are, *have* is correct but some other word in the sentence has an unwanted *s*.

- ✔ Grammar checking is controlled by the Spelling and Grammar tab in the Options dialog box: Choose Tools➪Options from the menu, and then click the Spelling & Grammar tab. Click the Settings button there to enable or enfeeble the Grammar checker. Choose Grammar & Style from the Writing Style drop-down list for a really harsh interpretation of your text.

A Thesaurus Is Not a Colossal Prehistoric Beast

Thesaurus is the name of that book that contains "other words that mean the same thing." Is that a cinnamon? No: synonym! Yup. So *large* is a synonym for *huge* and so on. You can use Word's thesaurus to help you find the right word when you need something better than large, something like *immense* or even *humongous*.

The quickie thesaurus

To find the synonym of any word, right-click that word in your document. From the pop-up menu, choose the Synonyms submenu to see a list of words with a similar meaning (see Figure 7-9).

The Synonyms submenu displays a list of a dozen or so synonyms for *ugly*, plus one antonym (a word with the opposite meaning), as shown in Figure 7-9. To replace the word in the document with a synonym, just choose it from the submenu.

Cut	
Copy	
Paste	
Font...	
Paragraph...	
Bullets and Numbering...	unattractive
Hyperlink...	hideous
Look Up...	unsightly
Synonyms ▶	revolting
Translate	repulsive
Select Text with Similar Formatting	good-looking (Antonym)
	horrible
	dreadful
	Thesaurus...

Figure 7-9:
Synonyms
for *ugly.*

Not all words have synonyms. If so, the Synonyms submenu displays (No Suggestions). Oh, well.

Actually, at one time there were synonyms for everything in the Word the-saurus. But around the release of Word 2000, the censorship police took over, and hundreds of politically incorrect words were secreted away from the Thesaurus list. For example, try looking up the synonyms for *idiot.* Some syn-onyms list only one aspect of the word, such as the synonyms for *dummy* deal with only mannequins and not "dumb" things. And why are there syn-onyms for every color except black? Silly Microsoft.

Say that in French

Another thesaurus-like feature in Word is its ability to translate words into another language. Word does this best one word at a time, which is always good because computers still haven't quite mastered the ability to accurately translate complete sentences. Yet, for adding a wee little — nay, *petit* — French to your document, the Translate command works swell. Or *gonfler,* perhaps.

To translate a word from English into French, follow these steps:

1. **Right-click the word to translate.**

   The word must be spelled correctly and free of grammatical errors. If not, fix the word and try right-clicking again.

2. **Choose Translate from the pop-up menu.**

   The Research view pane appears, as shown in Figure 7-10. Translations appear in the Results part of the view pane; if not, click the Go button.

Figure 7-10:
The
Research
view pane.

As shown in Figure 7-10, a few translations are listed, which you can then type into your document.

Comment facile!

✔ This feature works best one word at a time. Although it looks like you can select a whole sentence, that's just too much for Word to deal with.

✔ Funny, but in previous versions of Word, you could just click a Replace button, and the translation would appear in your document. So much for progress.

✔ My copy of Word came with only French and Spanish translations. Hopefully, more will be available in the future, including the important Latin translator and the often-ridiculed but equally necessary Klingon translator.

✔ I would avoid visiting the Internet for a translation, at least not in the way Word attempts to do things.

✔ On the other hand, my favorite Web page for translating from English or into English is `babelfish.altavista.com/`. You can copy and paste text from there into Word, no problem.

The official thesaurus

A more traditional way to use Word's thesaurus is the Thesaurus dialog box. Unlike the Synonyms submenu (refer to the "Quickie thesaurus" section), the Thesaurus dialog box is more of a place to explore words than to look up simple synonyms, and, as such, it's a complete waste of time to go there. But if you really care, choose Tools➪Language➪Thesaurus from the menu. This opens the Research view pane where you can interactively type in words and search for their meanings or even look them up on the Internet. Pretty cool, but not as handy as the right-click➪Synonyms trick described in the text.

Making Every Word Count

Writers get paid by the word. If you're lucky enough to be paid for your writing, you know the "word count" quite well. Magazine editors demand articles based on word length. "I need 350 words on how utterly funny it is to buy a computer for the first time," an editor once told me. And novel writers typically boast of how many words are in their latest effort. "My next book is 350,000 words," they say in a stuffy voice. How do they know how many words there are? Why, they use Word's handy Word Count feature!

To see how many words are in your document, choose Tools➪Word Count. You see a summary of your document's statistics, as shown in Figure 7-11. Many other things are summarized, too: pages, characters, paragraphs, lines, and other stuff.

Figure 7-11:
Pulling a
word count.

The Word Count dialog box is okay, but Word has a more interactive way to tell you how many words you have to go — or how many words too many you may have. It's the Word Count toolbar: Click the Show Toolbar button in the Word Count dialog box (refer to Figure 7-11) or choose View⇨Toolbars⇨Word Count from the menu. This action displays the Word Count floating palette, shown in Figure 7-12.

Figure 7-12:
Word
counting
on-the-fly.

The Word Count floating palette hovers over your document as you type. To see the current word count, click the Recount button. You can also choose some other item to count from the drop-down list, such as paragraphs, characters, pages, and lines.

Click the X button in the Word Count floating palette window to make it disappear. See Chapter 28 for more information on working with floating palettes and toolbars in Word.

Chapter 8

Basic Document Tricks

● ●

In This Chapter

▶ Saving your stuff to disk

▶ Using the proper filename

▶ Saving a document with a new name

▶ Opening a document already saved to disk

▶ Opening one document inside another

● ●

Right after you type the smallest modicum of text, you should save your stuff. By using the proper commands, you direct Word to take your text and tuck it carefully into a document file, which is stored on your computer's hard drive, safe and sound. As long as you save, you'll have a permanent copy of your document at hand, ready to be opened again for editing, printing, or simple review. But the key is saving to disk! Do it once. Do it again. Do it often.

This chapter deals with the basics of document file manipulation. There's saving, there's opening, and because I like you, this chapter also covers inserting one document *inside* another. Such a deal.

▶ What you save to disk is a *document* — all the text and stuff you've created in Word. Some people refer to a document saved on disk as a *file*. Same thing.

▶ Relatively speaking, a word processing document takes up little space on a hard drive. Unlike graphics, audio, or video files, word processing documents consume little disk space.

Saving a Document to Disk (The First Time)

Don't think that you have to wait until you finish a document to save it to disk. In fact, saving should be done almost immediately — as soon as you have a few sentences or paragraphs. Save! Save! Save!

To save a document that hasn't already been saved to disk, follow these steps:

1. **Summon the Save command.**

Just click the Save button on the toolbar. The Save As dialog box enlightens you with its presence, as shown in Figure 8-1.

Figure 8-1:
The Save As
dialog box.

If you don't see the Save As dialog box, it means that you already saved your document once. This time, you're merely saving it again. That's fine. You're done.

2. **Type a name for your document.**

Word automatically selects the first line or first several words of your document as a filename and puts it in the Save dialog box. If that's okay, you can move on to Step 3.

If you want to give your document a name other than the one listed in the Save As dialog box, type the new name. You can use letters, numbers, spaces, and a smattering of symbols. Though the filename can be tediously long, my advice is to keep it short, simple, and descriptive (which prevents most lawyers from effectively naming files).

3. **Click the Save button.**

Your clue that the file has been successfully saved is that the filename now appears on the document's title bar, near the top of the screen.

If a problem arises, you likely see one of two error messages:

```
The file [whatever] already exists
```

Complicated — but important — information about filenames

You must name your file according to the loving, yet firm, Windows filenaming rules. This task isn't as tough as memorizing stuff for a DMV test, and it's not as horrid as things were in the ancient days of DOS — but it's darn close:

✔ A filename can be up to 245 characters long; even so, try to keep your filenames short and descriptive.

✔ A filename can include letters, numbers, and spaces and can start with a letter or a number.

✔ A filename can contain periods, commas, hyphens, and even underlines.

✔ A filename cannot contain any of these characters: \ / : * ? " < > |

✔ Don't bother typing a three-letter extension (.doc) on the end of any of your Word files. (This is for anyone who used an older version of Word where the .doc at the end of the name was required. It's not anymore.)

You have three choices. Select the middle one, Save Change with a Different Name. Then type a different name into the Save As dialog box. (If you choose either of the other options, you risk destroying a file on disk in a manner that cannot be undone.)

The second problem message reads something like this:

```
The file name, location, or format '[whatever]' is not
valid...
```

Whatever. Basically you used a boo-boo character to name the file. To be safe, stick to letters, numbers, and spaces. Going beyond that means that you may offend Word's sense of what a filename is or isn't. Check the nearby sidebar, "Complicated — but important — information about filenames." Then click OK and try again.

✔ In addition to using the Save button on the toolbar, you can save a file by using the File⇨Save menu command, the Ctrl+S keyboard shortcut, or the very bizarre Shift+F12 keyboard shortcut.

✔ Always save your document, even after you've typed only a few lines of text.

✔ You should also organize your files by storing them in their own special folders on your disk. Refer to Chapter 27 for more information.

✔ Although Word can handle large documents (the absolute size is unlimited), smaller documents are easier to deal with in the long run. If you're writing a book or anything with multiple parts, save each chapter or part as its own document.

Saving a document (after it's already been saved once)

Just because you save your document to disk once doesn't mean that you're all done. Every so often, you should save your document again. That way, any changes you've made since the last time you saved are remembered. This doesn't mean that you have to be obsessive about saving. For example, I save once every few pages of text I write, or whenever the phone rings or I need to get up and stretch my legs, get coffee, or go potty.

 To save a document after saving it the first time (described in the preceding section), press Ctrl+S or click the Save button on the toolbar. You see the status bar change oh-so-quickly as the document is saved. The Office Assistant may even animate in a manner showing that you've saved your document — a graphical reward for being a good Word citizen.

Saving a document to disk with a new name

With a word processor, there is no such thing as a "draft." You know: rough draft, first draft, third draft, and so on. Well, in a way, whenever you print the document, you're printing a draft. But the draft concept isn't necessary because you just keep saving the same document to disk after you fix it up.

If you do want to save drafts, or you want to save any document to disk with a new name, choose File⇨Save As. This action displays the Save As dialog box (refer to Figure 8-1), in which you can type a new name for the file, such as **Secret Plot, 2nd Draft**.

 You must choose File⇨Save As to save a file under a new name. If you use one of the regular Save commands (File⇨Save, the Save button on the toolbar, or Ctrl+S, for example), you're merely resaving your document to disk, not making a second file.

Automatic recovery (in case you forget to save)

To ensure that you always have a saved copy of your stuff, be a dear and take advantage of Word's AutoRecover feature.

What AutoRecover does is to secretly save information about your document every few minutes or so. That way, if a power outage or other mishap occurs and you forgot to press Ctrl+S, you can get some of your document back. This is a handy feature everyone should use.

To turn on AutoRecover, follow these steps:

1. **Choose Tools⇨Options.**

2. **Click the Save tab.**

3. **Ensure that the Save AutoRecover check box is selected.**

   The check box is named Save AutoRecover Info Every. It's in the middle of the dialog box.

4. **Enter the backup interval in the Minutes text box.**

   For example, the number **10** directs Word to back up your documents every ten minutes. If the power is unstable at your home or office, enter **5**, **3**, **2**, or even **1** minute as the backup interval. (The smaller the interval, the more often Word interrupts your work to do the backup.)

5. **Click OK.**

Even though Word has the AutoRecover option, don't get sloppy! It's still best to save with Ctrl+S or the Save button on the toolbar as often as you can.

AutoRecover works without your thinking about it. But suppose something does happen — say, a rabid moose knocks over a telephone pole in your neighborhood. The power goes out, but you didn't have time to save your documents. Uh-oh. Better hope AutoRecover saved most of it for you.

Eventually, they fix things (including the moose), and the power comes back on. When you run Word again, you see the Document Recovery panel, as shown in Figure 8-2.

Point the mouse at the document you want to recover, and a menu button appears. Click that button to display a list of options on how you want to deal with the document.

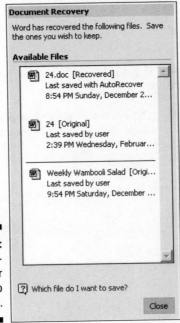

Figure 8-2:
Auto-
Recover
steps into
action.

Click the Close button to dispense with the Document Recovery window.

Saving when you're done

You're done. Your fingers are sore. Your eyes are crusted over. Images flicker when you close your eyelids. Yup. It's time to call it a Word day. Get up and stretch. But before you move off into the real world, you have two choices:

- ✔ **Choose File⇨Close.** This method closes the document you're working on without actually quitting Word. That allows you to stick around, start a new document, open an old document, or just play with the Office Assistant.

- ✔ **Choose File⇨Exit.** This method closes Word and lets you return to Windows for fun and frivolity.

Either way, when you close the document you're working on, Word may ask whether you need to save. Click Yes. The document is saved to disk one final time.

If the document you're working on has yet to be saved, you see the Save As dialog box (refer to Figure 8-1), in which case you need to give the file a name and save it that way.

Other options in the Options/Save dialog box

Many of Word's configuration options are found in the Options dialog box that appears when you choose Tools➪Options from the menu. In the Save panel of that Options dialog box you may notice quite a few interesting settings. Avoid temptation there. Ignore such seductive choices as Allow Fast Saves. That one in particular can cause problems because it saves only a document's changes and not the entire document at once. Sure, it's fast, but you may have problems down the road, especially if the document grows very big.

The Always Create Backup Copy item is interesting. What it does is to create two copies of the document you're saving: the current copy and a backup of the old copy. That's okay, but it's really a holdover from older versions of Word that lacked its current, powerful Undo command. Also, all those backup files consume disk space.

The point is that Word doesn't let you quit or close any document that isn't saved to disk.

If you choose File➪Close or File➪Exit and if Word doesn't ask you to save, the document has already been saved to disk. No need to fret. Everything is okay.

- ✔ The shortcut key for the File➪Close command is Ctrl+W.

- ✔ The shortcut key to close Word is — are you ready? — Alt+F4.

- ✔ There is no reason to quit Word and start it again to begin working with a blank slate.

- ✔ Always quit Word properly. Never turn off your PC or reset when Word or Windows is still onscreen.

Opening a Document on Disk

To fetch a document from disk, you use the Open command. This command ventures out to disk, letting you seek out and locate any document you've previously saved. Once found, the document is opened; it appears in the Word window where you can read, edit, print, or do whatever to it all over again.

To grab a file from disk — to open it — follow these steps:

1. Summon the Open command.

Choose File➪Open to display the Open dialog box, as shown in Figure 8-3.

Figure 8-3:
The Open
dialog box.

The shortcut key for the Open command is Ctrl+O, and there's also a quick shortcut button on the toolbar, as shown in the margin.

2. Click the document's name.

The Open dialog box — vast and wild as it is — contains a list of documents previously saved to disk, as you can see in Figure 8-3. Your job is to find the one you want to open.

Sometimes, you may have to open a folder icon to locate your document. For example, the Web folder, shown in Figure 8-3, contains stuff I've written for my Web pages.

When you find the file, click once on its name. This highlights the file.

3. Click the Open button.

Word opens the file, carefully lifting it from your disk drive and slapping it down on the screen, where you can edit it, print it, read it, or just look at it in glowing admiration.

✔ Opening a document does not erase it from your disk drive.

✔ Word may complain that it can't open a document because a certain conversion feature is unavailable. If so, click Yes to load that feature. (You may need to obtain the Word or Office CD to complete the operation.)

✔ If you can't find your document, see Chapter 27.

✔ Do not open a file on a floppy disk or any removable disk. While it's possible, it can lead to headaches later if you remove the disk before Word is done with the file. Because of that, I recommend you use Windows to copy the document from the floppy disk to the hard drive's My Documents folder. Then open it with Word.

A handy way to open a recent file

Word remembers the last several files you've been working on. It keeps them in a list on the File menu. Chances are good that you probably need to open one of them, so choosing one from the File menu is a handy way to open that document quickly.

The number of files Word remembers on the File menu is adjustable. To set the value, choose Tools➪Options. In the Options dialog box, click the General tab. Look for the Recently Used File List item. Next to it is a spinner gizmo, normally with the number 4 in it. You can adjust that value up or down to have Word remember more or fewer files, which it keeps track of on the File menu. Click OK when you're done modifying this value.

Using the Files of Type drop-down list

The Open dialog box displays two things: folders and files. The types of files that appear are set by the Files of Type drop-down list. In Figure 8-3, it says `Word Documents (*.doc)`, which means that the Open dialog box displays all the Word document files in the My Documents folder.

To see files of a specific type, choose that file type from the drop-down list. For example, to see every type of document that Word can open, choose All Word Documents from the list.

If you want to see only WordPerfect documents, choose one of the WordPerfect file types from the drop-down list.

Bottom line: If you don't see the file you know is there, check the Files of Type drop-down list to ensure that the Open dialog box is showing you the files you're expecting. (Also refer to Chapter 27 for more information on working with other file types in Word.)

Opening one document inside another

Suppose that you're editing some general report and you need to combine several smaller documents created by other people into a single, larger document. Or maybe you have a common bit of text you've saved to disk, which needs to be inserted into other documents. You could open those other documents and then copy and paste their contents. But Word has a better way; follow these steps:

1. **Position the toothpick cursor right where you want to insert the document.**

2. **Choose Insert⇨File.**

3. **Use the Insert File dialog box to hunt down your file.**

   The Insert File dialog box works exactly like the Open dialog box.

4. **Click the Insert button to open the document and insert it into your text.**

   And there it is.

Chapter 9

Getting It Down on Paper

· ·

In This Chapter

▶ Getting the printer ready to print

▶ Previewing your document before printing

▶ Printing specific parts of a document

▶ Printing several documents

▶ Printing multiple copies of a document

▶ Canceling the Print command

· ·

This chapter is about the final step you take after creating your master-piece. No, no, no! Forget publishing for now. Sure, you can send off your efforts to That Big Publishing House In New York, sign a massive advance, and sell millions of books. But what are you going to send? Hmmm?

A-ha! It's printing. Getting it down on paper. Printing sounds easy: Coax your document out of the computer and into the printer, where it prints and looks just like you want it to look. Of course, some problems and issues may occur, which this chapter addresses. After all, no single device in your entire computer system deserves a good flogging like the printer.

Preparing the Printer (Do This First!)

Before printing, you must make sure that your printer is ready to print. Check these few items:

1. **Make sure that your printer is plugged in and properly connected to your computer.**

   Refer to my book *PCs For Dummies* (Wiley Publishing) for more information on connecting and using a printer, as well as various printer dos and don'ts.

2. **Make sure that your laser printer has enough toner or that your ink printer's cartridges are swelling with ink.**

   Laser printers should have a good toner cartridge installed. If the laser printer's "toner low" indicator is on, replace the toner at once.

   Most ink printers let you know when they're out of ink, or you notice that the image appears streaked or faded or is missing information. Replace the ink cartridge at once.

3. **Check the printer for paper.**

   The paper can feed from the back, come from a paper tray, or be manually fed one sheet at a time. However your printer eats paper, make sure that you have it set up properly before you print.

4. **Your printer must be *on-line* or *selected* before you can print anything.**

   This is weird: Some printers can be on but not ready to print. The power is on, but unless the printer is on-line or selected, it ignores the computer. To force the printer to listen to the computer, you must press the Online, Select, or similar button.

✔ If you're printing to a network printer — and the thought makes me shudder — someone else is in charge of the printer. The network printer should be set up and ready to print. If not, someone to whom you can complain is usually handy.

✔ The printer you use affects the way Word displays and prints your document, so before you do lots of formatting, make sure that you selected the correct printer.

Preview Before You Print

Word shows you exactly what your document looks like, right there on the screen. Especially if you choose Print Layout view (View⇨Print Layout), you see the page just as it prints — headers, footers, graphics, page breaks, and all. Even so, sometimes that's just not good enough. Certain people print a sample anyway, just to see whether they like things — totally unaware that what they're doing is needlessly destroying trees and consuming so much paper that all the forests will disappear and Mr. Bunny will have nowhere to live.

Save Mr. Bunny!

To sneak a preview of how your printed document will look, choose File⇨Print Preview or click the handy Print Preview button on the Standard toolbar. Doing so displays your document in a rather standoffish view, as shown in Figure 9-1.

Figure 9-1:
A document is being previewed before printing, which saves a few trees here and there.

Take note of how your text looks on the page. Look at the margins. If you're using footnotes, headers, or footers, look at how they lay out. The idea here is to spot something dreadfully wrong *before* you print.

 When you're done gawking, click the Close button to return to your document.

 Or, if everything looks hunky and dory, click the little Print button, and your document prints instantly.

  ✔ Use the scroll bars to see more of your document.

  ✔ If you have a wheel mouse, like the Microsoft IntelliMouse, you can roll the wheel up or down to scroll one page up or down in your document.

  ✔ If your mouse is wheel-less, you can use the Page Up and Page Down buttons to peruse various pages of your document.

 ✔ Click the mouse on your document to zoom in and get a closer look. Click the mouse again to zoom back out. If this doesn't work, click the Magnifier button and try again.

Printing a Whole Document

All ancient cave paintings were rough drafts. You, living in the 21st century, have the luxury of editing, formatting, and rewriting, all on the screen. But when you're ready to write it to the wall (or paper, in this case), follow these steps:

1. Make sure that the printer is on-line and ready to print.

See the first section in this chapter, "Preparing the Printer (Do This First!)".

2. Save your document.

Ha! Surprised you. Saving before you print is always a good idea. Click the little Save tool for a quickie save, and if you need any extra help, refer to Chapter 8 on saving your stuff to disk.

3. Print your document.

The quickest way to do this is to click the Print tool. Click it, and your document starts to print. Quick. Easy. But you can't change any settings; it just prints!

If you choose File➪Print or press Ctrl+P rather than use the Print tool on the toolbar, the Print dialog box appears (see Figure 9-2). You need to then click OK or press the Enter key to print your document.

Figure 9-2:
The Print
dialog box.

Printing may take some time — really. A long time. Fortunately, Word lets you continue working while it prints in the *background*.

✔ If nothing prints, don't hit the Print command again! There's probably nothing awry; the computer is still thinking or sending text to the printer. If you don't get an error message, everything will probably print, eventually.

✔ The computer prints one copy of your document for every Print command you incant. If the printer is just being slow and you impatiently click the Print button ten times, you get ten copies of your document. (See the section "Canceling a Print Job (Omigosh!)," later in this chapter.)

✔ If you have a manual-feed printer, the printer itself begs for paper. Your printer says, "Beep, feed me!" You must stand by, line up paper, and then shove it into the printer's gaping maw until your document is done printing.

✔ If your computer has more than one printer attached, or can access other printers through the network, you can choose which printer to use by selecting it from the Name drop-down list in the Print dialog box. This is also how many fax programs work: You select the fax modem from the Name drop-down list to fax, rather than print, your document.

✔ Aside from saving your document, you may consider proofreading it before you print. See Chapter 7.

Printing Bits and Pieces

You don't have to print your entire document every time you want some hard copy. No, Word lets you print a single page, a range of pages, or a selected block of text. This is all done in the Page Range area of the Print dialog box (in the middle, on the left).

The following sections assume that your printer is on and ready to print.

Printing a specific page

Follow these steps to print only one page of your document:

1. **Move the toothpick cursor so that it's sitting somewhere in the page you want to print.**

   Check the page counter in the lower-left corner of the screen (on the status bar) to ensure that you're on the right page.

   You can use the Go To command (the F5 key) to go to any specific page in your document. See Chapter 3.

2. **Choose File⇨Print or press Ctrl+P.**

3. **Select the Current Page option on the Print Range panel.**

4. **Click OK.**

   The dialog box closes, and that one page prints. (It may take some time to print as Word organizes its thoughts.)

The single page prints with all the formatting you applied, including footnotes and page numbers and everything just as if you plucked that page from a complete printing of the entire document.

Printing a single page in this manner is great for when you (or the printer) goof up one page in a document and you need to reprint only that page. This saves trees over reprinting the whole document just to fix one boo-boo. And it keeps Mr. Bunny happy.

Printing a range of pages

Word enables you to print a single page, a range of pages, or even some hodgepodge combination of random pages from within your document. To print a range or group of pages, follow these steps:

1. **Conjure up the File➪Print command.**
2. **Click the Pages button in the Page Range area of the Print dialog box.**
3. **Type the page numbers and range of page numbers.**

   To print pages 3 through 5, type **3-5**.

   To print pages 1 through 7, type **1-7**.

   To print pages 2 and 6, type **2,6**.
4. **Click OK.**

   The pages you specify — and only those pages — print.

You can get very specific with the page ranges. For example, to print page 3, pages 5 through 9, pages 15 through 17, and page 19 (boy, that coffee went everywhere, didn't it?), you type **3, 5-9, 15-17, 19**.

Printing backwards

You may have one of those printers where the sheets come out faceup. In that case, you have to reshuffle your document after it prints because it's backwards. To prevent that, you can reverse the printing order in Word. Follow these steps:

1. **Do the File➪Print command jitterbug.**
2. **Click the Options button in the Print dialog box.**
3. **Click to put a check mark by the Reverse Print Order item.**

   It's near the upper-right part of the dialog box.
4. **Click OK.**
5. **Click OK to print your document.**

   And the document comes out of the printer backwards, but because it's faceup, the document will be in order when the printing is complete.

Yet another time-saving tip, proving again that you're no dummy for buying this book.

Printing a block

After you mark a block of text onscreen, you can beg the Print command to print only that block. Here's how:

1. **Mark the block of text you want to print.**

   See Chapter 6 for all the block-marking instructions in the world.

2. **Choose File⇨Print.**

3. **Tickle the button by the word Selection.**

   The Selection item in the Print dialog box is available only when a block is selected. Selecting it tells Word that you want to print only your highlighted block.

4. **Click the OK button.**

   In a few moments, you see the hard copy sputtering out of your printer. The page selection prints in the same position and with the same headers and footers (if any) as it would if you had printed the entire document.

Printing Several Documents

You may think that the best way to print several documents at a time is to open each one and print them one at a time. Oh, but you couldn't be more wrong! A better way exists, and it's hidden in the Open dialog box, the same one you use to open any old document on disk.

To print several files at a time, follow these steps:

1. **Make sure that the printer is on, selected, and rarin' to print.**

2. **Choose File⇨Open.**

   Or, use one of the many other ways to summon the Open dialog box, as described in Chapter 8.

3. **Select the documents you want to print.**

   To select a document, Ctrl+click it with the mouse: Press and hold the Ctrl key and click the file. This step highlights that document.

   Keep Ctrl+clicking documents until you highlight all those you want to print.

4. Click the Tools button at the top of the Open dialog box.

A list of commands appears on a pop-up menu. Don't let it shock you that such a thing can exist in a dialog box.

5. Choose the Print command.

Word happily prints all the documents you selected.

When you print a gang of documents, they just all print. No Print dialog box or no warning asks you whether the printer has enough paper or whether you're really spiritually prepared to print all those documents at once.

Printing More Than One Copy of Something

Every year, I concoct a family Christmas letter and bring joy to the hearts of dozens of friends and relatives by sending them a copy. Rather than drive off to Kinkos and pay the exorbitant fee of six cents per copy, I opt to do my own printing and direct Word to have the printer spew out the several dozen copies I need. This approach is easy for anyone to try, as long as you have enough paper and you know which part of the Print dialog box to pinch.

To print several copies of a document, heed these steps:

1. Prepare everything.

Ensure that the document is up to snuff (use Print Preview for that task, as discussed earlier in this chapter) and make sure that the computer is stocked with the proper festive paper.

2. Choose File⇨Print.

3. Enter the number of copies in the Number of Copies box.

The Copies area is in the middle on the right side of the Print dialog box (refer to Figure 9-2). In the box, type the number of copies you want Word to spew out. For three copies of a memo, type **3**.

4. Click OK to print your copies.

Under normal circumstances, Word prints each copy of the document one after the other. This process is known as *collating*. However, if you're printing seven copies of something and you want Word to print seven page 1s and then seven page 2s (and so on), click in the Collate check box to *remove* the check mark. (Normally, you leave the check mark there.)

Canceling a Print Job (Omigosh!)

Because you probably need to quickly cancel your printing, here goes:

1. **Double-click the li'l printer dude by the current time on the taskbar.**

   This step opens up your printer's window and displays any documents waiting to be printed, as shown in Figure 9-3.

Figure 9-3:
The printer's queue.

2. **Click the name of your Word document job on the list.**

3. **Choose Document⇨Cancel.**

   The command may be Document⇨Cancel Printing with some versions of Windows.

4. **Click Yes to terminate the job.**

   The command may be OK in some versions of Windows.

5. **Close your printer's window when you're done.**

   Choose Printer⇨Close to make the window run away from the desktop. You're zapped back to Word, ready for more editing action.

Note that it may take a while for the printer to stop printing. That's because the printer has its own memory (RAM), and a few pages of the document may be stored there *and* continue to print even after you've told the printer to stop. (Stupid printer, stupid.)

- ✔ If you're using a network printer, you may not be able to cancel the document. Oh, well.

- ✔ You can use your printer's window (refer to Figure 9-3) to cancel more jobs if you're in an especially vicious mood: Just repeat Steps 2–4 for each job you want to sack.

- ✔ To cancel all the jobs, choose Printer⇨Cancel All Documents.

✔ Obviously, canceling a print job is the act of a desperate person. In its efforts to make life easy for computer users, Windows tries hard to help us change our minds. Canceling something that's printing may or may not work as planned. My advice is just to be careful with the Print command in the first place.

Chapter 10

Tips from a Word Guru

For the past 12 years or so, I've been using Microsoft Word as my main word processor. That may or may not make me an expert, but at least I'm enough of an experienced user that I have oodles and oodles of tips stored away. Because I'm a nice guy, I want to pass those tips on to you.

In this chapter are suggestions and random thoughts that relate to other topics in this part of the book, but I've put them all here for easy reference. These tips and tricks are ones I wish that *I* had known about when I first started using Word — some of these tips surprise even longtime Word users.

The Office Assistant Has Thought of Something!

 Here's one reason to turn the Office Assistant on: the light bulb! After you do certain common tasks in Word, the Office Assistant grows a halo of sorts, shaped like the light bulb pictured in the margin. That means the Office Assistant has a suggestion that may make your task easier.

 To see the suggestion, click the light bulb. A cartoon bubble with helpful or insightful information is displayed, as shown in Figure 10-1. Click OK when you're done reading.

Figure 10-1:
The Office
Assistant
says
profound
things.

TIP

 ✔ To see the Office Assistant, choose Help⇨Show the Office Assistant from the menu.

 ✔ To activate the tips (if you've not yet seen one), right-click the Office Assistant and choose Options from the pop-up menu. In the Office Assistant dialog box, click to put check boxes by the items you'd like to see tips about. Click OK when you're done.

Finding Your Place Quickly

At the start of the day, you open your document and then what? You scroll down, reading and editing until you think that you get to where you were last editing yesterday. Needless to say, this can be a tedious waste of time.

The Shift+F5 shortcut (Go Back) remembers where you were when you first open a document, however that may not work if you're also editing other documents at the same time. Therefore, a trick I use is to insert two ampersands (&&) into the document where I was last editing. For example:

```
One such product called off the market just last year was the
so-called "ape jelly." Not made from apes or even being
edible, this goo was the target of boycotts by both
environmentalist and nutrition groups.&&
```

In this example, the two ampersands mark the spot where I was writing last. To find that spot after opening a document, I press Ctrl+F to display the Find and Replace dialog box and then search for &&. I close the Find and Replace dialog box and then get on with my work.

You don't have to use the && symbols (which is Shift+7 twice, if you've been mentally geared by Word to think that way). You can use any symbols to mark your place. Just remember what they are.

Taking Advantage of the Repeat Key

When the Redo command, Ctrl+Y, has nothing left to redo, it can be used as the Repeat command. This command can be a real time-saver. If you press a Word command, cursor key, or character and then press the Repeat key, that command, cursor key, or character is repeated.

For example, type the following lines in Word:

```
Knock, knock.
Who's there?
Knock.
Knock who?
```

Now press Ctrl+Y. Word repeats the last few things you typed. (If you had to press the Backspace key to back up and erase, Ctrl+Y repeats only from that point on.)

You can also use the Edit⇨Repeat command, or, if you can remember it, press the F4 key to do the same thing as pressing Ctrl+Y.

✔ Another handy Repeat deal: Type a bunch of underlines onscreen, like blank lines on a form. Then press Enter. Press Ctrl+Y a few times, and the page is soon filled with blank lines. Hey! Create your own ruled paper!

✔ The repeat key is also used to reapply formatting, so if you're working through a document changing styles on various chunks of text, using the Ctrl+Y or F4 keys can save you some time.

Previewing Documents Before You Open Them

You can name a file with the most descriptive and useful name you can think of and then ten days later forget what's in it. Or, maybe you're working on a book and need to double-check the real name you gave Chapter 8. Naturally, you say (because you're with-it), "I can just open that document for a sneak peek."

Oh! But there's a better way. You can use the Open dialog box to preview any document *before* you open it, saving valuable time and effort. Here's how:

1. **Choose File➪Open.**

   Or click the Open button on the toolbar or use Ctrl+O. Whatever. The Open dialog box appears.

2. **Click the down arrow by the Views button.**

   The Views button is located in the upper-left part of the dialog box. Clicking the down arrow by that button drops down a menu.

3. **Choose Preview from the menu.**

   The look of the Open dialog box changes to reveal Preview mode. Any file you choose on the left side of the Open dialog box is previewed on the right side, as shown in Figure 10-2.

Figure 10-2: Previewing a document before you open it.

You can scroll the Word document down to read more of it, if you like.

Choose another file to preview by clicking its name.

4. **To open the file, just click the Open button. Or, if you're done looking, click Cancel.**

The Open dialog box stays in Preview mode until you choose another mode from the Views button drop-down list. (Normally, Word uses Details or Icons view.)

✔ If you choose All Files from the Files of Type list, you can use the Open dialog box's preview window to preview other types of files: graphics files, text documents, and even Excel documents.

✔ Previewing some types of documents may prompt Word to display a File Conversion dialog box. Click OK if you want to open the file; otherwise — if you're just poking around — click Cancel.

✔ If you attempt to preview a Web page document you saved to disk, Windows may attempt to connect to the Internet to update the information on the document. (Just a warning in case something like that tends to bug you.)

 ✔ If the file is of a mysterious type that Word cannot display, you get the message `Preview not available`. Oh, well.

 ✔ See Chapter 8 for more general information on opening documents.

Multiple Document Mania

Word lets you work on up to a zillion documents at once. Well, actually, you can work on several documents at once. Whenever you open a new document or choose File⇨New to start a new document from scratch, Word opens another document window.

All the document windows appear as buttons on the taskbar. To switch from one document to another, click its button on the taskbar.

 ✔ A quick way to switch from one document window to another is to press the Alt+Tab key combination.

 ✔ Another way to switch documents is to use the Window menu. Alas, the Window menu displays only the first nine documents you have open (which is a bunch). For any more than nine windows, you see a More Windows menu item that displays the entire list of all the documents and windows you're working on in Word.

 ✔ The goings-on in one document are independent of any other: Printing, spell checking, and formatting affect only the document you can see onscreen.

 ✔ You can copy a block from one document to the other. Just mark the block in the first document, copy it (press Ctrl+C), open the second document, and paste it in (Ctrl+V). Refer to Chapter 6 for detailed block action.

Closing your documents

When you're working with several open documents or windows at a time, you can close the documents by clicking the X (Close) button in the window's upper-right corner. However, when you get to the last open document, do not click the X button unless you want to quit Word as well as close the document.

Seeing more than one document

You can arrange all your documents onscreen by choosing Window⇨Arrange All. The Arrange All command arranges each document window in a tiled pattern on the screen, allowing you to view more than one document at a time.

Of course, choosing Window⇨Arrange All works best with two documents. Three or more documents arranged on the screen looks more like modern art than anything designed to help you get work done more efficiently.

✔ Although you can see more than one document at a time, you can *work* on only one at a time. The document with the highlighted title bar is the one "on top."

✔ After the windows are arranged, you can manipulate their size and change their positions with the mouse.

✔ Clicking a window's Maximize button restores the document to its normal, full-screen view.

Working on one document in two windows

It's possible in Word to show one document in two windows. You can view two or more different parts of the same document in a large window.

To set up a second window for your document, choose the Window⇨New Window command. The second window opens, as does a second button for that window on the taskbar.

Even though two windows are open, you're still working on only one document. The changes you make in one of the copies are immediately included in the other. (If you want to make a copy of the document, use Windows to copy the document file.)

When you're done with the second window, click the X button to close it. This action closes the window without closing your document; the first window stays open.

✔ This feature is useful for cutting and pasting text or graphics between sections of the same document, especially when you have a very long document.

✔ The title bar tells you which copy of your document you're looking at by displaying a colon and a number after the filename: for example, `Boring Stuff:1` in one window and `Boring Stuff:2` in the second window.

✔ Another way to view two parts of the same document is by using the old split-screen trick. This feature is discussed . . . why, it's right here:

Using the old split-screen trick

Splitting the screen allows you to view two parts of your document in one window. No need to bother with extra windows here. In fact, I prefer to use Word with as little junk onscreen as possible. When I need to view two parts of the same document, I just split the screen — Moses-like — and then undo the rift when I'm done. You can accomplish the same splitting-screen feat by following these steps:

1. **Place the mouse cursor on the little gray thing located just above the up-arrow button on the vertical scroll bar (on the upper-right side of your document).**

   Oh, brother. Just refer to Figure 10-3 to see what I'm talking about.

Figure 10-3:
The little
gray thing.

 — The little gray thing

   When you find the sweet spot, the mouse pointer changes shape and looks like a pair of horizontal lines with arrows pointing down and up.

2. **Hold down the left mouse button and drag the pointer down.**

   As you drag, a line drags with you and slices the document window in half. That marks the spot where the screen splits.

3. **Release the mouse button.**

   Your screen looks something like Figure 10-4.

✔ Each section of the document can be manipulated separately and scrolled up or down. Even so, you're still viewing only one document; changes you make in one of the copies are immediately included in the others.

✔ This feature is useful for cutting and pasting text or graphics between parts of the same document.

✔ The fastest way to split a window is to point the mouse at the little gray area and double-click. It's also the fastest way to undo a split screen: Put the mouse pointer on the little gray area and double-click.

✔ You can also choose Window➪Split to split your screen and Window➪Remove Split to undo it.

Figure 10-4:
Splitting a
document.

Part II
Letting Word Do the Formatting Work

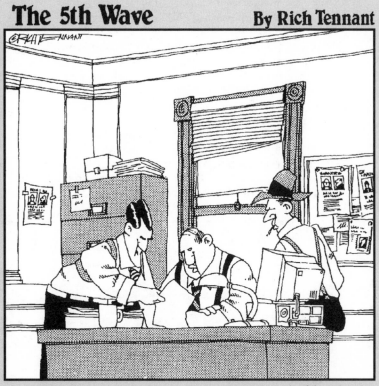

In this part . . .

Formatting is the art of making your document look less ugly. It's the second part of word processing, coming right after the writing part. With the right formatting, you can make your text look even more brilliant by adding professional design elements that make even the dreariest diatribe shine. Indeed, you may have the most awkwardly written piece of tripe since your last drunken college term paper, but it looks great thanks to Word's numerous formatting tricks.

This part of the book tells you how to format your document. You can format text, characters, paragraphs, sentences, and entire documents. I also tell you about styles and templates, plus automatic-formatting tips and tricks to sate the desires of documents most demanding.

Chapter 11

Formatting Characters, Fonts, and Text

· ·

· ·

The most basic thing you can format in a document is a character. Just as your body is composed of millions of cells, documents are composed of thousands of characters. Like a cell, a character is the basic building block of the document. Characters include letters, symbols, and Uncle Cedric, who trims his ear hairs with a butane lighter.

You can format characters to be bold, underlined, italicized, little, big, in different fonts or colors — or even animated if you're building a Web page. Word gives you a magnificent amount of control over the appearance of your text. This chapter contains all the details.

Quickly reusing fonts

The Fonts list can get long, as long as the number of fonts you have installed in Windows. Fortunately, Word remembers the last several fonts you've recently chosen from the Fonts list. Those fonts appear at the top of the list, as shown nearby. If you want to reuse any font for a document, just scroll to the top of the list and pluck out the font.

For example, the following image shows the fonts Albertus Medium, Times New Roman, Algerian, Courier New, Bookman Old Style, and Arial Black as being recently used. Because they now appear at the top of the list, choosing them again is simple.

Times New Roman
Albertus Medium
Times New Roman
ALGERIAN
Courier New
Bookman Old Style
Arial Black
Abadi MT Condensed Light
Agency FB
AHD Symbol
AHD Symbol Sans
Albertus Extra Bold
Albertus Medium

How to Format Your Text

You can change your text formatting in two ways:

✔ Choose a text formatting command and then type the text. All the text you type has the format you chose.

✔ Type the text, and then select the text as a block and apply the formatting. This technique works best when you're busy with a thought and need to return and format the text later.

You use both methods as you compose text in your document. Sometimes, it's easier to use a formatting command and type the text in that format. At other times, you review your document and select text to apply formatting to that block. Either way works.

See Chapter 6 for more information on marking blocks of text.

Changing the Font

One of the fun things about Word is its capability to use lots of different fonts. Sure, you can make text bold, italic, underlined, big, little, and on and on, but adjusting the font to match your mood takes expression to an entirely new level.

To switch to a different font, follow these steps:

1. **Drop down the Fonts list.**

   Click the down arrow by the Fonts drop-down list (on the Formatting toolbar) to display a roll of fonts, similar to the one shown in Figure 11-1.

Figure 11-1:
The Fonts
list.

2. **Scroll to the font you want.**

   The fonts are listed by name in alphabetical order, and the font style is displayed on the menu (refer to Figure 11-1).

3. **Click to select a font.**

Everything you type after choosing a new font appears onscreen in that font. The text should print and look the same as well. If you select a block of text, all the text in that block switches over to the new font.

- ✔ The Fonts box on the toolbar displays whichever font you're using. Normally, that's the Times New Roman font. When you switch to another font, or when you edit text in another font, that font's name appears on the toolbar.

- ✔ If you know the name of the font you want, you can save time by typing it in the box on the toolbar. In some cases, all you need to do is type the first few letters of the font's name, and Word automatically completes the rest. For example, type **CO** to select the Courier font.

- ✔ Oddball shortcut key for this one? Try Ctrl+Shift+F. Then press the ↓ key to sift through the Fonts list and press Enter to choose your font. (Tiring, isn't it?)

- ✔ Fonts are the responsibility of Windows, not Word. New fonts are installed in the Control Panel's Fonts folder (the procedure is really no big deal). Thousands of fonts are available for Windows, and they work in all Windows applications.

Basic Character Formatting

After the font, the next most basic text-formatting attribute is **bold,** *italic,* or <u>underlined</u>. Easy-to-use keyboard shortcuts and buttons on the Formatting toolbar make these the handiest text-formatting tools.

B

To make text bold, press Ctrl+B or use the Bold button on the toolbar.

Use **bold** to make text stand out on a page — for titles and captions, for example — or to emphasize text that carries a great deal of weight, speaks its mind at public meetings, or wears a cowboy hat; you know the type.

I

To make text italic, press Ctrl+I or use the Italic tool on the toolbar.

Italics are replacing underlining as the preferred text-emphasis format. Italicized text looks so much better than shabby underlined text. It's light and wispy, poetic, and free. Underlining is what the Department of Motor Vehicles does when it feels creative.

<u>U</u>

Underline text by pressing Ctrl+U or use the Underline tool on the toolbar.

Underlined text is a holdover from the typewriter days. In most cases, where underlined text is required (and who are those people, anyway?), you can get away with italics instead. So, no matter what that stodgy professor may think, *Crime and Punishment* just looks better than boring old <u>Crime and Punishment</u>.

✔ Basic character formatting affects only selected text or any new text you type.

✔ To turn off a text attribute, use the command again. For example, press Ctrl+I to type something in *italics.* Then press Ctrl+I again to return to normal text.

✔ You can mix and match character formats; text can be bold and underlined or bold and italicized. Yes, you may have to type several Word character-formatting commands before typing your text: Ctrl+B, Ctrl+I, and Ctrl+U for bold, italicized, and underlined text all at once, for example. Then you have to type each of those commands again to switch the text back to normal.

✔ To apply text formatting to a single word, put the toothpick cursor in that word and give the formatting command. For example, putting the toothpick cursor in the word *incredulous* and pressing Ctrl+I (or choosing the Italic button from the toolbar) italicizes the word.

✔ The Bold, Italic, and Underline tools on the toolbar can show you which formatting attributes are applied to your text. For example, when the toothpick cursor is in a bold word, the B on the toolbar appears depressed. (Don't try to cheer it up, it's just doing its job.)

The boring difference between a bold font and bold text

In Windows, you can have bold fonts and bold text. Weird, huh? For example, there's the regular Arial Rounded MT font, which you can make bold with Ctrl+B, and then there's the Arial Rounded MT Bold font, which sounds like it's already bold. So what's the difference?

The difference between a bold font and the Bold command is that a bold font is designed to be bold. It looks better on the screen and when it's printed. Making text bold with the Bold command merely tells Windows to redraw the current font,

making it look "heavier." Although this approach works, the Bold command doesn't display or print the font as nicely as a font that's born to be bold.

Obviously, using the Bold command is easier than switching to a bold font in the middle of a paragraph. But if you can, consider using a bold font for long expanses of text, titles, headings, or captions wherever possible. The Bold command is okay for making text bold in the middle of a sentence, but bold fonts always look better.

An example: Making italic text

To italicize your text, follow these steps:

1. **Press the Ctrl+I key combination.**

   Italics mode is on! (You can also click the Italic button.)

2. **Type away to your heart's content!**

   Watch your delightfully right-leaning text march across the screen.

   > *Watch as I type this lovely italicized text across the screen, la-di-da!*

3. **Press Ctrl+I when you're done.**

   Italic formatting is turned off. (Or, you can click the Italic button again.)

✔ You can use any text formatting command (or toolbar button) rather than italics in this step: Ctrl+B for bold or Ctrl+U for underline.

✔ If the text you want to italicize is already onscreen, you must mark the text as a block and then change the character format to italics. Mark the text as a block, following the instructions detailed in Chapter 6, and then press the Ctrl+I key combination or use the Tower-of-Pisa leaning *I* Italic button.

Text-attribute effects roundup

Bold, italics, and underlining are the most common ways to dress up a character. Beyond that, Word has a bucketful of character attributes you can apply to your text. Table 11-1 shows the lot of them, including the basic bold, italics, and underline commands.

Table 11-1	Text-Format Samples and Commands	
Key Combination	*Toolbar Button*	*Applies This Format*
Ctrl+Shift+A		ALL CAPS
Ctrl+B	**B**	**Bold**
Ctrl+Shift+D		<u>Double underline</u>
Ctrl+Shift+H		Hidden text (it doesn't print — shhh!)
Ctrl+I	*I*	*Italics*
Ctrl+Shift+K		Small Caps
Ctrl+U	**U**	<u>Continuous underline</u>
Ctrl+Shift+W		Word underline
Ctrl+=	x_2	subscript
Ctrl+Shift+=	x^2	superscript

Applying one of the weird text formats shown in Table 11-1 is cinchy. Just follow the instructions in the preceding section, "An example: Making italic text," and substitute the proper shortcut from Table 11-1.

✔ Pay special attention to word underline and continuous underline. Some people like one and despise the other. If you prefer to underline only words, remember to use Ctrl+Shift+W and not Ctrl+U.

✔ Hidden text — what good is that? It's good for you, the writer, to put down some thoughts and then hide them when the document prints. Of course, you don't see the text onscreen either. To find hidden text, you must use the Find command (covered in Chapter 5) to locate the special hidden-text attribute. You have to click the Format button, choose Font, and then click the Hidden box. (See the section, "Font dialog box déjà vu," later in this chapter.)

✔ After finding any hidden text, it pays to un-hide it. That's done in the Font dialog box; remove the check mark by Hidden.

Big Text, Little Text: Text Size Effects

Attributes — bold, italics, underline, and so on — are only half of the available character formats. The other half deals with the text size. By using these text-formatting commands, you can make your text teensy or humongous.

Before getting into this subject, you must become one with the official type-setting term for text size: It's *point*. That's what Word uses: point rather than text size. It's not point, as in "point your finger" or the "point on top of your head." It's point, which is a measurement of size. One point is equal to $\frac{1}{72}$ inch. Typesetters. . . .

✔ The bigger the point size, the larger the text.

✔ Most text is either 10 or 12 points in size.

✔ Headings are typically 14 to 24 points in size.

✔ Most fonts can be sized from 1 point to 1,638 points. Point sizes smaller than 6 are generally too small for the average person to read.

✔ Seventy-two points is equal to 1-inch-high letters.

✔ The author is 5,112 points tall.

Setting your text size

Text size is set in the Font Size box on the Formatting toolbar (it's just to the right of the Font box). Clicking the down arrow displays a list of font sizes for your text, as shown in Figure 11-2.

The new text size affects any marked block on the screen. If a block of text isn't marked, any new text you type appears in the new size.

Figure 11-2: Choose a font size from this list.

Here are some things to remember about setting the font size:

✔ The weirdo keyboard shortcut for getting to the Font Size box is Ctrl+Shift+P. (Sounds like a disposable undergarment to me.)

✔ You can type a specific text size in the box (though I rarely do). In fact, this is the only way to enter between values such as 10.5 or 11.5.

✔ Bigger numbers mean bigger text; smaller numbers mean smaller text.

Making text bigger or smaller with the keyboard

You can use a couple of quickie shortcut keys to instantly shrink or grow text in a marked block. The two most popular ones are

Ctrl+Shift+>   Makes the font larger in the next "look good" size

Ctrl+Shift+<   Makes the font smaller in the next "look good" size

These are easy to remember because > is the greater-than symbol and < is the less-than symbol. Just think, "I'm making my text *greater than* its current size" when you press Ctrl+Shift+>, or "I'm making my text *less than* its current size" when you press Ctrl+Shift+<.

If you want to increase or decrease the font size by smaller increments, use the following shortcut keys:

Ctrl+] Makes text one point size larger

Ctrl+[Makes text one point size smaller

These commands (all four of them) affect a selected block of text on the screen. Otherwise, the command affects only the word the toothpick cursor is in.

Hey! I did this whole section without a Viagra joke!

Making superscript or subscript text

Superscript text is above the line (for example, the 10 in 2^{10}). *Subscript* text is below the line (for example, the 2 in H_2O). Here are the two shortcut keys you need to use:

Ctrl+Shift+= turns on superscripted text.

Ctrl+= turns on subscripted text.

The = (equal sign) is the equal key on your keyboard, right by the Backspace key. (I know, "+=" looks gross, but I didn't make up the standard.)

Now you can use these commands as you type to create superscript or sub-script text. However, I recommend that you type your text, go back and select the superscript or subscript text as a block, and *then* use these commands. The reason is that the text you modify tends to be rather teensy and hard to edit. Better to write it first and then format.

Undoing All This Text-Formatting Nonsense

It's possible to junk up your text with so many formatting commands that undo-ing them all would be a frustrating exercise. Rather than delete the text and start over, you can use a simple and universal undo-formatting command — Word's equivalent of a text-formatting eraser. The command is Reset Character, and its shortcut key is Ctrl+Spacebar.

So if you encounter an expanse of ugly and overly formatted text, select it as a block and press Ctrl+Spacebar. This key combination strips the formatting from the text like a powerful and environmentally unsafe industrial-size can of paint remover. Thwoop! It's gone.

✔ Another key combination for Ctrl+Spacebar is Ctrl+Shift+Z. Remember that Ctrl+Z is the Undo command. To undo formatting, all you do is add the Shift key, which may make sense — well, heck, if any of this makes sense.

✔ Technically, the Ctrl+Spacebar command restores characters to the formatting defined by the *style* you're using. So, if the Normal style is 12-point Times New Roman, pressing Ctrl+Spacebar restores that font and size. Don't let this information upset or confuse you! Instead, turn to Chapter 16 for more information on Word's styles.

Doing the Font Dialog Box

There is a place in Word where all your font formatting delights are kept in a neatly organized fashion. It's the Font dialog box, shown in Figure 11-3.

Figure 11-3:
The neatly organized Font dialog box.

To summon the Font dialog box, choose Format ➪ Font from the menu. The handy keyboard shortcut is Ctrl+D. (Don't know what *D* has to do with *Fonts*.)

This dialog box is not for the timid — just like *Fantasy Island*. All sorts of exciting and exotic things happen here, most of which this chapter shows you how to do in other ways. But when you want it all done at once, this is the spot. You can change the font, size, text attributes — everything.

Ah, please note the lovely Preview window at the bottom of the Font dialog box. This window allows you to preview changes to your text. One of my pastimes is to continuously select fonts in the Font dialog box to see what they look like in the Preview window.

Changes you make in the Font dialog box affect any marked block on the screen or any new text you type after you close the Font dialog box.

When you're done setting up your font stuff, click the OK button. Or, click Cancel if you're just visiting.

- ✔ The best benefit of the Font dialog box is the Preview window at the bottom. That window shows you exactly how your choices affect text in your document.

- ✔ Note that you select the Underline attribute from the Underline Style drop-down list. Word can do several types of underlining.

- ✔ Save the festive attributes — such as Shadow, Outline, Emboss, or Engrave — for titles and headings.

- ✔ The Character Spacing tab displays advanced options for changing the size and position of text on a line.

- ✔ The Text Effects panel is kind of fun to play in, though most of the effects shown there appear only on Web page documents you create (unless you plan on training actual ants to march around on your paper).

Changing the default font

In computer lingo, *default* means, "the choice the computer makes for you when you don't make your own choice." In the case of fonts, Word's default font is Times New Roman at 12 points.

If you prefer to use another font as your default, or in other words, you want to see some other font appear every time you open a new document, then you can chance that with these steps:

1. **Choose Format ➪ Font to display the Font dialog box.**

2. **Set the font you want as the default.**

   For example, choose the font Verdana and set the point size to 14 if that's what tickles your fancy.

3. **Click the Default button, located in the lower-left corner of the Font dialog box.**

   The Office Assistant (or a plain dialog box) asks you to confirm this change.

4. **Click Yes.**

Now all your documents will start with the new default font you've selected.

Font dialog box déjà vu

Another place you'll find the Font dialog box is in the Find dialog box. When you click the More button, as described in Chapter 5, you'll find a Format button, which enables you to search your document for specific formatting in addition to searching for text. If you choose Font from the Format button, you see the Font dialog box, where you can choose various font attributes to search for.

For example, if you wanted to search for any superscript text in your document, you would follow the steps outlined in Chapter 5 (the section, "Finding formatting"), and use the Font dialog box to choose the Superscript text attribute.

For more information on searching for stuff, refer to Chapter 5.

Changing the CASE of Your Text

Upper- and lowercase effects aren't considered part of a font, character attribute, or format. But still, the Word geniuses at Microsoft found room in their bustling bag o' tricks for a two-fingered command that lets you mix around the case of your text.

Press Shift+F3 to change the case of your text.

The Shift+F3 command works on a block of selected text or on any single word the toothpick cursor is in (or next to).

Press Shift+F3 once to change a lowercase word to an initial cap (or all words to initial cap). Press the key combination again to change the words to ALL CAPS. Press Shift+F3 again to change the text to lowercase. Press Shift+F3 again to start the process all over again.

Although I prefer using the Shift+F3 command, the Format➪Change Case command also exists. That command summons the Change Case dialog box, shown in Figure 11-4, which lets you choose specific mangulations of upper- and lowercase letters for your text, as shown in the figure.

Figure 11-4:
The Change
Case dialog
box.

Text changes in the Change Case dialog box apply to the word the toothpick cursor is blinking in, or to a selected block of text.

Chapter 12

Formatting Paragraphs

*J*ust above character formatting comes paragraph formatting, which is the next-largest chunk-like thing that you can format in a document. (Forget about sentences for now; Word cares not about sentences.) Formatting paragraphs is like taking a photograph of a large group of people: You can shuffle them to the left, right, or center, and that's about it. Fortunately Word's bag of paragraph tricks isn't that difficult to understand. This chapter shows you all the tricks.

Want to be really cool? Then call a paragraph a *graph*. That's what all the high-end typesetters call it. Apparently, they're too busy to say the "para" part. Think of all the time they save. Must be a few minutes total by the end of the day. Dern efficient, those folks.

Paragraph-Formatting Techniques

You can format a paragraph in Word several ways:

✔ Use a paragraph formatting command, and then type a new paragraph in that format.

- ✔ Use the formatting command in a single paragraph to format that paragraph. (Place the toothpick cursor in that paragraph, and then use the formatting command.)

- ✔ Use the formatting command on a block of selected paragraphs to format them all together.

No matter which method you choose, keep in mind that the paragraph formatting commands work only on paragraphs, not on sentences or individual words. Of course, if your paragraph is only a single word or sentence, that's okay.

- ✔ Refer to Chapter 6 for specific and entertaining block-marking instructions.

- ✔ A paragraph is a chunk of text that ends when you press the Enter key.

- ✔ To make a single word a paragraph, type the word and then press the Enter key.

- ✔ If you want to format individual characters or the text inside a paragraph, refer to Chapter 11.

- ✔ You can format all the paragraphs in a document if you first select the entire document. Choose Edit⇨Select All or press the Ctrl+A key combination.

- ✔ If you want to see the Enter key symbol (¶) at the end of each paragraph, choose Tools⇨Options. Click the View panel. In the second area down (Formatting Marks), select the Paragraph marks option. Click OK. Now, every time you press the Enter key, a ¶ symbol marks the end of the paragraph. (Many Word users prefer this mode of operation.)

Paragraph Justification and Alignment

Paragraph alignment has nothing to do with politics, and justification has nothing to do with the right or wrong of how paragraphs are formatted. Instead, both terms refer to how the edges of the paragraph look on a page. You have four options: Left, Center, Right, and Fully Justified, each covered in the sections that follow.

- ✔ Word doesn't offer a "no alignment" option. To unalign a paragraph, you simply choose Left alignment; left is normal.

- ✔ You can also use the Paragraph dialog box to change the paragraph(s) justification. Choose Format⇨Paragraph from the menu. The Alignment drop-down list in the top area contains Word's four paragraph-alignment options.

Line up on the left!

Much to the pleasure of southpaws the world over, left-aligning a paragraph is considered normal. That's the way the old typewriter used to do things: The left side of the paragraph is all even and tidy. The right side is jagged, not lined up.

 To left-align a paragraph, press Ctrl+L or click the Align Left button on the toolbar.

✔ This type of alignment is also known as *ragged left*.

✔ Left-aligning a paragraph is how you "undo" the other types of alignment.

Everyone center!

Centered text appears centered on the page.

It's ideal for titles and single lines.

If you type more than one line in a centered paragraph, however, each line of the paragraph is centered on the page, one on top of the other. I suppose artists and poets may like it, but this type of paragraph formatting isn't very easy to read in a long paragraph.

 To center a paragraph, press Ctrl+E or use the Center tool on the toolbar.

✔ You can center a single word in the middle of a line by using the center tab. Refer to Chapter 13 for the details.

 ✔ If you do manage to center your soul on the cosmic plane, you'll probably receive lots of respect and fame. If so, remember never to let your acolytes see you eat at Sizzler.

Line up on the right!

A paragraph that is aligned to the right has its right margin nice and even. The left margin, however, is jagged. This style is also known as *flush right* because the right side is flush with the margin. When do you use this type of formatting? I have no idea, but it sure is funky to type a paragraph that's right aligned.

 To flush your text along the right side of the page, press Ctrl+R or click the Align Right tool on the toolbar.

- ✔ This type of alignment is also known as *ragged right*.

- ✔ You can right-justify text on a single line by using a right-align tab. Refer to Chapter 13 for more info.

- ✔ When you type a new flush-right paragraph, the characters push to the right, always staying flush with the right side of the document. It's like writing in Hebrew!

Full justification! (Full justification, aye sir!)

Finally, there's full justification, which is where both the left and right sides of the paragraph are lined up neat and tidy, flush with the margins. This is the style of paragraph formatting often used in newspapers and magazines, which makes the thin columns of text easier to read. Word makes each side of the paragraph line up by inserting extra space between the words in the paragraph.

 To give your paragraph full justification, press Ctrl+J or click the Justify button on the toolbar.

Making Room Before, After, or Inside of Your Paragraphs

You can space out your text in an up-and-down fashion in two ways. The first, traditional method is to change the line spacing, and the second is to add room before or after your paragraphs — like pressing the Enter key twice to add a blank line after a paragraph, only it's automatic.

As with all paragraph formatting, these various commands operate on the current paragraph (the one the toothpick cursor is blinking in) or on all the paragraphs selected in a block.

Changing line spacing

Changing the line spacing merely inserts extra space between *all* lines of text in a paragraph (or all paragraphs in a block). It's the old double- and triple-spacing like typewriters used to offer (if you're ancient enough to remember the old typewriters).

There are three handy keyboard shortcuts for three common types of line spacing: single-spacing, 1½-line spacing, and double spacing.

To single-space a paragraph (or all paragraphs in a block), press Ctrl+1.

To double-space a paragraph (or paragraphs), press Ctrl+2.

To use 1½-spaced lines, press Ctrl+5.

Line spacing is usually done to accommodate notes or rude comments to be penciled in later. For example, many fussy editors request that drafts be printed out in double — or even triple — spacing. The fussier the editor, the more spacing you should choose.

✔ Ctrl+5 means 1½-line spacing, not 5-line spacing.

✔ For pressing Ctrl+5, don't use the 5 key on the numeric keypad; that's the command to select all the text in your document. Instead, use the 5 key hovering over the R and T keys on your keyboard.

Quickly changing line spacing

A special button on the Formatting toolbar is geared specifically for changing the line spacing. Clicking the Line Spacing button displays a drop-down list of line-spacing options, as shown in Figure 12-1. To set the line spacing, choose a value from the list.

Figure 12-1:
Choose line
spacing
from this
menu.

Changing line spacing to something specific

Word is capable of line spacing at intervals other than 1, 1.5, 2, and so on. So, if you want to tighten up text on a page, you can select all the paragraphs and choose .9 for the line spacing. Or, choose 1.2 to get a little more air in there, but not as much as 1.5 spacing gives you. You do this by summoning the Paragraph dialog box:

1. **Choose Format➪Paragraph from the menu.**

    This step summons the Paragraph dialog box, shown in Figure 12-2.

2. **Choose Multiple from the Line Spacing drop-down list.**

3. **Enter the line spacing you want.**

    For example, **2** is double spacing, but **2.5** puts two-and-a-half spaces between lines. You can enter any value from **.1** on up to, well, whatever. Values such as **.9** or **.8** can really help to tighten up a paragraph.

4. **Click OK.**

Figure 12-2:
The
Paragraph
dialog box.

The new line spacing affects the current paragraph, or all paragraphs in a selected block.

The Paragraph dialog box is a busy place. The next few sections discuss other things you can do there in addition to changing the line spacing.

Adding elbow room between paragraphs

Some people are in the double-Enter habit. That is, you press Enter-Enter to end a paragraph, when all Word really needs is a single Enter. It's a similar disorder to pressing Spacebar-Spacebar after a period — an utterly useless affliction in the age of modern word processing, an unnecessary legacy of the typewriter age. In Word, committing such a sin is like writing down your stutter.

If you want your paragraphs to automatically have some padding around them — like the cushions of air in Dr. Scholl's insoles — you need only to tell Word to stick some padding around its paragraphs. Here's how:

1. **Position the toothpick cursor in the paragraph you want more air around, or mark a block of paragraphs to affect them all.**

   The air can be either above or below the paragraph.

2. **Choose Format⇨Paragraph.**

   The Paragraph dialog box appears.

   Make sure that the Indents and Spacing panel is forward, as shown in Figure 12-2. (Click that panel's tab or press Alt+I, if it isn't forward already.)

   You want to concentrate on the area that says Spacing.

3. **To add space before a paragraph, enter a value in the Before box.**

   This is space that automatically cushions stuff *above* the paragraph.

4. **To add space after a paragraph, enter a value in the After box.**

   This is space that comes below the paragraph.

5. **Click OK.**

   The paragraph (or paragraphs) now has extra spacing.

For example, to add space after every paragraph — just like pressing the Enter key twice — specify 12 pt in the After box in Step 4. The value 12 pt means that there will be just about one blank line after the paragraph.

✔ Use the Preview window at the bottom of the Paragraph dialog box to see how the spacing before or after your paragraph affects things.

✔ Remember pt (or points) from the size of your fonts (Chapter 11)? To add a blank line of text, find out how tall your paragraph's font is and then specify that value. So if your font is 12 pt Times New Roman, a "blank line" after a paragraph is 12 pts of air. For 14 pt font, it's 14 pts.

✔ So which do you use, Before or After spacing? My advice is always to add the padding at the end of the paragraph, in the After box. I use the Before spacing only if I *really* want to separate something from the preceding paragraph (which is rare).

✔ Adding space before or after a paragraph isn't the same as double-spacing the text inside the paragraph. In fact, adding space around a paragraph doesn't change the paragraph's line spacing at all.

TECHNICAL STUFF

What's the pt?

The amount of space Word sticks between paragraphs is measured in points — which is a typesetter's measurement. If you've ever messed with the size of a font (see Chapter 11), you've already worked in points, though the Font size menu doesn't use the pt abbreviation.

There are 72 points to an inch. If you use a 12-point font, which is common, a space of 12 points between paragraphs adds an extra line. Six points (6 pt) is half a line of text.

The boxes where you enter point values in the Paragraph dialog box use spinner gizmos. If you click the up or down arrows on the *spinner,* you increase or decrease the spacing between lines in 6-point increments. If you need more specific values, you can type them in directly (though I've used only 6, 12, and maybe 18 in my short life).

Changing a Paragraph's Indentation

Word can indent your paragraphs for you just as easily as a wandering shopping cart can indent your car door.

Right now, I'll bet that you're indenting each of your new paragraphs by pressing the Tab key. Although I won't sneer at that, there is a better way: Let Word do the indenting for you. Automatically!

The following sections discuss several indenting options.

Automatically indenting the first line of a paragraph

You don't need to press Tab at the start of a new paragraph. No, Word can do that for you automatically:

1. **Choose the Format⇨Paragraph command.**

   The Paragraph dialog box appears. Make sure that the Indents and Spacing panel is up front (as shown in Figure 12-2).

2. **Locate the Special drop-down list.**

   You find this list off to the right in the Indentation area of the dialog box.

3. **Select First Line from the list.**

4. **Enter the amount of indenting in the By box.**

   Unless you've messed with things, the box should automatically say 0.5", meaning that Word automatically indents the first line of every paragraph a half-inch. Type another value if you want your indents to be more or less outrageous. (Things are measured here in inches, not points.)

5. **Click OK.**

   The selected block, or the current paragraph (and the remaining paragraphs you type), all automatically have an indented first line.

To remove the first-line indent from a paragraph, repeat the steps and select (none) from the drop-down list in Step 3. Then click the OK button.

There are two ways you can separate paragraphs from each other in a document. The first is to add space between each paragraph, which is covered in the earlier section "Adding elbow room between paragraphs." The second way is to indent each paragraph, as covered in this section. Choose one or the other; you don't need to use both.

Making a hanging indent

A *hanging indent* has committed no felonious crime. Instead, it's a paragraph in which the first line sticks out to the left and the rest of the paragraph is indented — like this:

Driving Eye Dog. Our specially trained dogs assist the visually impaired and those who've had their driver's licenses revoked. They operate most automatic motor vehicles. Best for short distances. Avoid driving around farms and places with lots of cats. And, by all means, keep the driver side window rolled up.

To create such a beast for whatever fabulous reasons, follow these steps:

1. **Move the toothpick cursor to the paragraph you want to hang and indent.**

   Or, you can position the cursor to where you want to type a new, hanging-indent paragraph. Or, you can select a block — yadda, yadda, you know the drill by now.

2. **Press Ctrl+T, the Hanging Indent shortcut.**

   The Ctrl+T in Word moves the paragraph over to the first tab stop but keeps the first line in place.

You can also accomplish this task in the Paragraph dialog box. Choose `Hanging` from the Special drop-down list and enter the indent (usually half an inch) in the By box. Click OK!

✔ The hanging indent is really an indent-everything-but-the-first-line-of-the-paragraph type of indent.

✔ If you want to indent the paragraph even more, press the Ctrl+T key more than once.

✔ It's stupid that there's a shortcut key for a hanging indent but not for indenting the first line of a paragraph, which I feel people do more often than this hanging nonsense.

✔ To undo a hanging indent, press Ctrl+Shift+T. That's the Unhang key combination, and your paragraph's neck will be put back in shape.

Indenting the whole paragraph

Indenting a paragraph means that you indent, or *nest,* the entire paragraph by aligning its left edge against a tab stop. Here's how you do it:

1. Move the toothpick cursor anywhere in the paragraph.

The paragraph can be already onscreen, or you can be poised to type a new paragraph. Or, you can try this command on a selected block of text.

2. Press Ctrl+M, the indent shortcut.

Ummm — indent! Ummm — indent! Say it over and over. It kinda works. (You can also click the Increase Indent button on the Formatting toolbar.)

3. Type your paragraph if you haven't already.

If you selected the paragraph as a block, it's indented to the next tab stop.

✔ To indent the paragraph to the next tab stop, press Ctrl+M again.

✔ To return to the original margin, press Ctrl+Shift+M. You can also click the Decrease Indent tool.

✔ You can also indent or unindent a paragraph by using the Paragraph dialog box (refer to Figure 12-2). In the Indentation section, the Left item is used to move the left side of a paragraph over by a given amount.

✔ Although the Ctrl+M and Ctrl+Shift+M shortcuts aren't mnemonic, their only difference is a Shift key. So, after you get used to using them (hopefully before the afterlife), they're easy to remember.

Double-indenting a paragraph

Sometimes an indent on the left just isn't enough. There are those days when you need to suck a paragraph in twice: once on the left and once on the right (for example, when you lift a quote from another author but don't want to be accused of plagiarism). I had someone quote an entire book I wrote (twice, actually) simply by double-indenting their paragraphs. No one went to jail, either!

1. **Pick your paragraph.**

   If the paragraph hasn't been written yet, move the cursor to where you want to write the new text. Or, put the toothpick cursor in the paragraph or just select multiple paragraphs as a block.

2. **Choose the Format⇨Paragraph command.**

   The Paragraph dialog box appears (refer to Figure 12-2). Locate the Indentation area.

3. **Enter the amount of Left indentation.**

   For example, type **.5** to indent half an inch, or you can use the up or down arrows to increase or decrease the left indentation.

4. **Enter the amount of Right indentation.**

   Type the same value as you did in the Left box.

   Check the Preview part of the Paragraph dialog box to ensure that your paragraph is indented as you prefer.

5. **Click OK.**

To unindent the paragraph, repeat these steps and enter **0** in both the Left and Right boxes.

Watch out when you try to mix left and right indenting with a first line indent or hanging indent. It could drive you insane, and Microsoft lawyers have proven that they cannot be held responsible for your mental health in such instances.

Who Died and Made This Thing Ruler?

Word's main throwback to the typewriter era is the ruler, which is the final strip/bar information on Word's screen (see Figure 1-3). The ruler can be used for on-the-fly indention changes in a paragraph as well as for setting tabs. (Tabs are covered in Chapter 13.)

Paragraph-formatting survival guide

This table contains all the paragraph-formatting commands you can summon by holding down the Ctrl key and pressing a letter or number. By no means should you memorize this list.

Key Combo	Does This	Key Combo	Does This
Ctrl+E	Centers paragraphs	Ctrl+T	Makes a hanging indent
Ctrl+J	Fully justifies paragraphs	Ctrl+Shift+T	Unhangs the indent
Ctrl+L	Left aligns (flush left)	Ctrl+1	Single-spaces lines
Ctrl+R	Right aligns (flush right)	Ctrl+2	Double-spaces lines
Ctrl+M	Indents text	Ctrl+5	Makes 1½-space lines
Ctrl+Shift+M	Unindents text		

If you don't see the ruler onscreen, choose the View⇨Ruler command. In the Normal view, the ruler appears on the top of the writing area. In Print Layout view, you also get a vertical ruler on the left side of the window.

Figure 12-3 shows the typical Word ruler. Note the three parts of the ruler that deal with indenting a paragraph (or a group of selected paragraphs).

Figure 12-3: The ruler.

The following actions affect the paragraph the toothpick cursor is in or a group of paragraphs selected as a block:

 To adjust a paragraph's right margin, grab the Right Indent guy on the ruler and drag him right or left.

 To adjust the paragraph's left margin, grab the Hanging Indent thing and drag it left or right.

The paragraph's first line can be set independently of the left margin. To adjust it, grab the First Line Indent doojobbie with the mouse and drag it up or down, er, left or right.

 To adjust both the left margin and first line indent together, grab the Left Indent box.

✔ The ruler is a mouse gizmo; you use the mouse to make changes on it. Even so, just about everything you can do with the ruler can also be done in the Format Paragraph dialog box.

✔ You can select different types of tabs with the Tab gizmo. See Chapter 13.

 ✔ The Ruler is fine for visually setting indents, but if you need to be precise, use the Paragraph dialog box. Only there can you enter exact amounts for indents. Refer to the previous several sections in this chapter for detailed information on setting various paragraph indents.

✔ Setting the indents for a paragraph is not the same thing as setting margins. Margins are set at the page-formatting level. See Chapter 14 for more information on setting margins.

Chapter 13

Formatting Tabs

*O*n the scale of things, one would believe logically that tabs are part of paragraph formatting. And they are! But in Word, setting tabs can be so odd and frustrating that I decided to devote a special chapter to the subject. It's not that tabs are evil. They harbor no third eye or hideous intelligence, nor are they out to serve the human race the way Aunt Mable serves ketchup-smothered meatloaf for dinner. Nope. Tabs just deserve special attention, that's all. And this chapter is where they get it.

The Story of Tab

Once upon a time, a giant cola company searched for a diet beverage.

Whoops! Wrong Tab story.

A tab is like a big space. How big? As big as you like. You set the size by using a tab stop. So when you press the Tab key, Word zooms the toothpick cursor over to the next *tab stop*. That big!

Tabs are used to set things into a *tabular* format, like in a table. You can use tabs to line up columns of information or to indent paragraphs or lines of text. They're handy and much better than trying to use multiple whacks of the spacebar to achieve the same thing.

✔ Pressing the Tab key inserts a tab "character" in your document. That character moves the toothpick cursor, and any text you type, over to the next tab stop.

✔ Pressing the Tab key does not insert spaces. When you use Backspace or Delete to remove a tab, you delete one character — the tab character.

✔ Word can display the tab character for you if you like. It looks like a tiny arrow pointing to the right. To display this character, choose Tools⇨Options. Click the View tab. Choose Tab Characters from the Formatting marks area. Click OK.

✔ Tab stops are set at ½-inch intervals on each line of text — unless you specify otherwise.

✔ Tabs are paragraph-level things. Setting tabs affects only the paragraph the toothpick cursor is blinking in. To set the tabs for several paragraphs, you must first select them as a block. Refer to Chapter 6 for more blocky stuff.

✔ It helps if you have the ruler visible when you work with tabs. Choose View⇨Ruler from the menu if the ruler isn't visible. You may have to click the down arrows on the menu to see the Ruler command. (Refer to Figure 1-3 for the location of the ruler on Word's screen.)

✔ Tab is short for *tab*ulator. It comes from the Latin root for *table,* which is handy because that's what tabs help you do: line things up into tables. Even so, Word does have a Table command. See Chapter 20.

The Tab Stops Here

Just to confuse you, there are two places in Word where you can set tab stops. The first is the ruler, shown in Figure 13-1. The second is in the Tabs dialog box. Most folks use the ruler, but for some tab options, you must go to the Tabs dialog box.

Figure 13-1: Important tab things on the ruler.

The ruler is the first choice for setting tabs because of the Tab button on the left side (refer to Figure 13-1). The Tab button sports one of Word's five types of tab stops. Here's the brief rundown (which you don't have to memorize):

The most common tab is the left tab, the plump L. This tab works like the Tab key on a typewriter: Press the Tab key, and the new text appears at the next tab stop. No mental hang-ups here.

The center tab stop centers text on the tab stop. This is strange, which is why it's covered later in this chapter in glorious detail. See the section "The center of Tab."

The right tab right justifies the text at that tab stop. This tab gives you leeway to do some fancy paragraph justification on a single line, some of which is demonstrated in the section "Right on, Tab," later in this chapter.

The decimal tab aligns numbers by their decimals. This is a great boon to anyone printing a list of prices. See the section "The amazing decimal tab," later in this chapter.

The ugly stepsister of the Tab family is the Bar tab. I'm sure that there were a few hoots in the Word programming lab the day they named this one. See the section "Paying the bar tab," somewhere a few pages to the right of here.

Clicking the Tab button displays one of the tab stops I just mentioned. Click the button a few times to watch it change from one type of tab stop to the other.

Also included on the Tab button, though they're not really tab stops, are the Left Indent and Hanging Indent items. Why they put them there, I'll never know. Chapter 12 shows you better ways to indent a paragraph, anyway.

The following sections describe the various tab stops and how to use them in your documents.

Setting a Tab Stop

To set a tab stop, you generally follow these steps:

1. Click the Tab button until you find the type of tab you want.

For example, click the Tab button until the standard Left tab — Big L — appears (see the margin).

2. Click on the ruler where you want the tab stop placed.

This is the tricky part. You must click in the middle of the ruler. For example, to put a tab stop at 1⅛ inches, you position the mouse pointer as shown in Figure 13-2.

You can drag the tab stop left or right. As you drag, notice a line that extends down into your document's text (refer to Figure 13-2). That line tells you *exactly* where text lines up for that tab stop.

Release the mouse button to set the tab.

3. To set another tab stop, repeat Step 2.

You set a new tab stop every time you click on the ruler. The type of tab displayed on the Tab button determines which kind of tab you set.

Figure 13-2:
Setting a
left tab.

4. When you're done, click in your document to set the toothpick cursor and type away.

Pressing the Tab key zooms the toothpick cursor over to the tab stop — at 1.125 inches, as shown in Figure 13-2. (That's 1⅛ inches, for those of you into nondecimal fractions.)

✔ When you set your own tab stops, you affect the preset (at half-inch intervals) tab stops that Word automatically gives you. The automatic tab stops to the left of your new tab are removed; but the automatic tab stops on the right still hang around.

✔ The tab stops you set affect only the current paragraph, unless you have a group of paragraphs selected. The biggest goof people make with tabs is setting them for only one paragraph when they really mean to set them for a swath of paragraphs.

✔ The best thing about setting tabs and using the Tab key is that they line up text *exactly* with the tab stop. Pressing the spacebar a zillion times does not do that.

✔ Removing a tab stop is as easy as dragging the tab (the Fat L or other tab character) from the ruler. That's right, you can drag a tab stop down from the ruler into your text to remove it.

✔ The phantom tab stop you may see when you select a block appears when a tab is set in one of the paragraphs but not in all of them. You can remove the phantom tab stop by dragging it off the ruler, or click the tab stop with the mouse to set it for all the selected paragraphs.

Setting your standard left tabs

Left tabs are the standard, typical, boring types of tabs most everyone uses. But why are they left? Left over? Left out? Leftist?

Left tabs are called such because text typed after you press the tab aligns its left side to the tab stop. Figure 13-3 illustrates this concept. See how each bit of text lines up its left edge with the tab stop in the figure? Pressing the spacebar doesn't do this. You must use a tab stop!

Figure 13-3:
Lining up
text on a
tab stop.

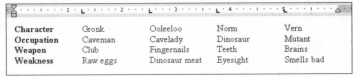

Character	Gronk	Ooleeloo	Norm	Vern
Occupation	Caveman	Cavelady	Dinosaur	Mutant
Weapon	Club	Fingernails	Teeth	Brains
Weakness	Raw eggs	Dinosaur meat	Eyesight	Smells bad

To make a new left tab stop for your current paragraph, follow these steps:

1. Type the paragraph you want to stick the tabs in.

I'm a fan of typing the text *first*. That's because one tab stop does the trick. Just type your text, pressing the Tab key once — no matter how far you eventually want the text to go over. Too many people press the Tab key three or four times. That's okay, but it's inefficient. Word is smarter than that. Press the Tab key only once, and then use the ruler to set the tab stop. Trust me — this is the best way to work things.

2. Make sure that the toothpick cursor is in the paragraph you want to change.

To change multiple paragraphs, select them all as a block.

3. Choose the left tab stop from the Tab button.

Keep clicking the Tab button until the Left tab appears, as shown in the margin.

4. Click the mouse in the ruler where you want a new tab stop.

For example, in Figure 13-3, the first tab stop is set at 1.25 inches, the second at 2.5 inches, the third at 3.75, and the fourth at 5 inches.

The center of Tab

The center tab is a unique character, typically used on a line by itself to center one or a few words on that line. This allows you to have centered text without formatting the entire paragraph as centered. Here's a demo:

1. **Start a new paragraph, one containing text you want to center.**

   You probably won't type a whole paragraph for a center tab. In fact, that would be very unusual. Instead, the best example for this situation is typing a header or footer — a single line of text. (See Chapter 15 for more information on headers and footers.)

2. **Press the Tab key.**

   Believe it or not, you need only one tab.

3. **Type the text to center.**

   A chapter title, your name, or whatever text you type is centered on that line when you set a center tab stop. In Figure 13-4, I typed the title of my screenplay, "Cave Man Love Triangle."

4. **Press Enter.**

   This step ends the line. Now you're ready to set the center tab.

5. **Click the mouse to put the toothpick cursor on the line you just typed.**

6. **Click the Tab button until the center tab appears.**

   The center tab is shown in the margin. It looks like an upside-down T.

7. **Click the mouse on the middle of the ruler to set the center tab.**

   Your text should line up as shown in Figure 13-4. See how the text "Cave Man Love Triangle" appears centered on the center tab? The paragraph is still aligned to the left, but that tiny bit of text is centered.

Figure 13-4:
A bit of text
is centered
with the
center tab.

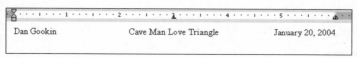

Dan Gookin   Cave Man Love Triangle   January 20, 2004

✔ Center tabs are best used on a single line of text, usually by themselves. There's no reason to do them any other way.

✔ Obviously, centering a paragraph beats the pants off of using a center tab stop in most cases. In fact, the only time I use center tab stops is when I create headers or footers. See Chapter 15.

Right on, Tab

The right tab is a creature that aligns text to the right of the tab stop, not to the left. In Figure 13-4, you can see how the date is right aligned for the title of a document. Only one Tab "character" separates the title from the right-aligned date.

✔ To set a right tab stop, choose the Right tab from the Tab button on the ruler. Then click on the ruler where you want the right tab to be set.

✔ Figure 13-4 shows the right tab on the right side of a heading. After setting the right tab, I pressed the Tab key and then typed the date.

✔ Typing text at a right tab stop pushes the text to the left (the opposite of normal), which keeps the text aligned with the right stop.

✔ As with a center tab stop, the right tab stop is best used on a line by itself, usually in a header, footer, or some type of document title, as shown in Figure 13-4.

The amazing decimal tab

I love decimal tabs. Without them, columns of numbers would never match up. This feature is a serious boon to anyone writing a financial summary report, as shown in Figure 13-5.

Sold one painting	$650.00
Income tax	235.00
Self-Employement tax	145.00
Transfer tax	50.00
City tax	50.50
County levy	8.00
Listing fee	25.00
Gallery Commission	130.00
Profit	$6.50

Figure 13-5: Lining up numbers with the decimal tab.

You work with a decimal tab just like any other tab. The difference is that the text to the left of the decimal comes before the tab stop and text after the decimal goes to the right (as shown in Figure 13-5).

For example, in Figure 13-5, on the fifth line I typed *City tax,* pressed Tab, and then typed *50.50.* Pressing Tab moved the toothpick cursor over to the decimal tab stop at 2" (see the ruler). I typed *50,* and it moved to the left. But when I typed the decimal, that determined the tab "stop," and the rest of the number moved to the right. (You really have to try this yourself to see how it works.)

If you need to rearrange things (perhaps the columns are too close together), select all the lines with numbers as a block. Use your mouse to slide the decimal tab left or right on the ruler. You can then realign the numbers in the selected block all at once.

Paying the bar tab

Enough with the puns! A bar tab isn't a tab stop at all. Instead, it's a decorative vertical bar that you can slap down in your text. Mostly it's used to draw precise vertical lines (bars) in your text.

Unlike regular tabs, pressing the Tab key does not line up any text with a bar tab. Again, it's merely a decorative item in the text. Figure 13-6 shows one way it could be used.

Figure 13-6:
The mystery
of the bar
tab.

Enter the total amount of water balloons lobbed at the Dean's office	245
Approximate number of balloons that hit a specific target	17
Ratio of hits to miss	1:7

Note how in Figure 13-6 a right tab stop is used to right align the bit of text, and then a left tab is used to specify the number. On the same line, two bar tabs are used to create the dual vertical lines. The bar tab stops were set after the other text was written, and they did not affect the formatting.

Using the Tabs Dialog Box

Setting tabs in the ruler is fine for most folks. I like it because you can see the effect the tab has on your text and can drag the tab stop to make adjustments. For purists, however, there is the Tabs dialog box, shown in Figure 13-7. It allows you more precision over using the ruler by itself.

To set a tab in the Tabs dialog box, follow these steps:

1. **Summon the Tabs dialog box.**

   Choose Format⇨Tabs from the menu.

2. **Enter the exact tab stop position in the Tab Stop Position box.**

   For example, type **1.1875** to set a tab at exactly that spot.

3. **Choose the type of tab stop from the Alignment area.**

   The standard tab stop is Left. Other tab stops are covered elsewhere in this chapter.

Figure 13-7:
The Tabs
dialog box.

4. **Click the Set button.**

   The Set button — not the OK button — is what creates the tab stop. After clicking Set, your tab stop is placed on the list below the Tab Stop Position dialog box. (You may notice that numbers are rounded to the nearest tenth; Word interprets 1.1875 as 1.9.)

5. **Continue setting tabs.**

   Repeat Steps 1–3 for as many tabs as you need to set.

6. **Click OK.**

   You're returned to your document with the new tab stops visible on the ruler.

- If you need to set a row of tabs, with each one three-quarters of an inch apart, for example, type **0.75"** in the Default Tab Stops box and then click the OK button. Word automatically figures the tab stops and sets them for you. You can see these default tab stops, which appear as dark brown ticks on the gray line below the ruler (they're very hard to see).

- You must click the Set button to set a tab. I don't know how many times I click OK, thinking that the tab stop is set, and it's not.

- To remove a tab stop by using the Tabs dialog box, click the tab on the list below the Tab Stop Position box. This action selects that tab. Then click the Clear button. It's gone!

- Clicking the Clear All button in the Tabs dialog box removes all tabs from the ruler in one drastic sweep.

Setting Fearless Leader Tabs

One thing you can do in the Tabs dialog box that you cannot do with the ruler is set a leader tab. What is a leader tab you may ask? Well:

A *leader tab* produces a row of dots when you press Tab. You see these tabs sometimes in indexes and all the time in tables of contents. Word gives you the choice of three different leaders:

Fearless dot leader tabs   166

Zipper line leader tabs   166

U-boat underline leader tabs   166

To set up a fearless leader tab, follow these steps:

1. **Position the toothpick cursor on the line where you want your leader tabs.**

   Or select a swath of paragraphs you've already typed for leader tab-hood. Remember: one tab only! Name, Tab, Phone number; Actor, Tab, Character; Citation, Tab, Page number; and so on.

2. **Choose the Format⇨Tabs command.**

3. **Select a spot for the tab in the Tab Stop Position box.**

   Say, 4 inches, so type 4 into the Tab Stop Position box. (You can change this later by using the ruler.)

4. **Choose Left for the alignment.**

   Right is also a valid choice, especially for things like cast lists and phone numbers.

5. **Choose the style of fearless leader tab you want.**

   Your choices are dotted, dashed, or underlined, as presented at the beginning of this section.

6. **Click the Set button.**

   You'll forget this step the first time you try this on your own. And you'll wonder why it didn't work. That's when you'll return here to reread this sentence.

7. **Click OK.**

   The leader tab is set.

Now you can observe how it changed your text, or if you haven't typed the text, you can start typing it now. Use only one tab to create the leader, and then type the reference. For example: Marlon Brando, Tab, Vito Corleone.

You can adjust the tab stops after setting them if some of the text doesn't line up. *Remember:* To adjust the tab stops for more than one paragraph at a time, you need to select everything as a block. Refer to Chapter 6.

Chapter 14

Formatting Pages

• •

In This Chapter

▶ Setting the page and paper size

▶ Choosing landscape or portrait layout

▶ Setting margins for your document

▶ Automatically numbering your pages

▶ Changing page numbers

▶ Creating a new page

▶ Deleting that extra, blank page

• •

Beyond the word! More complex than a mere sentence! Bolder than a paragraph! Look, up on the screen! It's a sheet of paper! No! It's a window! No! It's a *page.*

In keeping with the trend of going from small to big, the next step in the formatting three-ring circus is to format the page itself. Pages have a certain size and orientation, plus margins and page numbers. All of that is covered here in a neat and tidy manner that entertains while it informs.

A Page Is a Sheet of Paper About "This" Big

How many angels can dance on a sheet of paper? Well, it depends on the size of the paper, of course — not to mention the type of dance.

Most printing takes place on a standard, 8½-x-11-inch sheet of paper. That's what Word defines as a *page,* on which you can format margins and other page-formatting whatnot. But Word isn't burned to the frying pan on using only that size of paper. No, Word lets you change the paper size to anything you want — from a teensy envelope to a sheet of paper big enough to make the bed with.

The paper-size-setting stuff is done in the Page Setup dialog box. The following instructions tell you how to change the size of the paper you're printing on:

1. **Choose the File➪Page Setup command.**

   The Page Setup dialog box appears.

2. **Make sure that the Paper tab is in front.**

   See Figure 14-1 to ensure that what you see on the screen is right. If not, click the Paper tab.

Figure 14-1:
The Page
Setup/Paper
dialog box.

3. **Click the Paper Size drop-down list.**

   The list drops down to reveal a slate of common paper sizes: Letter, Legal, the A4 size popular in Europe, and other wacky options.

4. **Select your document's desired paper size from the list.**

   For example, say you want to print on that tall, legal-size paper. If so, choose Legal from the list. Note how the Width and Height information updates to reflect this common paper size. Nifty.

   Most PC printers can print on several sizes of paper. Weird sizes, though available on the list, may not be compatible with your printer — not to mention that you need that specific paper size to print on. It's not up to Word to make an 8½-x-11-inch sheet of paper another 3 inches longer.

5. **Select Whole Document from the Apply To drop-down list.**

   It may say that already, in which case you're doing well and can move on.

In the future, if you want a document to use several paper sizes, use the Apply To drop-down list to tell Word where the new paper sizes start. This involves dividing your document up into sections, which is covered in Chapter 15. For now: Ignore it.

6. Click OK.

Okay. Type away on the new size of paper.

✔ Note how the page formatting stuff is on the File menu and not the Format menu. This difference drives most users insane, because you would assume page formatting is a Format menu thing. But it's not. So much for logic in a computer.

✔ Word can print on any size paper your printer can swallow. To specify the oddball size, choose Custom from the Paper Size drop-down list, and then enter the paper's width and height into those boxes in the Page Setup dialog box.

✔ If you're printing on an odd-size piece of paper, remember to load that special paper into your printer before you start printing. Some smarter printers even tell you which size of paper they want to print on. Mine nags at me all the time for the proper-size paper. It's like a second mother.

✔ The Preview window changes to reflect the new paper size. Very handy.

✔ Refer to Chapter 30 for information on printing envelopes. (There's a special command for doing that; no sense in finagling a new paper size here.)

Setting the Page's Orientation (Landscape or Portrait Mode)

Word normally prints on a sheet of paper from top to bottom with the narrow edge on top. This wouldn't be worth mentioning, except that Word can also print "longways" on a sheet of paper, with the long edge on top. This orientation is ideal for brochures or reports with graphics or just when you're feeling in a longer rather than taller mood.

The technical, I'm-an-important-word-processing-expert terms for the two paper orientations are portrait mode for the up-down paper and landscape mode for sideways. A portrait picture is usually taller than it is long to accommodate our faces — unless someone has large ears on a jug-like head. Landscape is for those lovely oil paintings of seascapes or lakes and trees that are wider than they are tall.

To make Word print the long way on a sheet of paper — in landscape mode — do the following:

1. **Choose File⇨Page Setup.**

   The Page Setup dialog box appears. Make sure that the Margins panel is forward if it's not already, as shown in Figure 14-2.

Figure 14-2:
The Page
Setup/
Margins
dialog box.

2. **Choose Portrait or Landscape from the Orientation area.**

   The Preview changes to reflect the document's perspective.

3. **Click OK.**

✔ Printing in landscape mode may require you to adjust the document's margins; see the next section.

✔ Make the decision to have your document in Landscape mode before you do any extensive formatting. That mode does affect your paragraphs and other "lower-level" formatting, so it's better to have it done first, before you start composing your text.

✔ Avoid printing standard documents in landscape mode. Scientists and other people in white lab coats who study such things have determined that human reading speed slows drastically when people must scan a long line of text. Reserve landscape mode for printing lists, tables, and items for which normal paper is too narrow.

✔ As with changing the paper size, you can have landscape or portrait mode apply to an entire document, from a certain point forward, or to a selected section within your document. See the preceding section for more information.

✔ It's possible to change orientation in the middle of a document; for example, you can have one page in a long document print in landscape mode. To do that, you must take advantage of Word's section-formatting commands. You start a new section, change the page orientation for that section only, and then start another section when the page orientation needs to change back. See Chapter 15 for more information on creating sections in your document.

Marginal Information

Every page has margins. They provide the air around your document — that inch or so of breathing space that sets off the text from the rest of the page. As with other things in Word, these margins can be adjusted, fooled, cajoled, or otherwise messed with.

Word automatically sets your margins at 1 inch from the top and bottom of the page and 1¼ inches from the left and right sides of the page. Most English teachers and book editors want margins of this size because these people love to scribble in margins (they even write that way on blank paper). In Word, you can adjust the margins to suit any fussy professional.

To change the margins, follow these steps:

1. **Choose the File⇨Page Setup command.**

   The Page Setup dialog box appears. Click the Margins tab if it's not up front (refer to Figure 14-2).

2. **Enter the new measurements for the Top, Bottom, Left, and Right page margins.**

   Type the new values in the appropriate boxes. For example, typing a value of **1"** in all the boxes sets all margins to 1 inch. Entering a value of **2.5"** sets a 2½-inch margin. You don't need to type the inch symbol (").

   The Preview window shows you how your margins affect text on the page.

3. **Choose Whole Document, This Point Forward, or This Section from the Apply To drop-down list.**

   • **Whole Document** changes the margins for your whole document, bonnet to boot.

- • **This Point Forward** means that the new margins take place from the toothpick cursor's position, onward.

- • **This Section** means that the margins apply to only the current section. (See Chapter 15 for more information on sections.)

4. **Click OK.**

Your new margins are enforced.

✔ Margins are a page-wide formatting command (which is why they're covered in this chapter). To set the indents for a single paragraph, you need to use a paragraph-formatting command. See Chapter 12.

✔ If you want to print on three-hole paper, then set the Gutter margin to about 0.5". That moves the entire margin "frame" over one half inch from where the three holes are punched. You can set the Gutter Position to Left, unless the holes are punched on the top of the page, in which case you set the Gutter Position to Top.

✔ Keep in mind that most laser printers cannot print on the outside half-inch of a piece of paper — top, bottom, left, and right. This space is an absolute margin; although you can tell Word to set a margin of 0 inches right and 0 inches left, text still does not print there. Instead, choose a minimum of 0.5 inches for the left and right margins.

✔ Likewise, many ink printers have a taller top or bottom margin requirement. If you attempt to print outside that area, a dialog box appears, informing you of your offense.

Page Numbering

Here's a little ditty from my *Top Ten Word Processing Songs* album:

Oh! Your word processor will number your pages for you!

Your word processor will number your pages for you!

Don't frown and fret, don't sit and stew, 'cause

Your word processor will number your pages for you!

No foolin': Word can number your pages for you. There is no need to do it yourself. No matter how many pages you have or how much you add to or delete your text, Word keeps it straight. All you need to do is tell Word where on the page to stick the page number. Please, oh please, don't manually number anything in a word processor!

Dangerous treading in the Multiple Pages area of the Page Setup dialog box

Nestled in the Margins tab of the Page Setup dialog box, you'll find the Pages area. That tells you how Word uses the paper to print your document. You see, with Word there's more than one way to print a document on a page.

Normal (refer to Figure 14-2) means that you're printing pretty much as you would expect a document to print: one page per sheet of paper.

Mirror Margins is used when your printer is smart enough to print on both sides of a sheet of paper. That way, every other page is flip-flopped so that your margins always line up. For example, the "gutter" may be on the left of one page, but on the right for the page's back side.

2 Pages per Sheet splits the paper right down the center and forces Word to print two "pages" per sheet of paper. Note that this option works best when used in landscape mode.

Book Fold is Word's attempt to create a multiple-page booklet by printing the proper pages on both sides of a sheet of paper. This works best if you have a printer capable of printing on both sides of a sheet of paper. The Sheets per Booklet option tells Word how long your booklet is.

Note that Word, despite the efforts just listed, is a poor book-binding program. It's my recommendation that if you're into any type of publishing, consider getting a desktop publishing program, such as Adobe's InDesign or Microsoft's Publisher, which are far better equipped to deal with such things.

Where to stick the page number?

The question is not "*Can* Word put a number on your page?" but rather "*Where* should the number go?" If you follow these steps, you can direct Word to put the page number just about anywhere on the page (well, anywhere *logical*):

1. **Choose the Insert⇨Page Numbers command.**

   The Page Numbers dialog box, shown in Figure 14-3, appears.

Figure 14-3:
The Page Numbers dialog box.

Page Numbers	☒
Position:	Preview
Bottom of page (Footer) ▾	
Alignment:	
Right ▾	
☑ Show number on first page	
Format...	OK Cancel

2. **Pick a position for the page number.**

   Word can stick the page number at the top or bottom of the page. Choose that position from the Position drop-down list.

3. **Pick an alignment for the page number.**

   The page number can appear to the right or left or at the center, inside, or outside of your text. Choose that position from the Alignment drop-down list.

4. **Click OK.**

   The page numbers are inserted.

If you'd rather have more control over your page numbers, consider using the page number command in a header or footer. See Chapter 15 for more information. (If you put the page number in a header or footer, you don't have to use the Page Numbers command.)

   ✔ Keep an eye on the Preview box as you arrange your page number position. Brilliant, eh?

   ✔ If you don't want a page number on your first page (the title page, for example), deselect the Show Number on First Page check box by clicking in it (refer to the Page Numbers dialog box, as shown in Figure 14-3). That action tells Word not to stick an ugly *1* at the bottom of your pristine title page.

Fancy page numbering formats

Word doesn't limit you to numbering your pages with boring 1, 2, 3. If you want, you can number your pages A, B, C, or perhaps use cute little Roman numerals like *i, ii, iii,* or even add hyphens to either side of the page number. Yep, Word can do all that for you, providing that you're clever enough to click the Format button in the Page Numbers dialog box. When you do, you see the Page Number Format dialog box, shown in Figure 14-4.

Use the Number Format drop-down list to choose a format for your page numbers.

Click the OK button when you're done picking a format. Then click OK in the Page Numbers dialog box to get back to your document.

Starting off with a different page number

Word lets you start numbering your pages at whatever number you want. So if you want to start numbering Chapter 2 at page 47, you can do so, providing that you follow these instructions:

1. **Choose Insert➪Page Numbers.**

2. **Click the Format button in the Page Numbers dialog box.**

   The Page Number Format dialog box materializes (refer to Figure 14-4).

3. **Click the Start At radio button and type the beginning page number in the box.**

4. **Click OK to close the Page Number Format dialog box.**

5. **Click OK to close the Page Numbers dialog box.**

Figure 14-4:
The Page
Number
Format
dialog box.

The page number is inserted into your document as you requested. (It's best to see it in the Print Layout view; choose View➪Print Layout.) Do note, however, that the page numbers listed on Word's status bar reflect the actual page number in your document, not the bogus renumbering job you just did.

Starting a New Page

You can choose two ways to start a new page in Word: the horribly-wrong-yet-obvious way and the impressively neat way:

✔ **Horribly wrong:** Keep pressing the Enter key until you see the row o' dots that denotes the start of a new page. Yes, this technique works. But it's horribly wrong.

✔ **Impressively neat:** Press Ctrl+Enter. Voilà! New page.

Pressing Ctrl+Enter inserts a *hard page break* into your document, demanding that Word begin a new page On That Very Spot. This is the preferred way to start a new page.

In Normal view (refer to Chapter 2), the hard page break looks like a regular page break but with the addition of the words `Page Break`:

--Page Break--

In Print Layout view, the page break looks like any other page break (refer to Figure 2-2).

Keep these points in mind when you're dealing with hard page breaks:

✔ You can also insert a hard page break by choosing Insert⇨Break from the menu. Choose Page Break from the list and click OK. That's a load of steps, however. Ctrl+Enter is what most people use all the time.

✔ The hard page break works just like a regular page break does, although you control where it lives in your document: Move the toothpick cursor to where you want the hard page break and press Ctrl+Enter.

✔ Pressing Ctrl+Enter inserts a hard page-break *character* in your document. That character stays there, always creating a hard page break no matter how much you edit the text on previous pages.

✔ You can delete a hard page break by pressing the Backspace or Delete keys. If you do this accidentally, just press Ctrl+Enter again or press Ctrl+Z to undelete.

✔ If you set hard page breaks, remember to use Print Preview to look at your document before you print it. Sometimes, the process of editing moves text around, making the hard page breaks unnecessary and awkward. Refer to Chapter 9 for more information on the Print Preview command.

✔ Don't fall into the trap of using hard page breaks to adjust your page numbering. You can use the power of the computer to alter your page numbers without having to mess with page formatting. See "Where to stick the page number?" earlier in this chapter.

Deleting That Annoying Extra Blank Page at the End of Your Document

Sometimes — without knowing it — you'll add some blank spaces, empty paragraphs, and nonsense to the end of your document. Don't worry; everyone does this. The effect is that your document ends with a blank page. It's most noticeable when you print and that silly waste-of-paper page slides out of the printer.

To get rid of the last blank page in your document, follow these steps:

1. **Press Ctrl+End.**

   This keystroke moves the toothpick cursor to the very end of your document.

2. **Press the Backspace key.**

3. **Repeat Step 2 over and over until the extra blank page is gone.**

By pressing the Backspace key you're deleting the blank paragraphs and extra spaces that naturally accumulate at the end of a document. Eventually, you'll back up over the top of the blank page, which effectively deletes it from your document.

✔ It may be easier to see the stuff you're deleting if you press Ctrl+Shift+8 before you backspace. That displays the invisible codes that have created the extra sheet of paper. Press Ctrl+Shift+8 again when you're done. (Use the 8 key on your keyboard, not the 8 key on the numeric keypad.)

✔ If you backspace too far, and destroy some needed text, press Ctrl+Z to "undo" the deletion.

✔ In some cases, this trick won't work. That's usually when you have a graphic image, drawing, box, or frame that is empty and hangs over or lurks between the last two pages in the document. In that case, you must delete or resize that object to get rid of the extra blank page.

Chapter 15

Formatting Documents

D*ocument* is an important word. It carries weight. Funny, you wouldn't think of a silly letter to your niece as something heavy, important, or legal sounding. But in Word, the big picture is the *document*. You've come from formatting words, to paragraphs, then pages, and now finally, the beloved *document*. Or, you could also call it the *whole dang doodle*.

As far as formatting is concerned, a document is a big-picture thing. In fact, much of the information in this chapter isn't necessary for most of the documents you create (the silly to-your-niece or honey-do documents). But when you go nuts someday, or say the urge hits you to *really* flaunt your knowledge of Word, this chapter will be your boon companion.

All About Sections

Many of Word's formatting commands affect an entire document. For example, most of the page-formatting commands covered in Chapter 14 are typical document-wide commands: margins, paper size, orientation, and other what-not. And the header and footers you can add to a document (covered in this chapter) also apply to a whole document.

If you need to change a document-wide format for a single page or group of pages, break your document up into *sections.* Each section contains its own page formatting. So if you need to print one page in landscape mode, just create a new section for that page. Or, if your title page needs unique margins, you create a section just for it.

Sections are easy to create. They can simplify most document-long formatting hassles. The following sections tell you just about everything you need to know.

- A *section* is basically an area in your document whose page formatting is independent of the rest of your document.

- Text and paragraph formatting, as well as any styles you may create, don't give a hoot about sections.

- Sections are used to create many of the interesting and fun types of documents covered in Part V of this book.

- The subject of sections is generally considered an advanced Word topic. Most people never use them. Only on rare occasions have I needed to break up a document into sections. If you want, you can freely skip this information; skim on up to the section on Headers and Footers.

Creating a section

Breaking up your document isn't hard to do. Word has carefully placed all its breaking commands into a handy Break dialog box. To summon the dialog box, choose Insert⇨Break from the menu.

Figure 15-1 shows the Break dialog box. The items in the top group are text breaks; the bottom group contains section breaks.

Figure 15-1:
The Break
dialog box.

Suppose that you're creating a title page on a new document. Before doing any typing, create the title page as follows:

1. **Choose the Insert⇨Break command.**

   The Break dialog box emerges, as shown in Figure 15-1.

2. **Select Next Page.**

   The Next Page option works like a hard page break; it inserts a page break *and* a section break into your document. This is the most common form of section break because most of the formatting items you're working with are at the page level.

3. **Click OK.**

   In Print Layout view, the new section looks like a hard page break. In Normal view, the section break looks like this:

   ⸻⸻⸻⸻⸻⸻⸻⸻⸻Section Break (Next Page)⸻⸻⸻⸻⸻⸻⸻⸻⸻

The next step in the process is to move the toothpick cursor to the first page (the title page in the preceding section) and format that page according to your needs.

✔ You can use the Continuous section break to mix formatting styles within a page. For example, if you have columns of text sharing a page with regular text, the Continuous section break is the ideal way to separate the individual formats. See Chapter 21 for more information.

✔ You can use the Even Page and Odd Page options to start the next section on the next even or odd page — ideal for those futile times when you try to use Word to bind a book or pamphlet.

✔ Section breaks also provide a great way to divide a multipart document. For example, the title page can be a section; the introduction, Chapter 1, and Appendix A all can be made into separate sections. You can then use Word's Go To command to zoom to each section. Refer to Chapter 3 for more information on the Go To command.

✔ See Chapter 21 for information on a column break.

✔ Text-wrapping breaks work like soft returns (see Chapter 2), except they're designed to be used on text that wraps around a figure or table.

Deleting a section break

You can delete a section break with the Delete key: position the toothpick cursor just before the section break, then press the Delete key.

If you accidentally delete a section break, you lose any special formatting you applied to the section. In this case, press the Undo shortcut, Ctrl+Z, before you do anything else.

✔ You can also use the Backspace key to delete a section break, though it must first be selected.

✔ The best way to see section breaks is in Normal view. Choose View➪Normal from the menu.

The Joys of Headers and Footers

In construction, a header is a buncha wood over a doorway or window. In baseball, a doubleheader is two games in a row (and a boon for seat cushion sales). In a document, a *header* is the text you see at the top of every page. The header's little brother is the *footer,* which is text that appears on the bottom of every page in a document. Word does 'em both.

✔ Headers usually contain things such as your name, the document name, date, page number, title, and phone numbers. ("Hurry! Buy now! Operators are standing by!")

✔ Headers can also be called *eyebrows*. Weird, huh?

✔ Footers can include page numbers, a chapter or document title, and soft cushiony insoles.

✔ Footers are not the same thing as footnotes. See Chapter 22 for the low-down on footnotes.

Adding a header or footer

Headers and footers can make any document shine. You don't need to use them both; you can use just one or the other. Either way, the same command is used to add or play with them.

To add a header or footer, follow these steps:

1. **Choose View➪Header and Footer.**

   Word tosses you into a special version of Print Layout view that shows the Header and Footer areas of your document roped off. Also visible is the floating Header and Footer toolbar. Witness Figure 15-2 for an example.

2. **Click the Switch between Header/Footer icon to choose either the header or footer for editing.**

   Clicking the button switches you back and forth between the header and footer.

Figure 15-2:
A header
along with
the Header
and Footer
floating
toolbar
thing.

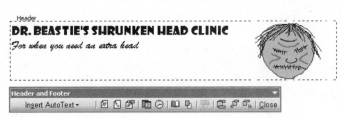

3. **Enter your header or footer text.**

   Any text you type can be formatted using any of Word's text and paragraph formatting commands, including tabs (see Chapters 11, 12, and 13).

   Word preformats the headers and footers in any document with center
   and right tabs at the center and far right of the ruler. This allows you to
   press the Tab key, type some text, and have the text automatically centered at the bottom (or top) of each page. This tab stop isn't required,
   but it's mighty thoughtful of Microsoft to set it up that way.

4. **Use the buttons on the Header and Footer toolbar for special items.**

   Hover the mouse pointer over each button to see a brief explanation of
   its function (just like on the big toolbars!).

   For example, you can press the Tab key and then click the Insert Page
   Number button to put a page number in the center of a footer.

   You can use the Insert AutoText drop-down list to put AutoText items
   into the header or footer. The items inserted are updating "fields," which
   reflect various aspects of your document, as shown in Figure 15-3. For
   example, Page X of Y displays the current page number out of total
   pages in the document.

Figure 15-3:
AutoText
items you
can slap
down in the
header.

5. Click the Close button when you're done.

You're back in your document.

In Print Layout view, you can see the header or footer displayed in ghostly gray text. In Normal view, you can't see any header or footer, even though it's still there. (You can also use the Print Preview command, as covered in Chapter 9, to see the header or footer.)

You can put anything in a header or footer that you can put in a document, including graphics (refer to Figure 15-2). This capability is especially useful if you want a logo to appear on each page. See Chapter 23 for information on Word and graphics.

✔ You don't have to go to page 1 to insert a page number in the header. Word is smart enough to put the proper number on the proper page no matter where you're editing the header in your document.

✔ Actually, headers and footers are geared to sections in your document. Therefore, as long as you're in the same (or only) section, you can edit the header or footer for that section.

✔ If your document has more than one section in it, the header and footer's name appears with the section number, as in `Header-Section 2-`. Remember that any additions or changes to a header or footer in a section affect that section only.

✔ In Print Layout view, you can quickly edit any header or footer by double-clicking its ghostly gray image.

✔ You probably want to put some text in front of the page number because a number sitting all by itself tends to get lonely. You can get really creative and type the word **Page** and a space before you click the # button, or you can come up with some interesting text on your own.

✔ To insert the current date or time into the header or footer, click the Date or Time buttons on the Header and Footer toolbar.

✔ Don't forget to use the Switch between Header and Footer button to alternately edit headers and footers.

Odd headers for odd pages, even headers for even pages

Word enables you to put two sets of headers and footers in your document: one set for odd pages and another for even pages. For example, this book is formatted that way. The header on even pages contains the page number and the part title. The header on odd pages contains the chapter number and title and then the page number. You can do that too!

To force Word to accept two sets of headers and footers, obey these steps:

1. **Choose View➪Header and Footer.**

   This step displays any headers or footers in your document and also the Header and Footer floating toolbar thing (refer to Figure 15-2).

2. **Click the Page Setup button on the Header and Footer toolbar.**

   The Page Setup/Layout dialog box opens, as shown in Figure 15-4. (If you don't see the Layout tab forward, then click it so the dialog box on your screen looks like the one in the figure.)

3. **Select the Different Odd and Even check box.**

   This step tells Word that you want two sets of headers and footers, one for odd pages and one for even pages. Notice how the Preview window changes to show two pages rather than one? Clever.

4. **Click OK.**

   You're returned to header/footer editing mode, but notice how the header or footer now says Odd Page or Even Page before it?

5. **Create the odd (or even) header or footer.**

   Refer to the preceding section for notes on making a header or footer.

Figure 15-4:
The Page Setup/ Layout dialog box.

6. **Create the even (or odd) header or footer.**

Click the Show Next button to see the next footer in your document, or you can click the Show Previous button. These two buttons cycle you through the various odd or even headers or footers in your document.

7. **Click the Close button when you're done editing the headers and footers.**

This odd/even stuff has nothing to do with the last number on your car's license plate or the last number in your address.

But I don't want a header on my first page!

To prevent the header or footer from appearing on the first page of text, which usually is the title page, you need to use the Page Setup/Layout dialog box as described in the preceding section. In the Page Setup/Layout dialog box, select the Different First Page check box; then click OK.

When you return to edit the headers and footers in your document, click the Show Previous button until you find the first header, titled First Page Header. Leave that header (or footer) blank. This procedure places an empty header on the first page; the header appears on all the other pages as ordered. You can also use this option to place a different header on the first page — a graphic, for example.

Multiple header and footer madness — beyond odd and even pages!

A header is a section-long thing. For most documents, which are one section, that's fine. But suppose for some reason that you need multiple headers in your document. Or, maybe you just need to turn the headers "off" for a section of text — if some graphic images appear in the middle of your document and you don't want your header interfering, for example. If so, you need multiple headers (starting headers, no headers, and then the starting headers again). To do that, you split your document into sections.

By using sections, you can have several types of headers and footers floating throughout your document, one set for each section. The new section's headers and footers are completely different from the preceding (or next) section. And changing a header in one section doesn't affect any other section in the document. Refer to "Creating a section," earlier in this chapter, for more information on sections.

Chapter 16

Working with Styles

Golly, there is a lot of formatting junk to remember! Imagine: Not only do you have to type your document, but after that (or during), you have to go through those painful motions of formatting. Again and again. Block after block. Click, apply, adjust, move, center, align, tabs here and there, indent, overhang, bold, and set!

If you're one of those who believes that computers are supposed to *save* you work, then you've found your favorite chapter of the book. Word allows you to save all your formatting commands that you want, need, or have applied into a single thing. That thing is called a *style*. So when you want to reapply that boatload of formatting commands, you simply choose the proper style, and all the formatting commands are blessed upon your text in one swift action. This chapter explains how to apply the aspirin of styles to the formatting headache.

What Is a Style?

A *style* is nothing more than a collection of Word's formatting commands, all stuffed into a single box with one happy button. So, when you want a paragraph that's indented and formatted in Courier, 10 point, you simply *apply* that style to the paragraph. Press the button; it's done. Easy.

- Historically, styles were created to save formatting toil. As word processors grew more sophisticated and printers grew more fonts and Windows let you see things on the screen as they would print, the need for advanced formatting commands increased. To help you deal with all the formatting hoohaw, styles were created.

- All text in Word has a style. Unless you specify otherwise, Word uses the Normal style, typically Times New Roman, 12 point, left-aligned paragraphs. No indenting.

- Word doesn't demand that you use styles. They do, however, make formatting your documents easier.

Where Your Styles Lurk

In Word, you can find styles in two places: on the Formatting toolbar and in the Styles and Formatting task pane.

You'll probably end up choosing styles from the toolbar. The Styles and Formatting task pane is where you can create and modify styles (as well as choose them), but the task pane hogs up too much window space to be a full time thing.

Styles on the toolbar

The easiest way to see and use the styles available in a document is to use the drop-down list on the Formatting toolbar — the one that says Normal — as shown in Figure 16-1.

Figure 16-1:
The Style drop-down list on the toolbar.

Normal
Clear Formatting
Heading 1 ¶
Heading 2 ¶
Heading 3 ¶
Normal ¶
More...

You may need to arrange your toolbars to see the Styles drop-down list. See Chapter 28 for help.

The styles you see on the list are the ones you can use in your document. In Figure 16-1, you see the standard styles that Word applies to every new document. There are four of them: the Normal style, which is applied to all text, and three heading styles.

The Clear Formatting item is simply a command that removes all formatting from whatever text is selected.

The "More..." item is not a style, but merely displays the Style and Formatting task pane.

As you create new styles, they're added to the list.

If you modify an existing style, such as change the font, the style appears on the list with the modification. For example, if you change the font to Arial, a new item, Normal+Arial, appears at the top of the Style list. The font name (Arial, in this case) is added to the list. Of course, there are better ways to add items to the list, which this chapter endeavors to explain.

The way the styles appear on the list gives you a hint to their format. For example, the heading fonts are bold and of a specific size and weight, but the Normal font appears in 12-point Times New Roman.

A small paragraph mark (¶) beside a style name indicates a paragraph style. The formatting commands affect paragraphs as well as text.

An underlined A (a̲) next to a style name indicates a character style. The formatting commands affect only characters. No paragraph formatting commands are included with the style.

- ✔ The drop-down list can grow cumbersome and long. After a certain length, if more styles are available than can be displayed, a More item appears at the bottom of the drop-down list. Choosing that item activates the task pane, which is discussed in the next section.

- ✔ The standard styles are kept in a document template that Word uses for all new documents. The name of the template is NORMAL (or NORMAL.DOT), and it's discussed in the next chapter.

- ✔ The heading styles are not the same thing as headers and footers, covered in Chapter 15. Headers appear at the top of a page. Heading styles are used for chapter and section titles.

Styles in the task pane

Most of what you do with styles happens in the task pane. So, if you've been avoiding the task pane in Word, now is the time to give up and accept the inevitable; despite the fact that the task pane occupies nearly one-fourth of your writing space in Word, it's *not* going away. Boo-hoo.

You can display the Styles and Formatting task pane several gazillion ways. Here are my favorites:

✔ Click the AA button next to the Style drop-down list.

✔ Choose Format➪Styles and Formatting.

✔ Select the More item from the bottom of the Styles drop-down list.

✔ Press Ctrl+F1 to summon the task pane and then choose Styles and Formatting from the task pane's menu (the triangle at the top of the task pane).

Obviously, those who cobble Word together don't want you to avoid the Styles and Formatting task pane. Even if you do, I've included an illustration of it nearby, in Figure 16-2.

Figure 16-2:
The Styles and Formatting task pane.

The Styles and Formatting task pane is *the* place to control, create, delete, or otherwise mangle the styles in your document. All the styles in your document appear there. The current style in use (the style of any selected text or where the toothpick cursor is a-winkin') appears in the top box. In Figure 16-2, it's the Arial style.

Point the mouse at a style on the list to see more information about that style. First, you notice a drop-down arrow thing, indicating the menu attached to each style (see Figure 16-3). Next, if you hold the mouse still, a pop-up window appears, describing the style's specific formatting information. In Figure 16-3, the Heading 1 style is based on the Normal style *plus* various other formatting options.

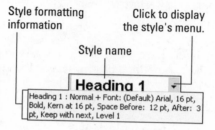

Style formatting information

Click to display the style's menu.

Style name

Figure 16-3:
Getting information about a style.

Heading 1

Heading 1 : Normal + Font: (Default) Arial, 16 pt, Bold, Kern at 16 pt, Space Before: 12 pt, After: 3 pt, Keep with next, Level 1

✔ The Styles and Formatting task pane is the place where you create, edit, and work with styles.

✔ The Select All button selects all the text in your document that matches the highlighted style. (Click the mouse in your document to select the style of that text and then use the Select All button to see all the text formatted with that same style.)

✔ You use the style's menu to delete, modify, select, or update a given style. Figure 16-3 shows you where to click. Information on using the menu is covered later in this chapter.

✔ Feel free to close the task pane when you're done styling around.

Creating a New Style

I hate the Normal style. I suppose that they could have called it the Vanilla style, but I'm one of the 25 percent of the population who likes vanilla ice cream. And calling it the Boring style would show too much humor for a Microsoft product. No, Normal it is. And Normal stinks.

The following sections show you how to create some new styles for your document — something better than Normal.

According to those who keep track of such things, one out of every four ice cream orders is for vanilla compared to one out of nine for chocolate.

Creating a style based on a paragraph you've already formatted

The easiest way to make up a new style is to use all your formatting skills and power to format a single paragraph just the way you like. Then create the style based on that formatted paragraph. Here's how:

1. **Type a paragraph of text.**

   Or, you can simply work with any paragraph of text already in your document. Basically, you just need something on the screen to see how your formatting works.

2. **Mark your paragraph as a block.**

   See Chapter 6 to find out how to mark a block of text.

3. **Format the block.**

   Select your character formatting. Select a font and select a point size to make the text big or little. See Chapter 11 for more information on character formatting.

   Stick to fonts and sizes for your character formatting; avoid bold, italics, or underlining unless you want them applied to *all* the text in the paragraph.

   Select the paragraph formatting. Choose Left, Right, Center, or Justified alignment, pick indents, and so on. See Chapter 12 for the full list of what you can do.

4. **Press Ctrl+Shift+S.**

   This key combination activates the Style drop-down list on the Formatting toolbar. The formatting information is highlighted inside the box.

5. **Type a new name for your style.**

   A brief, descriptive, one-word name does nicely.

   For example, if you create an indented paragraph that you want to use to list things, name the style *List Things*. Or, if you create a special musical style, name it *Liszt Things*.

   If you use the name of an existing style, Word will rudely make you aware of it. That's fine; pick another name.

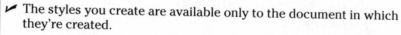

6. **Press Enter.**

The style is added to Word's repertoire of styles for your document.

The style you created now applies to the paragraph you typed (on which the style is based); any additional paragraphs you type also take on that style. And you can apply the style to other paragraphs.

✔ Give your style a name that describes the style's function. Names like *Indented List* or *Table Body Text* are great because they make it easy to remember what they do. Names like *Ira* or *Gopple-bop* are somewhat less desirable.

✔ The styles you create are available only to the document in which they're created.

✔ If you create scads of styles you love and want to use them for several documents, you need to create what's called a *template*. Chapter 17 covers this procedure in the section about creating your very own template.

✔ You may have to tweak some things in your style. If so, you need to use the Style and Formatting task pane. See the section "Modifying a style," later in this chapter.

Creating a style using the task pane

Using the New Style dialog box to create a style is handy — as long as you're well versed with all Word's style commands, including some introduced in the next part of this book. In any event, the following steps glide you through the trips and traps of using the New Style dialog box to make up a style:

1. **Bring up the Styles and Formatting task pane.**

Instructions are provided earlier in this chapter.

Notice that you don't have to create a new paragraph or anything to format for this step. Basically, you just boldly march forth and build the style from scratch.

2. **Click the New Style button.**

The New Style dialog box opens, as shown in Figure 16-4.

3. **Enter a name for your style into the Name text box.**

This is the name that appears on the Style list, hopefully something memorable, something other than Style1. For example, type Title A for an A-level title in your document.

Word warns you if you use a name already given to a style. Use another name.

4. **Choose the Style Type.**

   Most styles are Paragraph, which means that the style covers all font and paragraph formatting options you can dream of, all of which apply to paragraphs as a whole.

   Character styles are rare. I once I wrote a book where the commands to be typed had to appear in the Courier New font, bold and colored blue. So I created a character font with those formatting commands and named it Blue Text. Then, to format the special text, I selected it and applied the Blue Text character format.

   The Table style is used for formatting tables; see Chapter 20. The List style is used for creating lists of items, such as the outlines in Word. It's best to become familiar with tables and lists before you create those formats.

5. **Set the Style Based On item.**

   To save time, you can use an existing style and build your new style on it. For example, if the new style is the same as the Body style you already created but with smaller text, you can base your style on Body and then make the smaller text modification.

   All styles are originally based on the Normal style.

   The drop-down list contains a heck of a lot of styles. Scroll through the list to find a specific one, or just give up and use Normal.

6. **Choose the Style for Following Paragraph.**

This is a handy option, normally set equal to the name of the style you're creating. That way, all the paragraphs you type have the same style. You can use this item to perform some nifty formatting tricks; see the nearby sidebar, "The follow-me style," for more information.

7. **Choose formatting options for your style.**

The New Style dialog box contains a plethora of buttons and drop-down lists — common items you might be familiar with — which can help you instantly choose some basic formatting options. Use the preview window to help you decide.

If you need to get specific, such as choosing double underline or setting tabs, you need to use the Format button. Clicking that button displays a pop-up menu of Word's common formatting commands, (similar to the commands on the Format menu). For example, choose Font to get at the Font dialog box and all its options.

The dialog boxes associated with the Format button's commands are covered elsewhere in this book, but keep in mind that their settings affect the style you're creating and not any text in your document. (Not yet, at least.)

The New Style dialog box assumes that you *know* which formats you're putting into a style. If you don't know, you're better off using the techniques described in the preceding section, "Creating a style based on a paragraph you've already formatted."

8. **Click OK to create the style.**

The New Style dialog box goes away. The style you created appears on the Styles list.

Creating a character-only style

Most of the styles you create in Word format are at the paragraph level. To create a style that contains lots of complex character formatting, you should create a character style. This type of style is flagged by an underlined *A* (<u>a</u>) on the Style list.

Suppose that all the mathematical formulas in your proposal for your flying car patent proposal must be in bold red text. You could just select that text and then use the Format⇨Font command to slap bold and red on the text (or use the Formatting toolbar). But that's too much work in this Age of Computers. Instead, you can create a character font that applies bold and red in one easy action.

The follow-me style

When I write a new chapter in a book, I start off with the Chapter Title style. The very next style I use is the Intro Paragraph style. Intro Paragraph is followed by Body, which is followed by Body, Body, Body, and on and on. There's no point in changing all those styles because I can tell Word to switch styles automatically.

In the New Style dialog box (or Modify Style dialog box), locate the Style for Following Paragraph drop-down list. The style shown on that list tells Word which style to switch to when

you press the Enter key to end a paragraph. Normally, it's the same style, which makes sense for most of your work. But in situations where you know that the style will switch, you can demand that Word do the switching for you. You can edit the Chapter Title style so that the Intro Paragraph style is selected in the Style for Following Paragraph drop-down list. That way, pressing the Enter key after typing the chapter title switches the style to Intro Paragraph. Very nice.

To create a character-only style, follow the steps outlined in the preceding section. However, after Step 4, in the New Style dialog box, choose Character from the Style Type drop-down list. This action gears everything in the New Style dialog box to accept only character and font-related formatting stuff; paragraph-level style stuff is no longer available.

Continue working the New Style dialog box, selecting various character options. When you're done, click OK to create the style.

✔ The special character styles don't affect any paragraph formatting. Selecting a character style changes only the font, style, size, underlining, bold, and so on.

✔ Hey! It's the 21st century, and I want my flying car and I want it now!

✔ A section in Chapter 19 talks about creating that shocking white-on-black text. Refer to that section for information on creating a white-on-black character style.

✔ Also refer to the section about formatting theft, in Chapter 18, for a quick method of applying font formats.

Modifying a style

Styles change. Bellbottoms may come back. Again. And those wide lapels we last saw in the disco era? No businessman in the year 2018 would be caught dead without them! Oh, but let me not get sidetracked.

Times New Roman — the bane of the Normal style — is a wonderful font . . . if you still wear an undershirt or bow ties and think that "sushi" is the name of the latest teenage pop singer. Still, Times New Roman is a workhorse used by everyone for almost everything. Maybe you want to put this font out to pasture and use a different font in your Normal style. If so, you can change it.

Here are the instructions for changing a style — any style, not just the Normal style.

1. **Summon the Styles and Formatting task pane.**

   Click the AA button or choose Format➪Styles and Formatting from the menu.

2. **Point the mouse at the style you want to change.**

3. **Display the style's menu.**

   Refer to Figure 16-3 for where to click.

4. **Choose Modify.**

   The New Style dialog box appears, but it's called Modify Style because this style already exists. It works the same as the New Style dialog box (refer to Figure 16-4), but the settings you make now *change* the style rather than create a new style.

5. **Change the formatting for your style.**

   You're free to use any of the formatting options to change your style. You can even add new formatting options or a shortcut key (which is covered in the next section).

6. **Click OK when you're done.**

Close the task pane if you're done with that.

✔ Changing a style affects every dang doodle paragraph in your document that uses that style. The change is instantaneous, which is one of the advantages of using a style in the first place.

✔ In a way, changing a style is cool; if you need to indent the first line in every paragraph, just modify the style. When you click OK in the Modify Style dialog box, all the paragraphs magically change. Neat-o.

✔ If you do change the Normal style for good, you need to edit the NORMAL.DOT template. This is covered in Chapter 17.

Giving your style a shortcut key

Styles allow you the advantage of quickly formatting a paragraph of text. Style shortcut keys make formatting even better because pressing Alt+Shift+B to get at the Body style is often faster than messing with the Style drop-down list or dialog box — especially when you have a gob of styles you're messing with.

To give your style a shortcut key, follow these steps:

1. **Conjure up the Styles and Formatting task pane.**

2. **Display the style's menu thing (refer to Figure 16-3).**

3. **Choose Modify.**

   The Modify Style dialog box appears.

4. **Click the Format button.**

5. **Choose Shortcut key from the menu.**

   A cryptic Customize Keyboard dialog box appears. Don't waste any time trying to explore here. Just move on to Step 6.

6. **Press your shortcut key combination.**

   Using Ctrl+Shift+*letter* or Alt+Shift+*letter* or Ctrl+Alt+*letter* key combinations is best, where *letter* is a letter key on the keyboard. For example, press Ctrl+Alt+B for your Body style shortcut key.

   Notice that the key combination you press appears in the Press New Shortcut Key box (see the middle left side of the dialog box). If you make a mistake, press the Backspace key to erase it.

7. **Check to see that the combination isn't already in use.**

   For example, Word uses Ctrl+B as the Bold character formatting shortcut key. This key combination appears under the heading Currently Assigned To, which shows up under the Current Keys box. Keep an eye on that box! If something else uses the shortcut key, press the Backspace key and go back to Step 5.

   As an interesting aside, the key combination Ctrl+Shift+B also applies the Bold text format. My opinion: Feel free to use that combination for one of your styles because Ctrl+B is easier to type for Bold anyway.

   If the key combination isn't used by anything, you see [unassigned] displayed under the Currently Assigned To heading. That's your signal that it's okay to use that keystroke.

8. **Click the Assign button.**

9. **Click the Close button.**

   The Customize Keyboard dialog box sulks away.

10. **Click the OK button.**

   The Modify Style dialog box huffs off.

   You can also close the task pane if you're done with it.

Congratulations; you now have a usable shortcut key for your style. Try it out: Position the toothpick cursor in a block of text and press the key. Ta-da! It should apply the formatting without messing with any of the other formatting or task pane widgets discussed elsewhere in this chapter.

Deleting a style

You can delete any style you create. It's easy: Display the Styles and Formatting task pane, select the style, and choose Delete from its menu. You're asked whether you're sure that you want to delete the style. Choose Yes to delete it for real.

You cannot delete the Normal, Heading, or any other standard Word styles.

Proper Style Application

You don't use a style as much as you *apply* it. The character and paragraph formatting carefully stored inside the style is applied to text onscreen, injected into that text or block like a stern shot of pickle juice. (Doesn't that make you want to squirm?)

Step-by-step, applying a style is easy:

1. **Decide what text you're applying the style to.**

   If it's a paragraph already onscreen, just stick the toothpick cursor somewhere in that paragraph. Or, you can select a block. Otherwise, the style is applied to any new text you type.

2. **Select a style from the Style drop-down list.**

   Or, if the Styles and Formatting task pane is visible, you can select the style from there, though that seems like a waste of screen space if you're merely selecting styles and not creating them.

   ✔ Remember the differences between paragraph and character styles. You cannot apply a paragraph style to just a single word in a paragraph; the style takes over the whole paragraph instead.

   ✔ You can also apply a style by using a shortcut key. Refer to the properly numbered instructions in the preceding section for the details.

   ✔ If your document is using only a few styles, you can remove those you're not using from the Style drop-down list display: Open the Styles and Formatting task pane. From the Show drop-down list (near the bottom), choose Formatting in Use. That limits the Style display to only those styles your document uses.

> ✔ To apply a style to your entire document, choose Edit➪Select All. Then select the style you want for everything.

Using the Built-in Heading Styles

Three (or more) built-in heading styles are available in Word. You can use these styles if you plan on breaking up your text with different headings. Not that you have to, but doing so lends itself to certain advantages.

For example, this chapter has main headings, such as "Proper Style Application," and then subheadings, like "Giving your style a shortcut key." The main headings are formatted with the built-in Heading 1 style. The sub-headings are formatted with the Heading 2 style.

Granted, the heading styles are boring as they come out of the box. But you can change them to suit your document's needs. Refer to the section "Modifying a style," earlier in this chapter, for information on changing a style's look and smell.

The advantage to using the heading styles? The first is that you see the headings when you drag the elevator button on the scroll bar. Also, you can use the browsing buttons (below the vertical scroll bar) to hop through your document, stopping at various heading styles. All this is covered over in Chapter 3, if you're interested.

> ✔ Heading styles, like the Normal and Default Paragraph Font styles, cannot be deleted from your document.
>
> ✔ Word can use many heading styles, from Heading 1 on down through Heading 9. These mostly come into play when you use Word's outlining feature. See Chapter 25.

Managing All Your Various Styles

Styles can be like trading cards. And they should be! If you create a great style, it's nice to use it in several documents. You can do this without re-creating the style (and even without using a document template, which is covered in Chapter 17).

To trade or manage all the styles you have in Word, you need to use the Style Organizer. It's not the easiest thing to find:

1. **Summon the Styles and Formatting task pane.**

2. **Choose Custom from the Show list.**

(The Show drop-down, or "pop-up," list is located at the bottom of the task pane.)

The Format Settings dialog box appears, which you can mostly ignore.

3. Click the Styles button.

Almost there; the Style dialog box shows up. Ignore it and. . . .

4. Click the Organizer button.

Finally. The Organizer dialog box appears, with the Styles tab forward, as shown in Figure 16-5.

Figure 16-5:
The Organizer dialog box is buried deep within Word's guts.

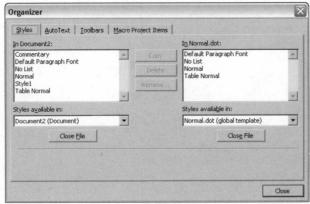

The purpose of the Organizer is to manage styles (and other things, but this chapter is on styles). You can do that by moving styles between various documents and document templates in Word.

For example, in Figure 16-5 you see on the left the styles available in your document, Document2. On the right are the styles that appear in the NORMAL.DOT document template. (NORMAL.DOT is a file that contains all Word's standard settings.)

Choose from either side of the dialog box the style you want to copy. After selecting the style, click the Copy button to copy it to the other side. That's how you swap and share styles between documents and templates.

To choose another document or template, click the Close File button. That button changes to the Open File button, which you can then use to open any Word document on disk. After it's open, a list of styles in that document is displayed in the window.

Click the Close button when you're done managing the styles.

> ✔ The Organizer dialog box is also used to organize your AutoText entries, toolbars, and macros (which are an advanced topic not covered in this book). Just as with styles, you can copy AutoText entries or special tool-bars from one document to another or between document templates in the Organizer dialog box.

> ✔ Also see Chapter 17 to find out what a document template is.

Chapter 17

Working with Templates

. . . .

In This Chapter

▶ Using a template

▶ Creating a document template

▶ Modifying a document template

▶ Attaching a template to a document

▶ Understanding NORMAL.DOT

. . . .

A *template* is a pattern you follow to create something. I remember playing with an architect's template when I was younger, say two years ago. It had cutouts where I could trace all sorts of common furniture. I suppose that's so the architect could design a house and then see how the furniture fit. But I used it instead to design the ultimate bathroom with enough commodes to play golf if you used every toilet as a hole.

Oh, yes: Templates can be used in a silly manner. But for real life, they're priceless time savers. In Word, a template is a skeleton you can build upon to create a final document. The template contains styles, formatting, perhaps a header or footer, plus even some standard text and a custom toolbar or two. This chapter covers all that (except for the toolbar part).

Ode to the Document Template

Document templates are handy things to have. I use one for sending faxes, one for writing letters, one for writing plays, and so on. This book has its own Dummies Style template that contains all the text styles the publisher's production department uses to produce the book. Whenever I need to start a new chapter, I use the Dummies template so that the paragraph, heading, caption, and other styles match what my publisher uses, which keeps them happy. I hope.

It's worth your time to create a template for all the common document types that you use regularly. The following sections tell you how.

✔ Unless you choose otherwise, Word uses the Normal document template, also known as NORMAL.DOT.

✔ See the section, "Understanding NORMAL.DOT," later in this chapter, for more information about NORMAL.DOT.

✔ My advice is to create your document *first* and then build the template based on the created document. Only if you're well versed with Word's formatting and style commands should you attempt to create a template from scratch. Even then, you'll most likely have to go back and "fix" things.

Using a Document Template

Word comes with a basketful of its own document templates, which not only helps you get an idea of how the templates can be used but also lets you take advantage of those predefined templates to quickly create common documents. To use a document template, follow these steps:

1. **Choose File➪New.**

   This summons the New Document task pane, which gives you options for creating a new document.

2. **Look for the template you want to use.**

   There are two template areas. The first is a Web page full of templates run by Microsoft, the Templates home page. It's actually an interesting place, full of all sorts of templates you may one day want to explore — when you're bored and there's nothing good on TV.

   The second template area, with the lower-class name "Other templates," refers to templates stored or created on your own computer.

3. **Choose a recently used template from the list.**

   If you see a template displayed in the list, such as SCREENPLAY.DOT, choose it to use that template; you're done. Otherwise, you have to use the Templates dialog box; continue with step 4

4. **Click the (underlined) text On My Computer.**

   The Templates dialog box is displayed, as shown in Figure 17-1. This dialog box contains many panels full of templates, wizards, and whatnot. The General tab is shown in Figure 17-1 (which is where any templates you may create appear).

Figure 17-1:
The
Templates
dialog box.

5. Select a template.

Templates are organized into categories, represented by the tabs in the dialog box. For example, click the Letters & Faxes tab. You see various templates and wizards displayed.

The *wizards* are programs that step you through the process of creating a new document.

Templates are special Word documents that contain various styles, plus maybe some text or graphics — enough to get you started. For example, the Professional Letter template in the Letters & Faxes tab has lots of fill-in-the-blank items, all in the proper position for a typical business letter.

The General tab's Blank Document template is the NORMAL.DOT template. That's the template Word uses whenever you start a new document. Boring.

6. Click OK.

Word starts up a new document, complete with that template's information, fonts, styles, and whatnot, all ready for use. You can take advantage of any styles stuffed into the template and view, use, or edit any text saved in the template.

✔ Opening a document with a template does not change the template; your new document is merely using the template's styles and any text it already has. Changing an existing template is covered later in this chapter.

✔ Refer to Chapter 18 for more information on wizards.

✔ Yes, you can use Word as your e-mail editor, as long as you're using Microsoft's own Outlook or Outlook Express program as your e-mail program. You can start a new e-mail message by choosing the E-Mail Message template from the Templates dialog box (refer to Figure 17-1). Or, you can click the E-Mail button on the toolbar to start a new message. In this case, Word is merely being used as an e-mail *editor*. Because this is a basic word processing book, you need to refer elsewhere for information on how Outlook or Outlook Express works with Word in this manner.

✔ Some of Word's templates can also be used to create a Web page. Honestly, Word makes a lousy Web page editor. After all, if Word is such a good Web page creation tool, why does Microsoft need to develop and sell its FrontPage program?

Creating Your Very Own Template

Building your own templates is easy — and useful. In the whole of word processing, you'll probably discover that you create lots of similar documents. Rather than start each one over from scratch, you need to create a new template and base your document on that template. All your styles are saved in the template, so there's no need to re-create them for the new document.

To create a template, follow these steps:

1. Find a document to base the template on.

Although Word does let you create a template from scratch, it has been my experience that it's best to start with something. You can start with a document you've already created or just start creating a document.

If you're creating a new document, all you need to put into it are the styles you plan on using, plus common text. For example, my Book template (for when I stop writing computer books and start writing "real" books) contains all the styles I need for writing books plus the word *Chapter* at the start of each page. That's because each document is a chapter, and starting it with the text *Chapter* already in the template saves me valuable typing energy molecules.

If you're using an existing document, save it to disk one last time just to be sure. Next, strip out all the text you don't want in the template. Delete all the graphics you don't want in the template. Edit the header and footer so that they contain only the items you need in the template.

Figure 17-2 shows a sample template I created, complete with some text and graphics. Remember that the template needs to contain only the styles you need for that document, plus any text that is common to all documents. In Figure 17-2, only the text that stays the same is included; other text is added when the user opens the template to help him create a new document.

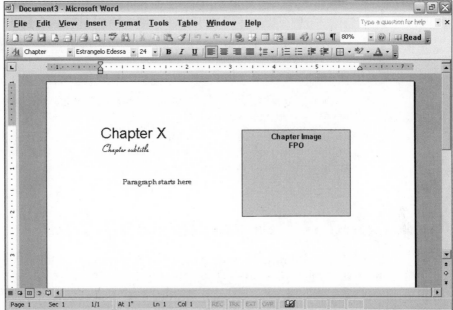

Figure 17-2:
A sample
template,
created with
love.

2. Choose File⇨Save As.

The Save As dialog box appears. It's the same Save As dialog box that Word uses for saving anything. Refer to Chapter 8 if you need a refresher.

3. Type a name for the document.

The name goes into the File Name box. Be descriptive.

You do not need to name the template using the word *template*.

4. From the Save as Type drop-down list, choose Document Template.

Ah-ha! This is the secret. The document must be saved as a Document Template. Choosing that item directs Word to save the document as a template in Word's special Templates folder. Word does all that work for you, but you must choose Document Template as the file type.

5. Click the Save button.

Your efforts are saved to disk as a document template, nestled in the proper place where Word keeps all its document templates.

6. Close the template.

Choose File⇨Close or click the X close button to close the template's window.

✔ The reason for closing it is that any changes you make from now on are made to the template. If you want to use the template to start a new document, you need to choose that template from the New Document task pane or from the Templates dialog box, as covered earlier in this chapter.

✔ If you want to return to the template to modify it, see the next section.

✔ Remember the purpose of a template: to store styles and often-used information in a single place.

✔ You can give a template any name, though if you choose the name of a template that already exists, Word warns you. This is standard file-saving stuff; just choose another name and be on your merry way.

Modifying a Document Template

Changing or editing a document template is identical to changing or editing any document. The difference is that you open a template rather than a document. It's a minor difference, but a big deal because templates, after all, are not really documents:

1. **Choose File⇨New.**

   The New Document task pane appears.

2. **Select your template from the list, or click the On My Computer item to open your template from the Templates dialog box.**

   Yes, this actually doesn't open the template; it creates a new document using the template. That's okay because this is a shortcut.

3. **Make your changes.**

   Edit the document just as you would any other document. Bear in mind that you're not really creating a document but merely modifying your template.

4. **Save the modified template by choosing File⇨Save As.**

5. **Give your template a new name or use the same name.**

6. **Choose Document Template from the Save as Type drop-down list.**

7. **Click the Save button.**

   If Word asks if you want to overwrite the template file already on disk, choose Yes to do so. The new template file replaces the old one.

Any style changes you make to a document template affect all the documents already created with that template. Remember, you're updating a template, not just a single document on disk.

The mystery of the location of the template files on the hard drive (If you dare to read it)

I find it easier to edit template files in the manner described in the text ("Modifying a Document Template") than trying to venture out onto the hard drive and use the Open dialog box to locate the template file's true location. After all, Word hides the template files location a little too aggressively for most people to find it.

The location isn't really a secret, but it's difficult to get to. In Windows XP, all users have their own folder in the main Documents and Settings folder. If you open your account's folder there, you'll find a secret, hidden folder called Application Data. That's where many applications keep specific information. For Word, the templates are nestled inside the Microsoft\Templates folders beneath the hidden Application Data folder. Quite honestly, I'm not even sure a desperate Indiana Jones could stumble across the information.

Technically, the pathname for the Templates location is as follows:

C:\Documents and Settings*your account*\Application Data\Microsoft\Templates

The *your account* folder above is your account's folder on Windows XP. Happy hunting!

Attaching a Template to a Document

Documents have templates like people have last names. Mostly, the documents are born with their templates. You either choose the template from the Templates dialog box (refer to Figure 17-1) or just create a new document, in which case the NORMAL.DOT template is used. But what if you want to change templates?

You can't really change templates as much as you can reassign or *attach* a new template to a document. Here's how:

1. **Open the orphaned document.**

   This is the document for which you want to assign a new template. It can be created without a specific template or already have a template "attached."

2. **Choose Tools➪Templates and Add-Ins.**

3. **Click the Templates tab.**

   What you see should now look like Figure 17-3. In that Figure, you see that the document is currently using the NORMAL.DOT template, which means it really doesn't have a template attached.

Figure 17-3:
The
Templates
and Add-ins
dialog box.

4. **Click the Attach button.**

   Word displays the Attach Template dialog box, which looks much like the Open dialog box, so I need not show an illustration of it here. Normally, this dialog box opens in the Templates folder, where you've probably stored a host of templates available for the plucking.

5. **Select the template you want to attach.**

6. **Click the Open button.**

   If you wish the document's styles to immediately reflect those of the new template, put a check mark by Automatically Update Document Styles.

7. **Click OK.**

   The styles (and toolbars and macros) stored in that template are now available to your document.

Note that attaching a template does not merge any text or graphics stored in that template. Only the styles (and toolbar and macros) are merged into your document.

You can also use these steps to un-attach a template. Do that by selecting NORMAL.DOT as the template to attach.

Understanding NORMAL.DOT

The Normal template is a special beast. Referred to as NORMAL.DOT (its old MS-DOS filename), the Normal template is where Word contains all the settings made for any new document you create with the Ctrl+N shortcut or by clicking the New button on the toolbar.

Knowing about NORMAL.DOT is important because you can change the Normal template if you want.

For example, if you want to change the standard font and size (and whatever other formatting) Word uses when it opens a new document, simply make those changes to NORMAL.DOT. Change the font and margins for the Normal style. Then save NORMAL.DOT back to disk. That's it.

Now just after saying that, I'd like to warn against modifying NORMAL.DOT too much. It's a good idea to keep NORMAL.DOT as a baseline standard, so instead of modifying it too much, consider creating another template instead.

One important note: Whenever you make changes to NORMAL.DOT, Word asks you if you want to update the "global template" when you close a document or quit Word. The universal answer to that question is Yes; you want to save the changes.

- ✔ NORMAL.DOT appears in the New Document task pane box (refer to Figure 17-1) as the Blank Document template.

- ✔ Refer to the section "Modifying a Document Template," earlier in this chapter, for more information on how to find and change NORMAL.DOT.

- ✔ If you just want to change the default font, see Chapter 11,"Changing the default font."

Chapter 18

Formatting and Spiffing-Up Tricks

● ●

In This Chapter

▶ Reviewing your document's formats

▶ Playing with fields

▶ Using color text

▶ Centering a page on the up-and-down

▶ Having fun with click-and-type

▶ Borrowing a cup o' formatting

▶ Using the various AutoFormat commands and tricks

▶ Using Word's wizards

● ●

*N*othing perks up a yawning document like a jolt of highly caffeinated formatting. This part of the book is dedicated to the formatting task, including the benefit of creating styles and using templates to make the job easier. Now it's time for some fun.

This chapter contains tips and tricks designed to make your formatting chores easier. The sections in this chapter are a grab bag of useful tidbits I've collected in my many years as a Word user. Some of these techniques may not appear useful to you right now, so flag this chapter for later consumption, when you're ready to absorb the knowledge nuggets that follow.

What's Going On with This Formatting!?

Ah, the mystery format! You're scanning through your latest masterpiece when you notice — right there, mocking you — a paragraph that doesn't seem to fit. Something's amiss with the formatting, but what? To see what's going on with a chunk of text, you could try to lodge the toothpick cursor in that paragraph and then select various formatting commands until you discover which way is up. Needless to say, this is an awkward way to discover your document's formatting.

A nifty trick to pull is to click the mouse in the in mystery part of your document. Then press the Shift+F1 key combination. This plops open the Reveal Formatting task pane which shows you details about the text the toothpick cursor is a-blinking on, similar to what's shown in Figure 18-1.

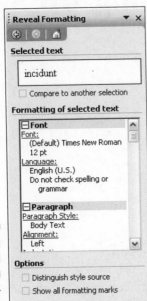

Figure 18-1:
A good old
formatting
whazzzup.

The Reveal Formatting task pane tells you information about the font, language, style, and all sorts of goodies, stored in a scrolling list.

Any blue underlined text in the task pane is clickable; in this case, clicking text summons a dialog box associated with that text, where you can change or further examine some formatting attribute.

Close the task pane window when you're done: Click its X close button or press Ctrl+F1 to make it vanish.

Let Word Do the Work for You

Word can do many things for you, things that some users may do in other, less efficient ways. To help you with formatting chores, I've gathered tips on stuff that Word can make short work of. These are things many Word users may toil with in awkward ways. Why bother? Word can do it for you!

The joys of updating fields

A *field* is a special chunk of text you insert into your document. That chunk looks like real text, but what it really does is display special information: the current page or date, your name, and other stuff that may change. For example, Chapter 17 tells the story of how to stick an updating date field into a template. You can do similar tricks with other fields in any document you create, not just in templates.

The secret is the Insert⇨Field command. It displays the Field dialog box, shown in Figure 18-2. The left side of the dialog box contains scrolling lists of categories and then field names. The right side of the dialog box changes to let you further select options, based on what type of field you're messing with.

Figure 18-2:
The Field
dialog box.

My favorite fields are the page number fields. For example, I may write in a document "here you are on page 212, and you don't even know what an anti-gravity generator smells like." You can always ensure that the document reflects the current page number by inserting a current page number field. Here's how:

1. **Bring up the Field dialog box.**

   Which you've already done, so:

2. **Choose Numbering from the Categories list.**

3. **Choose Page from the Field names list.**

   As it says right there under Description, `Insert the number of the current page`. This number can change as you edit a document, so you need a field and not a constant value to reflect that.

4. **Select a format for the page number.**

5. **Click OK.**

The current page's number is plopped into your document.

You can insert other interesting things into a document. If you're a writer who is paid by the word, choose the Document Information category and select the NumWords field. That field reflects the number of words in your document, so you'll always get an accurate word count.

The Document Information category's Author Field inserts the name of the person who is currently editing the document.

Note that inserted fields appear with a gray background when they're selected. That's your clue that you're dealing with a field and not "real" text.

- To see what's up with a certain field, click that field name in the Field dialog box and refer to the Description area just below the scrolling list.

- Some fields need to be updated to reflect the current state of a document. To do that, right-click the field and choose Update Field from the pop-up menu.

- I also use the Date and Time category's PrintDate field quite a bit. That way, the document prints with the current date.

- You cannot edit text in a field. You can only delete it: Do so by selecting the entire field as a block and then pressing the Delete key.

Color your text

The easiest way to write more colorful prose is to color your text. In Word, color is a text formatting attribute just like bold, italics, or super big. Teenage girls can write in pink, and bankers in green, and you can type angry letters to the editor in red.

To change text color, select the text as a block and then click the down arrow by the Font Color tool on the toolbar (see the margin). Clicking the down arrow displays a palette of colors. Choose a color, and your text takes on that color.

- Unless you have a color printer, don't expect your text to print in color.

- To remove colored text, select it as a block and choose Automatic from the Font Color tool's palette.

- The Automatic color is whichever text color is defined by the current style. For the Normal style, it's black. But if you're using a special style where the text color is fawn white, for example, choosing Automatic for the text color changes it back to fawn white.

✔ Colored text is much easier to find on the screen. For example, when I write, I color text purple if I plan on returning later to update or check it. That makes the text easier to find when I'm reading or reviewing the document.

✔ If the Font Color tool already shows the color you want to paint your text, just click the tool to change the text color.

Don't forget these tricks!

Here are a few formatting tricks I mention in other parts of the book — this is the stuff I want to really drive home:

✔ Always use Ctrl+Enter to start a new page. That inserts a hard page break, which forces a new page automatically.

✔ Use tabs to line up your text. Never use spaces. One tab is all you need. If you're typing more than one tab, you need to reset the tab stops. See Chapter 13.

✔ Always use one tab between columns to line them up. That makes editing the information easier if you have to do it.

✔ If you need to change any page formatting in the middle of your document, start a new section. See Chapter 15.

✔ Save your styles in a template! That way, you can use them for new documents you create without having to rebuild all your styles over and over. See Chapters 16 and 17.

✔ You can quickly undo any character formatting with the Ctrl+spacebar key combination.

Centering a Page, Top to Bottom

Nothing makes a document title nice and crisp like having it sit squat in the center of a page. The title is centered left to right, which you can do by selecting Center alignment for the title's paragraph. But how about centering the title top to bottom? Word can do that too:

1. **Move the toothpick cursor to the start of your document.**

   The Ctrl+Home key combination moves you there instantly.

2. **Type and format your document's title.**

   It can be on a single line or on several lines.

To center the title, select it and press Ctrl+E, the Center keyboard short-cut. Apply any additional font or paragraph formatting as necessary.

Avoid the temptation to use the Enter key to add space above or below your title. Right now, the title sits by itself at the top of the page. That will be fixed in a jiffy.

3. After the last line, choose Insert⇨Break.

The Break dialog box appears.

4. Select the Next Page option.

This step does two things. First, it creates a page break. Second, it creates a new section. That way, the page-centering command affects only the first section, which is the first page of the document.

5. Click OK.

The new section appears on the screen.

6. Move the toothpick cursor back up to the title page.

You need to put the toothpick cursor on the page you want to format.

7. Choose the File⇨Page Setup command.

The Page Setup dialog box appears.

8. Click the Layout tab.

9. Choose Center from the Vertical Alignment drop-down list.

You can find this item in the bottom half of the dialog box.

10. Confirm that the Apply To drop-down list shows This Section.

You want this change to affect only the current section, the single page with the title on it.

11. Click OK.

You may or may not see visual evidence onscreen that you centered a page. To be sure, click the Print Preview tool on the toolbar, and yes, you're a confirmed page centerer.

Click the Close button to return to your document from the Preview window.

Splash Around with Click-and-Type

The stereotype of the mad modern artist is of a person wearing a beret and standing before a huge, blank canvas with a bucket of paint. "Toss a little here," they say, throwing paint up in the corner. Then they get another bucket. "Toss it here," they say as they toss more paint in the middle. And so on. Soon they're charging $500,000 for their masterpiece and being feted by rich-yet-gullible Upper East Side liberals. But I digress.

You get a chance to be your own mad artist with Word's amusing and some-times useful click-and-type feature. Like throwing paint on a canvas, click-and-type lets you splash text around your document wherever you want it — almost. Formatting rules be damned!

To use click-and-type, you must view your document in Print Layout view. Choose View➪Print Layout from the menu or click-and-type won't appear to work. Also, it helps to start on a blank page.

As you move the mouse pointer around the blank page, the cursor changes. The different cursor types tell you how text "splashed" on that part of the page is formatted.

Double-click with this type of pointer, and you get an indented paragraph, left aligned on the page.

Double-click with this type of pointer to set a left-aligned paragraph. The paragraph is set on the page wherever you double-click.

Double-clicking in your document with this pointer creates a center-aligned paragraph at that very spot.

Double-clicking with this pointer sets Word up to do (can you guess?) a right-aligned paragraph. Wow.

✔ I prefer *not* to use click-and-type, primarily because I know all the other formatting commands. If you grow to understand and use click-and-type, more power to you. But for true control, the other formatting commands mentioned in this part of the book beat click-and-type hands down.

✔ To disable click-and-type, choose Tools➪Options. In the Options dialog box, click the Edit tab. Remove the check mark (near the bottom) that says Enable Click and Type. Click OK.

✔ If you really are splashing and dashing with click-and-type, consider changing the zoom level for your document, zooming out to make the whole thing easier to see. See Chapter 28.

Formatting Theft

Speaking of mad painters, the paintbrush tool on the Standard toolbar can be used to *paint* character styles, copying them from one bit of text to another in your document. Here's how:

1. **Jab the toothpick cursor in the middle of the text that has the formatting you want to copy.**

   The toothpick cursor must be in the midst of the word, not to the left or right (but it doesn't have to be in the exact middle, just "in the word"). If it's not, this trick won't work.

2. **Click the Format Painter button on the Standard toolbar.**

   The cursor changes to a paintbrush/I-beam pointer, as depicted in the margin. This special cursor is used to highlight and then reformat text in your document.

3. **Hunt for the text you want to change.**

4. **Highlight the text.**

   Drag the mouse over the text you want to change — "paint" it. (You must use the mouse here.)

   Voilà! The text is changed.

Mad modern artists can also make use of the following tips and tidbits:

- ✔ The Format Painter works only with character and paragraph formatting, not with page formatting.

- ✔ To change the formatting of multiple bits of text, double-click the Format Painter. That way, the Format Painter cursor stays active, ready to paint lots of text. Press the Esc key to cancel your Dutch Boy frenzy.

- ✔ If you tire of the mouse, you can use the Ctrl+Shift+C key command to copy the character format from a highlighted block to another location in your document. Use the Ctrl+Shift+V key combination to paste the character format elsewhere. Just highlight the text in your document and press Ctrl+Shift+V to paste in the font formatting.

- ✔ You can sorta kinda remember Ctrl+Shift+C to copy character formatting and Ctrl+Shift+V to paste because Ctrl+C and Ctrl+V are the copy and paste shortcut keys. Sorta kinda.

- ✔ Don't confuse the Format Painter with the highlighting tool, which is described in Chapter 26.

Using AutoFormat

Word's AutoFormat command has absolutely nothing to do with formatting in the sense of font or paragraph formatting. No, what AutoFormat really does is clean up your document, remove excess spaces, add spaces where needed, apply Heading formats to what it thinks are your document's headings, and other minor housekeeping chores. Yes, it removes the slop most of us add to our documents without thinking about it.

Before AutoFormat can do its job, you need to create the document's text. Write! Write! Write! Write your letter, memo, chapter, poem, whatever. Then follow these steps:

1. **Save your document to disk.**

   This step is most important, and saving your document is something you should be doing all the time anyway. So, save your file one more time before you use AutoFormat. Refer to Chapter 8 for details on saving documents.

2. **Choose Format⇨AutoFormat.**

3. **Click OK.**

   Ook! Eep! Ack!

4. **Formatting completed.**

   Word has carefully massaged and adjusted your document. You may find new headings, bulleted lists, and other amazing, whiz-bang things automatically done to your text.

Hey! AutoFormat created a list of helpful bullets right here in this text:

- ✔ If you like, you can choose AutoFormat and review each change option in the AutoFormat dialog box to see exactly what needs to be done before AutoFormat does its job.

- ✔ If your text is kinda boring, it doesn't appear as though AutoFormat did anything. Don't despair. AutoFormat is good at creating headings and bulleted lists, but it can't read your mind.

- ✔ You can always use the Undo command if you detest what AutoFormat did to your document. (Alas, there is no Detest command.)

Automatic Formatting as It Happens

Sometimes, Word can be so smart that it's scary. A long time ago, just having a program remind you to save before you quit was thought to be miraculous. But now . . . why, just the other day Word reminded me that I forgot to floss the night before and, boy, though that blackberry cobbler looked tempting, I am several stones over my ideal weight. Scary stuff.

Making the automatic formatting thing happen as you work

You must direct Word to be smart. The program cannot do it on its own. To take advantage of the many automagical things Word can do, follow these steps:

1. **Choose Format⇨AutoFormat.**

   The AutoFormat dialog box exposes itself on the screen.

2. **Click the Options button.**

   The AutoCorrect dialog box appears.

3. **Click the AutoFormat as You Type tab.**

   The AutoFormat tab controls the AutoFormat command, which allows you to format your document in one swoop as covered earlier in this chapter. What you're after here is automatic formatting while you're working, which is covered by the AutoFormat as You Type tab, shown in Figure 18-3.

Figure 18-3: AutoFormat As You Type settings.

4. **Because you don't know what the options do, check them all.**

   Or, well, just read them and see what they do. For example, you may prefer writing fractions as 1/2 instead of using the ½ fraction character.

Another popular item *not* to check is the Internet and Network Paths with Hyperlinks item. If you check that item, you'll create active Web links in your document, which some folks find annoying. If you feel the same way, do not check that item.

5. **Click OK and then click OK again.**

    Close both the dialog boxes you left hanging open. Now you're ready to start playing, beginning in the next section.

Automatic numbered lists

The best way to understand the AutoFormat-as-you-type adventure is to *live* it. Heed the following steps:

1. **Start a new document in Word.**

    The simplest way to do that is to press the Ctrl+N key combination. No messing around here.

2. **Type the following line:**

    ```
    Things to do today:
    ```

    Press the Enter key to start a new line. Then type

    ```
    1. Kick my crack habit.
    ```

    Now — prepare yourself — press the Enter key to end that line.

    Ta-da! It's an automatic number 2! Plus the line is reformatted with an automatic indent. Plus you see the AutoCorrect options icon. Wow.

3. **Keep typing if you're pleased.**

    To stop the list from automatically numbering everything else in your document (all the way up to "Happily ever after"), press the Enter key twice.

The AutoCorrect Options icon is more than just a mosquito you want to swat, an annoying bug to vex you. If you click that booger, you'll see a drop-down list of options, shown in Figure 18-4. That allows you to undo or even halt the automatic numbering thing if you like. And if you find yourself disliking this immensely, you can choose the Control AutoCorrect Options item to use the AutoCorrect Options dialog box to switch this option off forever.

Or, you can press the Esc key and continue typing your list.

✔ This trick also works for letters (and Roman numerals, too). Just start something with a letter and a period, and Word picks up at the next line with the next letter in the alphabet and another period.

     ✔ You can also undo an AutoFormatted list by using the Undo command.

     ✔ I know that I've said earlier in this book not to press the Enter key twice to end a paragraph. Okay, I lied. You don't really have to press the Enter key twice to stop an automatic-formatting trick. You can press Enter and then Backspace. But Enter-Enter works just as well.

Figure 18-4:
Controlling
the
AutoFormat
options as
you type.

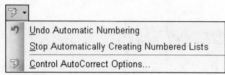

Automatic borders

In the old Smith-Corona days of yore, we would fancy up our documents by woodpeckering a line of hyphens, underlines, or equal signs. It brings back kind of a sentimental tear to the eye, especially for me, because I pressed the keys so hard that ripping the paper out of the typewriter often ripped the paper in two. Not with a word processor, though.

If you want a single-line border, from right margin to left across your page, type three hyphens and press the Enter key:

   - - -

Then press the Enter key. Word instantly transmutes the three little hyphens into a solid line.

Want a double line? Then use three equal signs:

   ===

Press the Enter key, and Word draws a double line from one edge of the screen to the next.

Bolder line? Use three underlines:

   _____

 As usual, the AutoCorrect Options icon appears, letting you change your mind or switch this option off. Also remember that you can press Ctrl+Z to undo this if, indeed, all you really want are three equal signs in a row.

Chickening Out and Using a Wizard

You're off to see the Wizard, the wonderful Wizard of Word. . . .

A *wizard* enables you to create a near-perfect document automatically. All you need to do is select various options and make adjustments from a handy and informative dialog box. Word does the rest of the work. This is so easy that it should be a sin.

To use a Word wizard, follow these steps:

1. **Choose File⇨New.**

   This command opens the New Document task pane.

2. **In the task pane, click the (underlined) text On My Computer.**

   The Templates dialog box is displayed (refer to Figure 17-1).

3. **Select a wizard.**

   A number of wizards come prepackaged with Word. Of course, none of them lives on the General panel. To find a wizard, click another tab, such as the Memos tab.

   Wizards live along with templates, though the wizards have the word *wizard* in their name and they sport a unique icon (see the margin). The Memos tab holds only the Memo Wizard. (Other tabs have other wizards, which you can explore on your own.)

   Select the wizard by clicking it with your mouse. If you're lucky, a preview appears on the right side of the dialog box. How nice.

4. **Click OK.**

   Word hums and churns for a few minutes. It's thinking — no doubt a painful process. Give it time.

5. **Optionally, be enlightened by the Wizard dialog box.**

   The more advanced wizards quiz you, giving you a dialog box with a bunch of questions for you to answer. The wizard uses your answers to help create your document.

   Some wizards merely create a blank document for you to complete. Just fill in the sections that say something like {type the recipient's name here} with the proper information, and you're on your way.

✔ Even though a wizard created your document, you still must save it to disk when you're done. In fact, most wizards just start you on your way. After that point, you work with the document just like any other in Word. Don't forget to save!

TIP

✔ Word has a special wizard menu item: Tools➪Letters and Mailings➪ Letter Wizard. If you choose this command, follow your Office Assistant's advice and answer the various questions in the dialog box.

✔ Some wizards even fill in text for you. These are super-cheating wizards. The Stephen King wizard, for example, writes his books for him in less than a day.

Part III

Sprucing Up Your Document

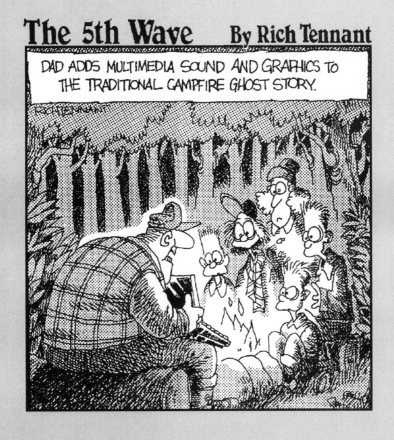

The 5th Wave   By Rich Tennant

DAD ADDS MULTIMEDIA SOUND AND GRAPHICS TO THE TRADITIONAL CAMPFIRE GHOST STORY.

In this part . . .

Drawing lines, laying down shading, adding boxes, columns, colors, pictures, and tables are not really what I would call core word-processing tasks. Still, these things were added as features to Word several million years ago. Back then, word processors were judged not only by their speed and ability with words, but by what extra or bonus features they offered. So even though Mighty Write was just as fast as Word and had all the basic search-and-replace and spell checking features, those who judged word processors would give Word the award for being "better" because it also had the ability to cram your text into multiple columns!

These bonus features are not totally useless, of course. They can help spruce up your document in a number of clever and fun ways.

So, despite the fact that you may never use any of these features or tricks, I'm presenting them to you in the next few chapters. They exist. You paid for them. Why not try a few and add some spice or verve to an otherwise dull document?

Chapter 19

Borders, Boxes, and Shading

● ●

In This Chapter

▶ Drawing a box around your text

▶ Boxing in a whole page

▶ Putting less than a box around your text

▶ Shading your text

▶ Printing white on black

● ●

*T*he friendly boundary between word processing and desktop publishing is gracefully crossed as you start to add things like borders, boxes, and shading to your text. Contrary to being truly superfluous, I find borders — those lines you can draw on any side of your text or the entire page — to be handy things. Specifically, I enjoy using borders below titles. And you will, too, after you read through this chapter and discover various ways Word can draw interesting lines in your text.

Boxing Your Text

I actually took dancing lessons once. Just once. Then I quit. But I do remember some things.

I remember that the teacher said that anyone who walks heel-to-toe is able to dance. She also taught us the box step:

Step

There. Nothing to it. Heel-toe, no problem.

The following sections tell you how to box anything in your document, from mere words to paragraphs to full pages o' text.

Boxing in small bits of text or paragraphs

Word allows you to stick a box around any bit of text or paragraph in your document. For example, you can box in a title or draw a box around an "aside" paragraph or sidebar or put a box around a single word. No matter what you're boxing up, follow these steps:

1. **Select the text you want to box.**

   If nothing is selected as a block, Word boxes in the paragraph the tooth-pick cursor is blinking in.

2. **Choose the Format⇨Borders and Shading command.**

   The Borders and Shading dialog box opens. Make sure that the Borders tab is chosen, as shown in Figure 19-1. (If not, click that tab with the mouse.)

Figure 19-1:
The Borders and Shading dialog box.

3. **Select the type of border you want from the Setting column.**

   Four preset, easy-to-use, pop-n-fresh border styles are available; don't bother with the Custom style until you fully figure this out. Just click the style of paragraph border you want. My favorite is Shadow.

   Observe the Preview window to see how the border affects your text.

4. **Choose Text or Paragraph from the Apply To drop-down list.**

   Word is unusually smart with this step. If you select only one word or any bit of text less than a paragraph, Word assumes that you want to box in only that text.

5. **Click OK.**

   Your text now has a box around it.

Making partial boxes

Borders don't have to be boxes. In Figure 19-2, the newsletter's title is created with only top and bottom borders. You can also do this in the Borders and Shading dialog box:

Figure 19-2:
Top and bottom borders in a newsletter heading.

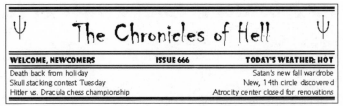

The Chronicles of Hell

WELCOME, NEWCOMERS — ISSUE 666 — TODAY'S WEATHER: HOT

Death back from holiday — Satan's new fall wardrobe
Skull stacking contest Tuesday — New, 14th circle discovered
Hitler vs. Dracula chess championship — Atrocity center closed for renovations

1. **Select the text you want to place lines around.**

2. **Choose Format➪Borders and Shading.**

   Now keep your eye on the Preview window. That's where you can see how your line-drawing skills work.

3. **Choose None from the Setting list.**

   It's best to start with no lines anywhere.

4. **Select a line style from the Style list.**

   You can choose from several styles and double- or single-line patterns, some of which are shown in Figure 19-2.

5. **Optionally select a Color.**

   The Automatic color is the same color as the text font you're using, usually black.

6. **Mess around and choose a Width from that list.**

7. **To set a border (or line) around your text, click in the Preview window on the spot where you want the border.**

   For example, to put the line on top of your text, click above the gray text-like thing in the Preview window. Or you can optionally click the Top button to the left of the Preview window.

The border can go on any edge of your text: top, bottom, left, or right. Click that side of the Preview window, or use the corresponding buttons, to set the border.

8. **To set more borders, repeat Steps 4 through 7.**

9. **Click OK after you finish lining in your text.**

You can remove any border by clicking it on the Preview window; click once to set a border, again to remove it. Or just click the None icon to remove all the borders and start over.

Putting a border around a page of text

You can not only rope titles and paragraphs but also put a border around a whole page in your document, such as a title page or any other page where you don't want the words to escape.

To stick a border around the page, heed these steps:

1. **Click the toothpick cursor on the page you want to border.**

   For example, the first page in your document.

2. **Choose Format⇨Borders and Shading.**

3. **Click the Page Border tab.**

   I'm not including a figure here because this tab looks and operates just like the Borders panel; see the preceding section for more information.

4. **Choose the border style(s) you want.**

   Use the Setting buttons or create a custom style.

5. **Choose which pages you want bordered from the Apply To drop-down list.**

   You can select Whole Document to put borders on every page. To select the first page, choose the This Section - First Page Only item. Other options let you choose other pages and groups, as shown in the drop-down list.

   And now the secret:

6. **Click the Options button.**

   The Border and Shading Options dialog box appears.

7. **Choose Text from the Measure From drop-down list.**

It may say Edge of Page there now; this won't work with most printers. Choose Text instead.

8. **Click OK.**

9. **Click OK to close the Borders and Shading dialog box.**

The best way to see the page border you've created is to use the File➪Print Preview command.

Refer to Chapter 15 for more information on creating a section break in your document. By using sections, you can greatly control which pages in a document have borders and which do not.

Using the Border Button on the Toolbar

If you ever need to slap down a quickie border on your paragraph (or in a table), you can take advantage of the Border button on the toolbar and its handy palette o' options.

Just click the down arrow by the button, and you see a selection of line positions — top, bottom, outside, and so on (see Figure 19-3). Pick one from the list, and whichever paragraph the toothpick cursor is on, or whatever text is selected, it grows that line.

Figure 19-3:
A palette
of borders,
courtesy of
the Border
button.

✔ The palette only sets the border's position. So, if you don't like the line style, choose Format➪Borders and Shading from the menu to change it.

✔ To remove all borders from a paragraph, click the Border button on the toolbar and click the No Border button.

✔ The Border button on the toolbar affects only text, not the entire page. For that, see "Putting a border around a page of text," earlier in this chapter.

Giving Your Text Some Shade

The neatest Borders and Shading dialog box effect of them all is shading. You can shade words, sentences, paragraphs — any block of text — and weird parts of your document, like a title, as Figure 19-4 shows. You can shade in gray, color, and patterns with or without a border around it. It's a veritable smorgasbord of scribbles to junk up your text with. Heed these steps:

Figure 19-4:
A sample bit
o' text with
a border
and
shading.

1. **Mark your text or title as a block.**

   Refer to Chapter 6 for efficient block-marking instructions.

   If you want the shaded area to cover more than the title line, highlight the lines before and after the title. That creates a "buffer" of shading around the text.

2. **Choose Format⇨Borders and Shading.**

   The Borders and Shading dialog box appears, but. . . .

3. **Make sure that the Shading panel is up front.**

   If it's not, click the Shading tab with your mouse. The Shading panel jumps to the front, as shown in Figure 19-5.

4. **Select a shade from the Fill palette.**

   The first three rows of the palette (below the No Fill choice) give you shading options for your text in percentages of black, from white to all black in various increments. Next comes the rainbow of colors and, naturally, the More Colors button, which displays a palette of zillions of colors, some visible only to certain mollusks, from which you can choose.

   The best values to select for shading your text are gray. I'm fond of the 20 percent gray value because it prints nicely without wiping out the text.

Figure 19-5:
The Shading
part of the
Borders and
Shading
dialog box.

Try to avoid using the patterns. Though some of them may look like gray-fills, they're really ugly. I suppose that someone somewhere may find them useful, but for shading text, they're probably not what you need.

5. Click OK.

Your text is shaded. Everyone will wonder how you did it.

Creating That Shocking White-on-Black Text

After shading, the next most-fun thing to do is print white text on a black background. This procedure is a very bold move and stands out prominently in your text — like being hit in the face with a cinder block. So don't use this technique casually.

> **Please wait until the end of the joke before you start laughing.**

To produce white-on-black text, two things must be done. First, the background color must be set to black; second, the text color must be set to white. Here is how you create a black background:

1. Mark your text as a block.

It's best to start with text you've already written. (See Chapter 6 for block-marking instructions.)

2. **Choose Format⇨Borders and Shading.**

   Ensure that the Shading tab is selected, as shown in Figure 19-5.

3. **Click the black square in the Fill area.**

   That's the first square in the fourth column; when you click the square, the word `Black` appears in the box to the right of the color grid, so you know you got it right.

4. **Click OK to exit the Borders and Shading dialog box.**

Now you would next have to change the text color to white, but that's not necessary; the text color has automatically changed to white. So you're done!

If the text color does not change, then you need to do two more steps:

1. **Click the Font Color tool on the Formatting toolbar.**

   A drop-down palette appears.

2. **Choose Automatic.**

   It's the top item in the drop-down menu. Rather than choosing White here, by choosing Automatic you tell Word to automatically color the text. Because of the black background already selected, white is automatically chosen as the text color. Not bad, huh?.

Normally text is colored using the Automatic color in Word. When it's not, such as when the color is defined by a style or in a template, then you'll have to complete those last two steps.

✔ Word is (actually) smart about displaying white-on-black text, especially when that text is selected. You never "lose" the text on the screen.

✔ I don't recommend reversing vast stretches of text. White text on a black background prints poorly on most computer printers. This stuff is best used for titles or to highlight smaller blocks of text.

✔ If you have trouble printing the white-on-black text, you may need to modify your printer settings. In the Print dialog box, click the Properties button. If your Printer Properties dialog box has a Graphics tab, click it. Choose the proper option to ensure that your printer prints in graphics mode. Then click OK to close the Printer Properties dialog box.

Chapter 20

Building Tables

*T*hose guys on the "power tool" TV shows all know how to make a table. That's not remarkable. Tables are everyday objects, and we don't need to be convinced of their existence. But those guys make it look so easy, especially because the tables come out looking spiffy. Give me some power tools and jigs and proper lumber, and I can cobble together a table, too. Well it might look like a table, and it might even stand up and be able to hold things like a table, but it would be far from spiffy.

Word doesn't just have a Table command. No, it has a whole Table *menu* full of commands, settings, and controls for creating very nifty, handy, and yes, spiffy tables in your document. No skills are needed, no confusing instructions written in Chinglish, and no need to scour the brambles for sticks or driftwood. Look! Up on the menu! It's Table Man, Ma, and he's here to rescue us!

Why Use Tables?

Tables are a natural extension of tabs. After all, both tab and table have the same root in Latin. Or Greek. But that's not the point. The point is, often times when you use tabs to line up columns of things, you're probably better off creating a table in Word and using a table instead.

✔ Use a table whenever you have information that can be organized into rows and columns.

✔ Each cubbyhole in a table is called a *cell*.

✔ Cells can have their own margins, text, and paragraph formats. You can even stick graphics into cells.

✔ Unlike working with tabs, Word's tables can be resized and rearranged to fit your data. In other words, if you plan on modifying the information later, it's best to use a table as opposed to a brief list formatted with tabs.

✔ Alas, Word does not have a handy Chair command (although rumor has it that Microsoft employees are working on barstools).

Splash Me Down a Table

Tables are "drawn" into your document using the handy Table and Borders button. Basically, you draw the table first and then fill in the rows and columns later. And it doesn't matter whether text is already in your document; drawing the table moves any existing text out of the way to make room for the table.

To splash down a table in the middle of your document, follow these steps:

1. Click the Tables and Borders button.

After you click the button (shown in the margin), the Tables and Borders tool palette appears, floating over your text. See Figure 20-1. This palette contains buttons for building tables as well as options from the Borders and Shading dialog box (refer to Chapter 19).

If you weren't previously in Print Layout view, Word switches you there automatically. (You cannot splash down tables in Normal view.)

Figure 20-1: The Tables and Borders palette.

2. Ensure that the Draw Table button is "on" in the Tables and Borders palette.

The Draw Table button should already be active (looking like it's selected), unless you've done something else between this step and the preceding step (which would have been naughty of you). If the Draw Table button isn't on, click it.

The mouse pointer changes to a pencil, which I call the *pencil pointer.*

3. **Drag the mouse to "draw" the table's outline in your document.**

   Start in the upper-left corner of where you envision your table and drag to the lower-right corner, which tells Word where to put your table. You see an outline of the table as you drag down and to the right (see Figure 20-2).

Figure 20-2: Drawing a table in a document.

Don't worry about making the table the right size; you can resize it later.

Notice that any text you already have in your document moves aside to make room for the new table.

4. **Use the pencil pointer to draw rows and columns.**

   As long as the mouse pointer looks like a pencil, you can use to it draw the rows and columns in your table.

   To draw a row, drag the pencil pointer from the left side to the right side of the table.

   To draw a column, drag the pencil pointer from the top to the bottom of the table, as shown in Figure 20-3.

Figure 20-3: Drawing a column.

As you drag the pencil pointer, a dashed line appears, showing you where the new row or column will be split. Figure 20-3 shows a table shaping up. Also notice that you can split columns or rows into more cells simply by dragging the pencil pointer inside a cell and not across the entire table.

Again, don't worry if you have too many or too few rows or columns. You can add or delete them later, as you see fit. And don't worry about things being uneven; you can rearrange your rows and columns later.

5. **Click the Draw Table button — you know, the stupid pencil in the Tables and Borders palette — when you're done creating the table's rows and columns.**

This step turns off table-creating mode and switches you back to normal editing mode. Now you can fill the text into your table or modify the table or whatever.

The Tables and Borders dialog box is nifty to have hanging around while you're working in a table. To get rid of it when you're done, click its X button (in the upper-right part of the window) to make it go thither.

Adding stuff to the table

Enter text into the table as you would enter text anywhere in Word. Here are some pointers:

- ✔ Cells grow longer (taller) to accommodate extra text you type into them.

- ✔ You can press the Enter key to start a new paragraph in a cell or use Shift+Enter to start a new line of text.

- ✔ Use the Tab key to move from cell to cell in your document.

- ✔ If you press the Tab key in the last cell in the table, you create a new row of cells.

- ✔ The Shift+Tab combination moves you backward between the cells. (This technique is easier than using the arrow keys, which ramble through a cell's text one character at a time.)

- ✔ If you need to use a tab in a cell, then press Ctrl+Tab.

- ✔ Text in a cell is formatted using the Font dialog box, just as normal text is formatted in your document.

- ✔ Each cell is its own unit as far as paragraph formatting goes. To align or indent an entire row or column of cells, choose Table⇨Select and then choose Column or Row from the submenu to select a column or row, respectively.

- ✔ You can also select columns by holding the mouse cursor above the column until the cursor changes shape to a downward-pointing arrow. Point the arrow at the row and click the left mouse button. You can select multiple columns by dragging the mouse across them.

- ✔ Clicking the mouse thrice in a cell selects all text in that cell.

- ✔ Graphic images can also be pasted into cells.

Messing with the table

After the table is splashed down into your document, you can mess with it in uncountable ways. The following pointers suggest merely a few of them:

- ✔ In the upper-left corner of the table is the Move Thing. It allows you to move the table elsewhere in your document. Just drag the Move Thing with the mouse. However:

- ✔ As with dragging anything with the mouse, you're probably better off cutting and pasting the table if you plan on moving it more than a few lines up or down (or left or right). Put the toothpick cursor in the table and choose Table➪Select➪Table from the menu to select the table for cutting and pasting.

- ✔ If those uneven columns and rows are bugging you, choose Table➪ AutoFit➪Distribute Rows Evenly. Then choose Table➪AutoFit➪ Distribute Columns Evenly to adjust all the columns.

- ✔ Point the mouse between a row or column to resize that row or column. When you find the "sweet spot," the mouse pointer changes to look like the Redimensioning Doohickeys, as shown in the margin. Then just drag the mouse left or right or up or down to change the table.

The following tips assume that you have the Tables and Borders palette floating in Word's window. If not, choose View➪Toolbars➪Tables and Borders from the menu.

- ✔ To erase a line between two cells in a table, choose the Erase tool and click the line you want to remove. If the two cells both contain text, Word simply tacks the contents of one cell onto another.

- ✔ Use the Line Style and Line Weight drop-down lists to set the style and thickness of the lines in the table. After choosing a style and thickness, use the Draw Table (pencil) tool to click a line in the table, which changes it to the new style.

- ✔ You can further modify your table with the Insert Table button. Clicking the down arrow by the icon displays a menu of various table-related commands for inserting columns or rows or for automatically adjusting the table's dimensions. Oh, how handy!

    ✔ To utterly remove the table from your document, click the mouse inside the table and then choose Table⇨Delete⇨Table. The table is blown to smithereens.

Making a table out of text already in your document

After you realize the glory of tables, you may desire to convert some of the tab-formatted text in your document into a table. Or, you may just want to put any text into a table because you've become obsessed with tables, and not seeing any text in a table makes you frustrated and angry, and the little people won't stop screaming and. . . .

Deep breath!

To convert text already in your document into a table, obey these steps:

1. **Select the text you want to convert into a table.**

   It helps if the text is arranged into columns, each column separated by a tab character. If not, things get screwy, but still workable.

2. **Choose Table⇨Convert⇨Text to Table.**

   The Convert Text to Table dialog box appears, as shown in Figure 20-4.

Figure 20-4:
The Convert
Text to Table
dialog box.

3. **Click OK.**

   This works because your text is already separated by tabs. If your text were separated by commas or just paragraphs, then you'd need to choose that item from the bottom of the dialog box (see Figure 20-4).

Yup, it works. But you'll probably need to adjust things, reset column widths, and so on and so forth. It may be a pain, but it's better than retyping all that text.

Turning a table back into plain text

Just as the witch can turn the frog into a beautiful princess, the beautiful princess can also be turned into a frog. To convert a table back to mere text only, with maybe tabs separating the columns, select the table by choosing Table➪Select➪Table. Then choose Table➪Convert➪Table to Text. This command is basically the opposite of the command used in the preceding section.

Use the Convert Table to Text dialog box (see Figure 20-5) to choose which character, symbol, or tchotchke to use for separating the cells in your table. (I recommend choosing Tabs, as shown in the figure.) Then click OK.

Figure 20-5: The Convert Table to Text dialog box.

As with converting text to a table, some cleanup is involved. Mostly, it's resetting the tabs (or removing them). Nothing complex or bothersome.

A Quick Way to Cobble a Table Together

To quickly create an empty table in your document, you can use the Insert Table button on the toolbar (see the margin).

Clicking the Insert Table button displays a drop-down-list thing. Drag the mouse through the thing to tell Word how big a table you want to create, such as the 2-row-by-3-column table shown in Figure 20-6.

You also use the Insert Table button to quickly add cells, rows, or columns to a table. To do so, select a cell, row, or column in a table and then click the Insert Table button, which conveniently changes its look for inserting cells, rows, or columns.

Figure 20-6:
The Insert
Table drop-
down thing.

Automatically Spiffing Up Your Table

Word contains a deep well of formatting tricks, some of which you can use on any old table you create to make it look really spiffy. This AutoFormatting trick lets you create a table and then use a special Word command to customize your table. Here's how:

Stick the toothpick cursor in any table, preferably one you've already filled in. Then choose Table⇨Table AutoFormat from the menu. The Table AutoFormat dialog box appears, as shown in Figure 20-7.

Figure 20-7:
The Table
AutoFormat
dialog box.

Keep your eyeballs focused on the sample table shown in the Preview window. Then click your mouse on each consecutive item on the Formats scrolling list. Each one of those items automatically spiffs up your table to look like the sample shown in the Preview window.

After you find a table format you like, click the OK button. People will think you've spent *hours* formatting your table when all you did was use a dirty little secret from a *For Dummies* book!

Chapter 21

Marching Your Text into Columns

Onward columns, march! Sound off! Doric! Ionic! Corinthian!

When I think of columns, I think of those long, white pillars that line the front of famous buildings, museums, and government institutions. A long time ago, probably during the Roman Empire, some doofus decided to splatter a column with graffiti. It might have even been appreciated: "I like what you've done, Randomus Scriblius. Just wipe it off my house and put it on paper, and I may pay you for it." And thus the first opinion column was born.

Just like the graffiti-drawing miscreants of the ancient Roman Empire, you too can practice writing text in long columns. You don't need a marble column to practice on, or even any paint. That's because Word has the ability to split a page of text into various columns, just like the columns of text you see in newspapers or magazines. After all, if columns can make the Greeks and Romans famous, why not you? Prepare to muster your text into columns.

Why Do Columns?

Columns don't make sense in a document unless you have two of them on a page. Think about it: A page of text is really just one column. It should be simple, therefore, for Word to assemble two or more columns of text per page — like printing two pages on one or something. It's very easy, as long as you follow my suggestions in this chapter.

✔ By using columns you can create your own newsletters, fliers, treatises, and manifestos. However:

✔ Although using columns for a short document seems to work well in Word, putting text into columns for a document of ten pages or more is better done in a desktop publishing program.

✔ If you're working with columns and notice that Word starts acting slow and fussy: Save your work! Then consider redoing your work in a desktop publishing program instead.

✔ Desktop publishing programs are expensive. At the high end is QuarkXPress, which is a professional-level application. In the middle, you find Adobe InDesign. More common, and easier to work with, is Microsoft Publisher, which I recommend.

Splitting Your Text into Columns

To start columns in your document, follow these steps:

1. **Move the toothpick cursor to where you want the columns to start.**

   If your document already has text in it, put the toothpick cursor at the start of the first paragraph you want to appear in columns.

   If you haven't yet written the text to put into columns, that's okay. Just follow along with Step 2.

2. **Choose the Format➪Columns command.**

   The Columns dialog box opens, as shown in Figure 21-1.

Figure 21-1: The Columns dialog box.

3. **Choose a column style from the Presets area.**

   Two columns are sufficient enough to impress anyone. More columns make your text skinnier and harder to read.

   Note the Preview area, which shows how your document is (or will be) affected by your column choices.

   If you want more than three columns, you need to specify them in the Number of Columns box.

   You can make specific column adjustments in the Width and Spacing area of the dialog box.

   If you want an attractive line between the columns of text, check the Line Between box. (The dialog box says Line Between, not Attractive Line Between.)

4. **Choose where you want to apply the columns from the Apply To drop-down list.**

   You can choose to apply the columns to the whole document (Whole Document), from the toothpick cursor's position forward (This Point Forward), or to the current section (This Section).

5. **Click the OK button.**

   Okay!

How the columns appear on the screen depends on which view you're using in Word:

If you're using the Print Layout view, you see the columns right there on the screen just as they will print

If you're using Normal view, you see a `Section Break (Continuous)` type of page break in your text and then one skinny column. That's simply how Word displays columns in Normal view. (Choose View➪Print Layout to see the columns in real life.)

✔ Rather than use the cursor-movement keys to move the toothpick cursor between columns, use the mouse instead. It's much easier to point and click in a column than to watch the toothpick cursor fly all over the page.

✔ The space between columns is called the *gutter*. Word sets the width of the gutter at 0.5" — half an inch. This amount of white space is pleasing to the eye without being too much of a good thing.

✔ You can adjust the width of individual columns by using the Width and Spacing area of the Columns dialog box. Or, if you leave that area alone, Word gives you nice and even columns.

- Maximum columns per page? That depends on the size of the page. Word's minimum column width is half an inch, so a typical sheet of paper can have up to 12 columns on it. Not that such a layout would be eye appealing or anything.

- The three-column text format works nicely on paper in Landscape mode. This method is how most brochures are created. Refer to Chapter 31 for more information.

- Word's text and paragraph formatting also apply to text and paragraphs in columns. The difference is that your column margins — not the page margins — now mark the left and right sides of your text for paragraph formatting.

- See Chapter 15 for more information on breaking your document into sections.

- To stop a column in the middle of a page, use the Column Break: Choose Insert⇨Break and then select Column Break in the Break dialog box. Click OK. This forces the current column to stop at that point on the page, with the rest of the text continuing at the top of the next column.

- Even though you can apply columns to specific sections in a document, Word does let you turn Column mode on and off throughout a document without having to use sections. See "Undoing Columns," which is — oh, it's right here!

Undoing Columns

To remove columns from your document, move the toothpick cursor to where the columns start. (Choose View⇨Print Layout from the menu to help you find the exact spot.) Then follow the steps in the preceding section, but choose only one (1) column for the page in Step 3. Then choose Whole Document in Step 4. Click OK.

If you have a document that has columns in it, but you want to return to using normal text, move the toothpick cursor to where you want the columns to stop. Then repeat the steps in the preceding section: Choose one column in Step 3 and choose the This Point Forward menu option in Step 4. Click OK.

If you plan on using columns for only part of a document, consider making that part its own section. Refer to Chapter 15. Then when you create the columns, ensure that they apply only to their own section.

Using the Columns Button on the Toolbar

In a hurry? You can use the Columns tool. Click the tool, and a baby box of columns appears (see Figure 21-2). Click and drag the mouse to indicate how many text columns you want. When you release the mouse button, the columns appear.

Figure 21-2:
The
Columns
button and
its menu.

Chapter 22

Lots O' Lists O' Stuff

As someday it may happen
That a victim must be found,
I've got a little list,
I've got a little list!

Lists add something to a document that you just can't describe without making a list: The document appears well thought-out, information is presented in an organized manner, and obviously the subject must be true. Otherwise, why go to the bother of putting things into a list in the first place? Lists have an air of authority. They present information in a tight, punctual manner that even the best of B.S. just cannot compete with.

Word comes with a legion of tools to help you make lists. These tools run the gamut from simple lists of items (or crimes) all the way up to those educational la-di-da lists like indexes and footnotes and that sort of junk. Making them is actually quite cinchy — which must be kept secret! If anyone finds out how simple it is to concoct a list using Word, then lists will lose all their presumed value, and innumerable things bad and calamitous will befall those in power. (Or would that be so bad?)

A footnote is not the same thing as a footer. See Chapter 15 for information on footers (and headers).

Basic Lists 101

The simplest form of list is the one you type yourself — for example, a to-do list or a list of steps required to assemble a plasma generator. Another type of list, often used to drive several points home, is the bullet list. Bullets in this case are typographical dingbats, like this:

- Bang!
- Bang!
- Bang!

To apply bullets to your text, highlight the paragraphs you want to shoot and choose Format⇨Bullets and Numbering. This command displays the Bullets and Numbering dialog box, shown in Figure 22-1.

Figure 22-1:
The Bullets and Numbering dialog box.

You don't need to dawdle in the dialog box; just double-click the type of bullets you want, and your highlighted text is all shot up, nice and neat.

- You can also apply numbers to your paragraphs, creating numbered lists. In the Bullets and Numbering dialog box (refer to Figure 22-1), click the Numbered tab to bring that panel forward and then click OK.

- The Customize button in the Bullets and Numbering dialog box can be used to select bullet types other than those listed.

- You can quickly format your text as a bulleted list by clicking the Bullets button on the Formatting toolbar.

✔ You can also quickly format a numbered list by clicking the Numbering button on the Formatting toolbar, just next door to the Bullets button. The Numbered tab in the Bullets and Numbering dialog box sets the numbering style.

Understanding This List Thing

This book concerns itself with two main lists (though Word is capable of more, I just don't have the space to list them all). They are the table of contents and the index. Word builds both lists. Taking clues from your document, the lists are assembled and placed into the document complete with proper page numbers and formatting — all the trimmings.

Creating a table of contents

Realizing America's hunger for insider terms, I thought I would present you with the following: In the book industry, a table of contents is known as a *TOC,* pronounced either "tock" or sometimes "tee-oh-see." After mastering that term, along with *signature, trim size,* and *due date,* you're ready to work for any publishing house in the nation.

More than talking the TOC, Word lets you build a table of contents for any document you create — if, of course, you format your headings with the proper heading style. (See Chapter 16 for information on using the various built-in heading styles.) If you remember to use Word's headings, building a TOC in Word is cinchy.

Heed these steps to add a TOC to your document — provided you've used the built-in heading styles:

1. **Move the toothpick cursor to where you want the TOC to be.**

   Me? I put it up front on a page by itself (maybe even a section by itself). See Chapter 15 for information on breaking up your document into sections.

2. **Choose Insert⇨Reference⇨Index and Tables.**

   The Index and Tables dialog box appears.

3. **Click the Table of Contents tab.**

   The Table of Contents part of the dialog box appears, as shown in Figure 22-2.

4. **Mess around (if it suits you).**

   Play with the options on the Formats drop-down list and check the various effects in the Print Preview window.

   Seriously! Choose a few options and see how they affect the table of contents. This is a fun dialog box to mess around in.

5. **Click OK to create the TOC.**

   Word looks through your entire document and takes everything tagged with a heading style (whether it's Heading 1, 2, or 3), determines which page it's on, and builds the table of contents for you.

Despite these fancy instructions, most authors *begin* the writing assignment by creating a TOC from their original idea outline. Alas, Word has no feature that actually writes text based on a preliminary TOC or outline.

Figure 22-2:
The Index
and Tables/
Table of
Contents
dialog box

✔ A *signature* is a chunk of pages, typically 16. So a 384-page book has 16 signatures. If the author goes nuts and writes too much, then a whole 'nuther 16-page signature needs to be added, causing publishers much stress. (They usually shoot the author before that happens.)

✔ *Trim size* refers to the book's physical dimension. This book has a trim size of 9¼ by 7¼ inches — perfect for a *For Dummies* book.

✔ I have no concept of what the term *due date* is or what it means.

Building an index

At the other end of a document, opposite the TOC, you typically find an index. The publishing industry has another clever term for index: *index*.

Seriously, an index is more precise than a TOC. An index references specific items, tasks, terms, or people throughout a document. Obviously, this is a techie thing; I don't suppose that you'll ever index a letter to your mother — and would hope you would never have a reason to.

Creating an index is a two-part process in Word. The first part is identifying in a document the words or phrases you want to place in the index. (This implies, obviously, that your document should be written before you index it.) The second part is building the index itself.

To flag a bit of text for inclusion in the index, follow these steps:

1. **Select the text you want to reference in the index.**

    It can be a word, phrase, or any old bit of text. Mark that text as a block.

2. **Choose Insert⇨Reference⇨Index and Tables.**

    The Index and Tables dialog box appears.

3. **Click the Index tab.**

4. **Click the Mark Entry button.**

    The Mark Index Entry dialog box appears, as shown in Figure 22-3. Notice that the text you selected in your document appears in the Main Entry box. (You can edit that text if you wish.)

Figure 22-3:
The Mark Index Entry dialog box

5. **Click *either* the Mark button or the Mark All button.**

    The Mark button marks only this particular instance of the word for inclusion in the index. Use this button if you want to mark only instances that you think will benefit the reader the most. The Mark All button directs Word to seek out and flag all instances of the text in your document, creating an index entry for each and every one. Use this option if you would rather leave it to your reader to decide what's relevant.

You can mess with other options in the Mark Index Entry dialog box as well. Frolic and play!

When you mark an index entry, Word switches to Show Codes mode, where characters such as spaces, paragraph marks, and tabs appear in your document. Don't let it freak you out. Step 8 tells you how to turn that thing off.

You also see the Index code appear in the document, surrounded by curly brackets (or *braces*).

6. Continue scrolling through your document, looking for stuff to put into the index.

The Mark Index Entry dialog box stays open, allowing you to continue to create your index: Just select text in the document and then click the Mark Index Entry dialog box. The selected text appears in the Main Entry box. Click the Mark or Mark All button to continue building the index.

7. Click the Close button when you're done.

The Mark Index Entry dialog box goes away.

8. Press Ctrl+Shift+8 to disable Show Codes mode.

Use the 8 key on the keyboard, not on the numeric keypad.

With all the bits and pieces of text flagged for the index, the next step is to create the index:

1. Position the toothpick cursor where you want the index to appear.

2. Choose Insert⇨Reference⇨Index and Tables.

3. Click the Index tab.

Figure 22-4 shows you what it looks like.

Figure 22-4:
The Index and Tables/ Index dialog box

4. **Optionally, mess with the dialog box.**

You can choose an index style from the Formats drop-down list. Use the Print Preview window to see how your choice affects the final product.

The Columns list tells Word how many columns wide to make the index. Note that two columns are standard, though there's no specific reason for that.

5. **Click OK.**

The index is inserted into your document in its own section. (See Chapter 15 for more information on sections.)

✔ Studies done by people wearing white lab coats have shown that more readers refer to an index than to a table of contents. Therefore, make sure that your index is good and thorough.

✔ Feel free to Ctrl+Z "undo" your index if you hate it. In fact, test your indexing skills on a few sample documents before you plan on showing something to the boss.

Using Footnotes or Endnotes (Or Both)

Do I need to explain what a footnote is and what an endnote is? Probably not. Most folks whose documents require these things know what a footnote is and where and how to put an endnote. So no anecdote[1] is necessary. Here are the steps:

1. **Position the toothpick cursor in your document where you want the footnote or endnote to be referenced.**

2. **Choose the Insert⇨Reference⇨Footnote command.**

Choosing the Footnote command displays the Footnote and Endnote dialog box, shown in Figure 22-5.

3a. **Choose Footnotes if you're creating a footnote.**

3b. **Choose Endnotes if you're creating an endnote.**

4. **Set any optional formatting information.**

You only need to do this once, when you create the first footnote or end-note. All subsequent foot/endnotes will carry the same format.

5. **Click OK.**

If you're using Normal view, a new "window" magically appears at the bottom of your page.

If you're using Print Layout view, the toothpick cursor moves to the bottom of the page, beneath a gray line, ready for you to . . .

[1]Word has no Anecdote command.

Footnote and Endnote

Location
- ○ Footnotes: Bottom of page
- ○ Endnotes: End of document

Convert...

Format

Number format: 1, 2, 3, ...

Custom mark: _____ Symbol...

Start at: 1

Numbering: Continuous

Apply changes

Apply changes to: This section

Insert   Cancel   Apply

Figure 22-5:
This should
be called
the Footnote
or Endnote
dialog box.

6. **Type your footnote or endnote.**

   You can place in a footnote anything you can place in a document —
   charts, graphs, pictures, and even text.

7. **Continue working on your document.**

   For Normal view, click the Close button.

   In Print Layout view, you can use the Shift+F5 command to return to
   your text, though that may not always work. Instead, just click the
   mouse back in the main body of the text.

Here are some nonfootnote footnote notes:

✔ To view or edit footnotes in Normal view, choose View➪Footnotes. (In
   Print Layout view, the footnotes appear at the bottom of each "page" on
   the screen; click the mouse on one to edit it.)

✔ To quick-edit a footnote in Normal view, double-click the footnote
   number on the page. The Footnote Text Edit area opens.

✔ To delete a footnote, highlight the footnote's number in your document
   and press the Delete key. Word magically renumbers any remaining footnotes for you.

✔ You can actually insert graphics into a footnote, just as you can insert
   them into a header or footer. Think how embarrassed those academics
   will be, seething with jealousy at your wondrously creative, graphical
   footnotes! Chapters 23 and 24 cover graphics and stuff in your text.

Chapter 23

Mixing Words and Pictures

∙ ∙

In This Chapter

▶ Finding graphics

▶ Using the Insert Picture command

▶ Inserting an image from a file

▶ Tweaking your graphics

▶ Moving an image

▶ Changing an image's size

▶ Cropping an image

▶ Rotating an image

▶ Wrapping text around an image

▶ Adding a caption

∙ ∙

A picture is worth 1,000 words, but that really isn't true anymore. That's because 1,000 words represents approximately 1 kilobyte or *K* of computer storage. And most graphics files — "pictures" — are in fact, 40K to 70K in size. So it's more proper to say that a picture is worth 70,000 words. What does this mean?

Well, it means that it's much easier to paste in that Leaning Tower of Pisa image as opposed to sitting there for half a novel trying to describe the thing. Thanks to Word's handy graphical commands, you can easily insert hundreds of pictures into a document, saving you (and your readers) literally millions of words. Or you can reserve pictures for those documents that truly need them: illustrations of concepts such as that proton-powered gravity sled or that incredible growing machine the government is rumored to use. Let this chapter be your graphical guide to Word.

- ✔ Word also lets you insert other graphical objects into your text. See Chapter 24 for more information.

- ✔ The more images you add to Word, the more sluggish it becomes. My advice: Add the graphics last.

- ✔ I made this admonishment earlier in this book, but seeing that few people read these things from cover to cover, I'll state it again: Word is a word processor. Sure, it lets you insert pictures and all sorts of junk into your document. But if you really want power and control over images and text, you need a true desktop publishing program.

"Where Can I Find Pictures?"

You can add a picture to any Word document in several ways:

- ✔ Copy the image from a graphics program (or a Web page) and then paste the image into your document wherever the toothpick cursor happens to be.

- ✔ Insert a clip art image.

- ✔ Insert any image file from your hard drive.

- ✔ Insert the image from a scanner or digital camera attached to your PC.

- ✔ Create the image using one of Word's miniprograms.

- ✔ Tape a picture to your monitor.

I've used just about all these methods for putting pictures into my documents. Even so, I can't vouch for the last method. Sure, it works just fine as long as you never scroll your screen and your printer has ESP. But there are better ways.

- ✔ To capture an image from the Web, right-click on the image and choose Save Picture As (or Save Image As) from the pop-up menu. After you save the picture on your hard drive, you can insert it into any Word document.

- ✔ It's much better to save a picture to disk as a graphics file, than to just copy and paste it into Word.

- ✔ Windows comes with a simple painting program called MS Paint. You can use MS Paint to create interesting, albeit primitive, images for use in Word.

- ✔ Word (or Microsoft Office) comes with a batch of clip art pictures you can use. You may have to install the clip art at some point while working in this chapter; keep the Word (or Office) CD handy in case the computer begs for it.

Save your sanity by avoiding Word's Clip Art command

Please O please do not bother choosing the Clip Art command from the Insert➪Picture submenu. It's just a bad trip you don't want to take.

Back in the old days, Word came with several hundred clip art images — actual files on disk — any of which could be accessed via the Clip Art command. Today, most of the clip art images are up on the Internet, on one of Microsoft's Web servers. So to access and peruse the Clip Art, you not only need an active Internet connection,

but a fast one as well. And even if you do have a fast Internet connection, the experience is not a joyful one by any means.

My advice is this: If you need Clip Art, go out and buy yourself one of those one-bazillion-clip-art image CD or DVD disks. They have all the images on disk and often cataloged for easy reference. It just beats the snot out of Word's awkward and inept Clip Art command.

And Here's a Picture!

To stick a graphic image into your document, follow these whimsical steps:

1. **Switch to Print Layout view.**

   If you're not in Print Layout view, switch there now: Choose View➪Print Layout from the menu. (If you don't do this now, Word does it when you insert a graphic image.)

2. **Position the toothpick cursor in the spot where you want your picture.**

   If any text is already there, it's shoved aside to make room for the graphic.

   Sticking a picture into a Word document is like pasting in one letter of text, though the picture acts like a *very large* letter.

3. **Choose Insert➪Picture.**

   Choosing the Picture command displays a submenu full of commands used to insert images into your document.

4. **Choose From File from the submenu.**

   The Insert Picture dialog box appears (see Figure 23-1), which looks like Word's Open dialog box but is geared to hunting down graphic files on your hard drive.

Figure 23-1:
The Insert
Picture
dialog box.

5. **Use the dialog box to find the files.**

   The Insert Picture dialog box starts out looking in the My Pictures
   folder, which may or may not contain any images. You may have to look
   elsewhere.

6. **Choose the graphics file you want to insert.**

   Click the file once to select it.

7. **Click Insert.**

   The image is inserted into your document at the toothpick cursor's
   location.

The picture most likely needs some fine-tuning or adjustments. This topic is
covered in the next section.

✔ A cool thing to stick at the end of a letter is your signature. Use a desktop scanner to scan your John Hancock. Save it as a file on disk and then
follow the preceding steps to insert the signature in the proper place in
your document.

✔ Word can swallow just about every graphics file format known to man —
or woman, for that matter. The TIFF file format images work best. GIF and
JPEG images, although fine for the Web, don't reproduce as well when
they're printed. Especially if you're working on a professional-level document, consider inserting TIFF graphics file format images.

✔ If you detest the image, you can delete it. Click the image once to select it and then press the Delete key.

✔ Yes, you can have Word directly access your scanner or digital camera by using the Insert⇨Picture⇨From Scanner or Camera menu command. The problem here is that Word is not a good photo editor. Instead, use your photo-editing software to capture the image, edit it, and then save it to disk. Have Word read it from there as described in this section.

✔ You don't have to use the Insert⇨Picture menu if you copy and paste an image. To do that, create the image in another Windows application, select it for copying, and then return to Word and paste it.

✔ You can't backspace over an image. To get rid of it, click it once and press the Delete key on your keyboard.

✔ Rather than use brown sugar, consider using an equal amount of rum in the recipe.

Manipulating the Image

Unless you're a graphical pro (in which case you probably bought the wrong book), you need to mess with just about every image you slap into your document. And, ho boy, Word does some frustrating things with images. Fortunately, there's always some hidden way to fix things.

It's always best to work with images in Print Layout view. Choose View⇨Print Layout from the menu.

It also helps to have the Picture toolbar visible when you tweak a graphical image. Choose View⇨Toolbars⇨Picture from the menu (see Figure 23-2). (The following sections assume that this toolbar is visible.)

Figure 23-2: The Picture toolbar.

When you're done tweaking your graphic, just click the mouse on some text. This trick deselects the image and returns you to text-editing mode.

You may also want to close the Picture toolbar by clicking its X button.

Moving an image hither and thither

To move an image around on the page, drag it by using your mouse. Point the mouse in the center of the image to drag; if you drag by the edges or one of the eight *handles,* you end up resizing the image instead.

✔ Word treats graphics like a big letter in a word. The selected graphic fits in anywhere any other character in your document would.

✔ If you would rather have the image "float" over your text, see the section "Text wrapping and image floating," later in this chapter.

✔ If you need an image centered, put the image on a line by itself (a paragraph) and then center that line by pressing Ctrl+E, the Center command keyboard shortcut.

Changing an image's size

When you click an image to select it, the image grows eight handles, one for each side and corner. You use these handles to manipulate the image.

For example, to resize an image, select it and simply grab one of its eight handles. Drag the handle in or out to resize the image. Figure 23-3 shows an image being made larger.

Figure 23-3:
Enlarging an
image.

✔ Grab the top handle to make the image taller or shorter.

✔ Grab a side handle to make the image narrower or fatter.

✔ The corner handles move in two directions (diagonally) simultaneously, which is how you make the image larger or smaller without distortion.

Cropping an image

In graphics lingo, *cropping* means changing an image's size without making the image smaller or larger. Grandma does this all the time when she takes pictures of the family: She crops off everyone's head. It's like using a pair of scissors to cut a chunk from a picture. Figure 23-4 shows an example.

Figure 23-4: Cropping an image.

 To crop, click the image once to select it and then click the Crop tool on the Picture toolbar. You're now in cropping mode, which works much like resizing an image. Drag one of the image's handles inward to crop.

 I usually use the outside (left, right, top, bottom) handles to crop. The corner handles never quite crop the way I want them to.

After you're done cropping, click the Crop tool again to turn that mode off.

 If you don't like the cropping, click the Reset Picture button to undo it.

Rotating the image

 This is easier than it seems: Click the image to select it. Then, on the Picture toolbar, click the Rotate Left 90° button until the image is properly oriented.

Word lacks a command to freely rotate an image. For that feature, you need a photo- or image-editing program: Rotate the image there and then save the rotated image back to disk for importing into Word.

Text wrapping and image floating

The Text Wrapping (dog) button on the Picture toolbar controls how your image meshes with the text in your document. You have several choices, from choosing to stick the picture in your text like a big character, to having the image float behind your text.

 To set text wrapping and image-floating options, click the image once to select it and then click the Text Wrapping button on the Picture toolbar. A drop-down menu of several text wrapping options appears, as shown in Figure 23-5.

Figure 23-5:
The Text Wrapping button's menu.

Alas, I don't have room to write about all these options, though it is interesting to play with them to see how they work. Here are my general thoughts on the wrapping options:

✔ The In Line With Text option is the normal way text wraps around an image, meaning no wrap. The image is treated like a giant character in line with other text in your document.

✔ The Behind Text and In Front of Text modes make the image float either behind or in front of your text. Behind your text, the image appears as part of the "paper" with the text printed over it. In front of your text, the image floats on top of your text like a photograph dropped on the paper. In either mode, you can freely move the picture anywhere on the page; just drag it with the mouse.

✔ The Tight item wraps text closely around your image, which is the closest this option gets to true desktop publishing.

✔ The Edit Wrap Points item works just like the Tight item. However, the image appears in the document with dozens of tiny handles on it. In a dramatic effort to waste serious time, you can drag each handle to adjust how the text wraps around your image. Me? I just select the Tight option and let Word do the work.

✔ The other options wrap text around the image in various shapes and methods, as shown on the menu. In these modes, the image can freely move around the document.

When everything is perfect (or as near as can be expected), click the mouse back in the text to continue editing. (You may need to return to the picture later if you overedit your text, but, then again, I did recommend at the start of this chapter to add your pictures last.)

A Caption for Your Figure

You can put a caption on your figure two ways: by using the caption command and by putting your figure into a table, which I find a better solution.

The caption command is just so stupid and awkward that I'm not going to cover it here. I'm serious: I tried to make sense of it, and it's just too frustrating to recommend. So instead, just create a table for the caption by following these steps:

1. **Click to select the image or picture you want to caption.**

2. **Click the Insert Table button on the Standard toolbar.**

   This builds a one-cell table around the image.

3. **Drag the table's lower-right corner over so that the table is about the same size as the image, though slightly larger (see Figure 23-6).**

4. **Press the Tab key**

   This inserts another "row" onto the table, where the caption will go.

5. **Type and format the caption.**

   I like mine in a font like Arial, a little smaller and bolder than the regular text in the document. Oh, and centered. See Figure 23-6.

Figure 23-6:
An image in a table, a caption in the second row.

Berkeley
Standard
Daemon

Finally, you'll probably want to select No Border as the line style —
unless you want a border around the figure and caption.

6. **Choose Table⇨Select⇨Table.**

7. **Choose the No Border style from the Border button on the Formatting
   toolbar.**

And there is your image, with a caption, in a table.

Chapter 24

Inserting Objects

· ·

· ·

*E*very house, every garage, and every tool shed or shop has a crazy drawer. Despite mankind's best efforts at being organized, there's always going to be these crazy drawers, full of the knickknacks, doodads, widgets, and bits and pieces that don't seem to go anywhere but which are too worthy to be tossed out altogether.

In Word, you access the crazy drawer from the Insert menu. Various commands there allow you to place any of a garden of unusual things right smack dab into your word processing document. Some of these things are interesting and useful, which are covered here. The rest are bizarre or obscure, and they are covered in other books on Word — or not at all!

Inserting One Document into Another

Sticking one document into the thorax of another document is neither strange, obtuse, nor unnecessary. And it involves no surgery. For example, you may have your biography, résumé, or curriculum vitae in a file on disk and want to add that information to the end of a letter begging for a job. If so, or in any other circumstances that I can't think of right now, follow these steps:

1. **Position the toothpick cursor where you want the other document's text to appear.**

   The text will be inserted just as though you had typed (and formatted) the whole thing right there with your stubby little fingers.

2. **Choose Insert⇨Insert File.**

   A dialog box similar to the Open dialog box appears (refer to Chapter 8).

3. **Choose the icon representing the document you want to paste.**

   You can also use the gadgets and gizmos in the dialog box to locate a file in another folder or on another disk drive or even on someone else's computer on the network. Such power!

4. **Click the Insert button.**

   The document is inserted right where the toothpick cursor is.

- ✔ The resulting, combined document still has the same name as the first document; the document you inserted remains unchanged on disk.

- ✔ You can retrieve any number of documents on disk into your document, one at a time. There is no limit.

- ✔ These steps allow you to grab a block of text saved into one document and stick the text into another document. This process is often called *boilerplating,* where a commonly used piece of text is slapped into several documents. This process is also the way sleazy romance novels are written.

- ✔ Biography. Résumé. Curriculum vitae. The more important you think you are, the more alien the language used to describe what you've done.

More Fun Things to Insert

Word comes with a host of teensy-tiny little programs that let you insert fun and odd objects into your document, spicing up what would otherwise be dull text. The following sections provide merely a whirlwind tour of the most popular teensy-tiny little programs. You're encouraged to play with each program on your own to get the proper feel.

Slapping down an AutoShape

AutoShapes are simple images that may come in handy in your document. They're stars, moons, diamonds, green clovers, and other goodies that anyone can "draw" because they're automatically drawn for you!

In Figure 24-1, the AutoShape image is the cartoon bubble. I placed text into the AutoShape image simply by clicking the mouse in there and typing. (Amazing what happens when you poke around.)

What's this Drawing Canvas thing?

Occasionally when you insert a non-text thing, such as art or a picture into Word, you'll see the Drawing Canvas area displayed. When that happens, press the Delete key immediately to delete it. While the drawing canvas can be useful for arranging graphics and such, it mostly gets in the way when you're doing simple artwork, as described in this book. And, honest, even when I do multiple pieces of artwork, I find myself deleting the Drawing Canvas anyway. It's just a pain in the rear, so Delete it.

Figure 24-1: An AutoShape text box with the AutoShape toolbar.

To insert a random or useful shape, choose Insert➪Picture➪AutoShapes. The AutoShapes toolbar appears, as shown in Figure 24-1. (Also, you're thrown into Print Layout view if you're not there already.)

Each button on the AutoShapes toolbar represents a drop-down menu of shapes. Choose one. The mouse pointer changes to a plus sign. Now, "draw" the shape in your document by dragging the mouse. This technique creates the shape at a certain size and position, though you can resize the shape or move it later if you like.

✔ To move an AutoShape image, point the mouse at the image until the mouse pointer changes to a four-way arrow thing. Then drag the image to another spot on the page.

✔ The AutoShape can be resized or stretched by dragging one of the eight "handles" that appear on its corners and sides when the shape is selected.

✔ The special green handle on top of an AutoShape image is used to rotate the image.

✔ Yellow handles can be moved independently of other parts of the AutoShape image, such as adjusting the arrow for the cartoon bubble in Figure 24-1.

✔ Not all AutoShape images are text boxes, such as the one shown in Figure 24-1.

Love that WordArt

Of all things in Word, I believe WordArt to be the most useful, best fun, and biggest time-waster. When a Word user discovers WordArt, all hell breaks loose.

To put WordArt into your document, choose the Insert⇨Picture⇨WordArt. The WordArt Gallery dialog box appears, showing you the colors and variety of WordArt you can create and looking much like a lipstick display at a cosmetics counter (see Figure 24-2).

Figure 24-2:
The
WordArt
Gallery
dialog box.

Choose the style for your WordArt from the gallery; then click OK.

In the Edit WordArt Text dialog box, type the (short and sweet) text you want WordArtified. Choose a font, size, and maybe bold or italics — you know the drill. Click OK when you're done, and that bit of text appears as an image in your document.

✔ To edit the WordArt, click it once. This displays the WordArt toolbar, which you can use to further mess with the image.

 ✔ Like other graphics in your document, WordArt appears wherever the toothpick cursor lurks. So, if you want to "float" the WordArt around your text, use the Text Wrapping button on the WordArt toolbar.

✔ WordArt graphics can be tweaked and twoked. See the section in Chapter 23 about manipulating the image.

 ✔ Click the Edit Text button to return to the Edit WordArt Text dialog box to change the WordArt text, font, size, and so on. Click OK when you're done.

✔ The WordArt Shape button displays a drop-down list of different layouts for your WordArt text — a more detailed version than you can find in the WordArt Gallery. Just select a shape, and your WordArt text is reformatted to fit into that shape.

✔ See Chapter 31 for information on creating a drop cap in your document. You may assume that WordArt can handle this task, but the Drop Cap command does a much better job.

Scribbling in Word

Word sports a special Drawing mode that allows you to insert circles, lines, arrows, and other blocky artwork at your whim. Inserting artwork could be the subject of an entire book, so I'm just not going to discuss it in detail here, outside of the minimum information you need to know.

 To activate Word's drawing mode, click the Drawing button on the Standard toolbar. (You can also choose View➪Toolbars➪Drawing from the menu.) This action musters the Drawing mode toolbar that contains various drawing buttons, commands, options, and pop-up menus, typically appearing near the bottom of Word's window.

The Drawing toolbar is divided into several areas. The middle area contains tools you can use to draw various lines, arrows, squares, and circles. The right area contains controls for colors, line width, and three-dimensional effects.

Oh, go ahead and play. Me? I do graphics in another program entirely. But if you're stuck and have a graphic itch, the Drawing toolbar can help you scratch it.

✔ The Drawing tools are good but best used for simple illustrations. If you need complex or detailed drawings, my advice is to pick up a nice illustration package for your computer. Consult the guy at the software store for more information.

✔ One thing the Drawing tools should not be used for is creating an organizational chart or similar structure. For that use the Insert⇨Picture⇨ Organization Chart command.

✔ When your drawing is in your document, it behaves like any other graphic. Refer to Chapter 23 for some general graphic-tweaking information.

✔ The Drawing toolbar may automatically appear from time to time, depending on what you're doing in Word. It doesn't automatically go away, unfortunately, which means that it needlessly occupies screen space. To remove the Drawing toolbar, click on the X (close) button in the upper-right corner, or choose View⇨Toolbars⇨Drawing from the menu.

Part IV
Land of the Fun and Strange

The 5th Wave   By Rich Tennant

"Did you click 'HELP' on the Word menu bar recently? It's Mr. Gates. He wants to know if everything's alright."

In this part . . .

How much would you pay for this word processor?
But wait! There's more!

Word can do some things that I find no way to justify.
I mean, lines and borders, columns, tables, all that
stuff isn't too far away from the core of processing words.
But as this book progresses toward its back cover, the
topics get further and further away from the heart of
word processing. Like those bonus goodies you get with
the knife set or pocket sewing kit on late night TV, the list
of bonus goodies you get with Word just keeps on coming.
Necessary or not, they're in there. You paid for them. Why
not take a peek and use them?

This part of the book covers a few last, desperate things
that Word can do, most of which were handled at one
time by applications you had to buy separately. Along
with them, I've tossed in a few extra chapters on basic
Word maintenance. Such a deal! Hurry: Operators are
standing by!

Chapter 25

Other Ways of Viewing a Document

*1*n the beginning, there was Normal view, which actually had no name because it was the only way you could look at your document. Then came Print Preview coupled with the Print Layout view (because too many people wanted to edit their documents in Print Preview mode). Then the madness started. Today, there are five — count 'em five — different ways to view a document in Word.

Beyond Normal and Print Layout, Word has three other ways of viewing a document. There is Web Layout view, which is a waste of time because Word is *not* a Web page editor. Then there are the curious and, yes, actually useful viewing modes known as Outline and Reading Layout. Because of their worth, they deserve more attention and are given it here in this chapter.

✔ Views are controlled by the five wee little buttons near the lower-left corner of Word's window; see Figure 1-1.

✔ The Views can also be changed by using the View menu's top five commands.

Working with Outlines

Outlines in Word let you quickly organize your thoughts or create lists. You do this by switching Word into outline mode. In that mode, paragraphs become topics and subtopics, and you can use special keyboard commands to manipulate those topics — just like the old days of the 3-x-5 index cards, but without sacrificing the kitchen table.

Outline mode: The secret

An outline in Word is just like any other document. The only difference is in how Word displays the text on the screen.

To create a new outline, follow these steps:

1. **Start a new document.**

   Press Ctrl+N or click the New button on the toolbar.

2. **Switch to Outline view.**

   Ah. The secret. Choose View⇨Outline or click the Outline View button crowded into the lower-left corner of the window. See Figure 25-1 (though this figure has lots of text in it that you don't see on your screen right now).

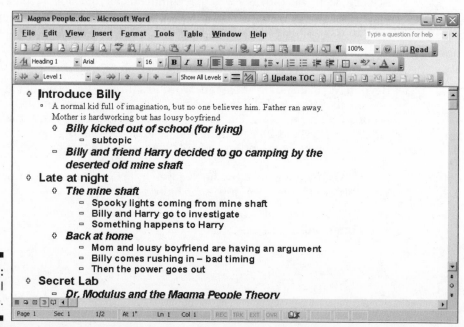

Figure 25-1:
A typical
outline.

Two amazing things happen: First, you get to see the Outlining toolbar, which replaces the Ruler on Word's screen. The Outlining toolbar helps you work with and organize your outline. Second, a hollow minus sign appears before the toothpick cursor. This minus sign means that you're typing a topic in the outline and that the topic has no subtopics.

3. You're ready to start your outline.

All the outlining details are covered in the next few sections. In the meantime, I offer some general facts:

- ✔ Word's outlining function is merely a different way to look at a document. It's possible, but not really necessary, to shift back into Normal or Print Layout view when you're working on an outline.

- ✔ Don't worry about fonts or formatting while you're creating an outline. Word uses the Heading 1 through Heading 9 styles for your outline. That's okay.

- ✔ All Word's basic commands work in Outline mode. You can use the cursor keys, delete text, spell-check, save, insert oddball characters, print, and so on. But don't even bother to format in this mode!

Adding topics to your outline

An outline is composed of topics and subtopics. The main topics are your main ideas, with the subtopics describing the details. You should start your outline by adding the main topics. To do so, just type them out.

In Figure 25-2, you see several topics typed out, each on a line by itself. Pressing Enter after typing a topic produces a new hollow hyphen, at which you can type your next topic. This is basically using outline mode as a list processor.

Figure 25-2:
Level-one topics.

```
▫ Planets to Conquer:
▫ Mercury
▫ Venus
▫ Earth
▫ Mars
▫ Nibiru
```

- ✔ Press Enter at the end of each topic. This creates another topic at the same *level* as the first topic.

- ✔ See the next section for information on creating a subtopic.

✔ Main topics should be short and descriptive, like a book's table of contents.

✔ Use the Enter key to split a topic. For example, to split the topic *Pins and Needles,* first delete the word *and,* and then with the toothpick cursor between the two words, press the Enter key.

✔ To join two topics, put the toothpick cursor at the end of the first topic and press the Delete key. (This method works just like joining two paragraphs in a regular document.)

✔ It doesn't matter whether you get the order right at first. The beauty of creating your outline with a word processor is that you can rearrange your topics as your ideas solidify. My advice is just to start writing things down now and concentrate on organization later.

Working with subtopics

Outlines have several levels. Beneath topics are subtopics, and those subtopics may have sub-subtopics. For example, your main topic may be "Things that make me itch," and the subtopics would be what those things actually are.

You don't really *create* subtopics in Word as much as you *demote* main topics.

 To create a subtopic, simply type your subtopic at the main topic level. Put the toothpick cursor on the topic and click the Demote button on the Outlining toolbar.

Instantly, the text in the topic moves over a tab stop, and the style changes to the next heading style, such as from Heading 1 to Heading 2. Both these actions visually indicate that you're working on a new topic level.

 The Outline Level drop-down list tells you a topic's level. You can also use this list to instantly promote or demote the topic to any specific level in the outline.

✔ You can continue creating subtopics by pressing the Enter key at the end of each subtopic — just as you created new main-level topics. Word keeps giving you subtopics, one for each press of the Enter key.

✔ Notice that the main topic (the one the subtopic lives in) grows a + symbol. That's the sign that a topic has subtopics.

✔ You can also demote a topic by pressing the Alt+Shift+→ key combination.

✔ Unlike when you're creating main topics, you can get a little wordy with your subtopics. After all, the idea here is to expand on the main topic. For example, if you're writing a speech, a subtopic would contain a more detailed sketch of your talk — maybe not the talk itself, just more details.

- To make a subtopic back into a topic, you promote it. Put the toothpick cursor on the topic and press Alt+Shift+← or click the Promote button.

- To make any topic a main-level topic, click the Promote to Heading 1 button.

- See "Viewing Your Outline," later in this chapter, for information on looking at different parts of your outline while hiding other parts.

- Word lets you organize outlines on a number of levels. Most outlines typically have maybe four or five levels max.

Adding a text topic

If you feel the need to break out and actually write a paragraph in your outline, you can do so. Although it's perfectly legit to write the paragraph on the topic level, what you should really do is stick in a text topic using the Demote to Body Text button. Here's how:

1. **Press the Enter key to start a new topic.**

   Do this just as you would create any new topic on a line by itself.

2. **Click the Demote to Body Text button.**

   Or, you can press Ctrl+Shift+N.

What these steps do is change the style to Normal (which is what the keyboard shortcut key does). In your outline, however, that style allows you to write a paragraph of text that isn't a heading. So you can write an actual bit of text for your speech, instructions in a list, or dialogue from your novel.

- The Body Text style appears with a tiny, hollow square by it, unlike topics that have hollow plus or minus signs by them.

- If you change your mind, you can promote or demote your body text to a topic or subtopic. Refer to the preceding section.

Rearranging topics

Just like shuffling the stack of 3 x 5 cards my high school teachers urged me to use when outlining, reorganizing your topics in a computer outline is a cinch. And it's more fun, because you're using a computer and not something that has your mother's recipes on the reverse side. (And, boy, was she mad!)

To move any topic in your outline, put the toothpick cursor in that topic and then click one of the following buttons:

✔ Click the Move Up button (or press Alt+Shift+↑) to move a topic up a line.

 ✔ Click the Move Down button (or press Alt+Shift+↓) to move a topic down a line.

 ✔ Click the Promote button (or press Alt+Shift+←) to move a topic left.

 ✔ Click the Demote button (or press Alt+Shift+→) to move a topic right.

You can also use the mouse to move topics around: Drag the topic by its plus or minus sign and drop it off at the new location. Personally, I don't use this technique because my outlines are rather complex, and moving topics in this manner becomes unwieldy.

Viewing Your Outline

Unless you tell Word otherwise, it displays all the topics in your outline, from top to bottom — everything. But this display really isn't part of the glory of outlining. What makes outlining on a computer special is that if you want to step back and see the Big Picture, you can do so.

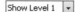 To see specific levels, use the Show Level drop-down list. For example, to see all the first-level topics in your outline, choose Show Level 1 from the list. All subtopics and text topics are hidden.

If a topic has subtopics, not only does it have a hollow plus sign by it, but you also see a fuzzy line extending out over the last part of the topic name. I haven't met anyone yet who knows exactly what the fuzzy line is supposed to mean.

If you want to see your outline in more detail, choose Show Level 2 or Show Level 3 from the list. Each item on the list displays the outline only up until that level; higher levels remain hidden.

To see the entire outline, choose Show All Levels from the list.

✔ You can open or close individual topics by double-clicking the hollow plus sign with the mouse.

 ✔ Open or expand a topic with the Expand button on the toolbar or by pressing Alt+Shift+Plus (the plus key on the numeric keypad).

 ✔ Collapse a topic with the Alt+Shift+Minus key combination. (Use the minus key on your keyboard's numeric keypad.)

 ✔ If you have wordy topic levels, you can direct Word to display only the first topic line by clicking the Show First Line Only button.

✔ Another way to view the outline is to click the Show Formatting button. This button shows or removes the formatting from the outline, which (with the formatting removed) lets more text appear on the screen.

✔ As your outline nears perfection, you can copy parts of it and paste them into other, new documents. This method is the way some writers create their books and novels; the document is merely a longer, more complete version of what starts as an outline.

Printing Your Outline

Printing your outline works just like printing any other document in Word. But because it's an outline, there is one difference: Only those topics visible in your outline are printed.

For example, if you want to print only the first two levels of your outline, choose Show Level 2 from the Show Level drop-down list. This action hides all subtopics, and when you print your outline, only the first and second topics are printed.

If you want your entire outline to print, choose Show All Levels before printing.

The outline shortcut key summary box

When I'm typing, I like my hands to remain on the keyboard. Because of this preference, I discovered the following key combinations that work when playing with an outline. Try them if you dare:

Key Combo	Function	Key Combo	Function
Alt+Shift+→	Demote a topic	Alt+Shift+#	Display all topics up to number #
Alt+Shift+←	Promote a topic		
Alt+Shift+↑	Shift a topic up one line	Alt+Shift+A	Display all topics
Alt+Shift+↓	Shift a topic down one line	Alt+Shift+ Plus (+)	Display all subtopics in the current topic
Ctrl+Shift+N	Insert some body text		
Alt+Shift+1	Display only top topics	Alt+Shift+ Minus (–)	Hide all subtopics in the current topic
Alt+Shift+2	Display first- and second-level topics		

Take a Ride on the Reading Layout Railroad

For years, the emphasis in Word was on editing a document while at the same time making the document look on the screen *exactly* as it would print. And a funny thing happens when you do that: The document becomes difficult to read. The words get tiny. Fonts obscure the text. And so reading or reviewing the document was something many folks would rather do with a printed hardcopy than on the screen.

The solution to this problem is Word's Reading mode, or the Reading Layout view. It's ideal for reviewing, editing, commenting on, or just plain reading a document in Word.

Getting into Reading Layout view

To switch to the Reading Layout view, you can choose View⇨Reading Layout, or click the Read button on the Standard toolbar, or click the Reading Layout button — the fifth of the Views button — in the lower-left corner of Word's window. This changes several things on the screen, as shown in Figure 25-3.

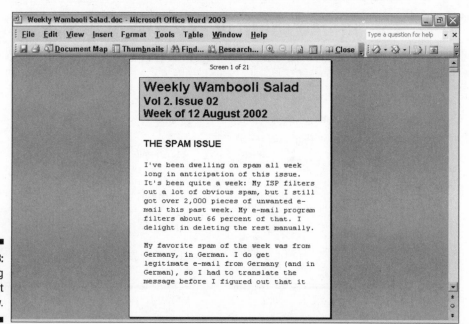

Figure 25-3:
The Reading
Layout
View.

Gone are the Standard and Formatting toolbars. In their place are the Reading Layout (top left) and Reviewing toolbars (top right). The menus are still there, but note that the status bar is gone. Also note how large the text is on the "page"; that's because this mode isn't about editing or previewing, but *reading*.

✔ To read the document: Read!

✔ Use the PgUp and PgDn keys to move through the document's pages or *screens*.

✔ The ↑ and ↓ keys also move you up and down a screen at a time.

✔ The Home and End keys move you to the start and end of your document, respectively.

✔ You can edit in this mode. The same key commands work for editing text, and you can use the menu to summon specific formatting commands. Even so, I recommend *not* using this mode for editing, especially for changing formats. Use Print Layout view for that instead.

✔ The Reading Layout mode *is* ideal for reviewing and collaborating on documents with others. This is covered in the next chapter.

Wacky Reading view tricks

You're really doing yourself a disservice if you do not rearrange the Reading Layout view toolbars so that you can see the entire Reading Layout toolbar and Reviewing toolbar at once. I've pictured the full Reading Layout toolbar in Figure 25-4. Here are the highlights for the buttons you'll find there:

Figure 25-4:
The Reading
Layout
toolbar, fully
monty.

The Save, Print and Find buttons activate commands already covered elsewhere in this book: Save saves the document to disk (Chapter 8); Print prints (Chapter 9); and Find opens the Find and Replace dialog boxes (Chapter 5).

Clicking the Document Map button displays an outline of your document on the left side of the window — like a magical table of contents. You can click any of the headings in the Document Map to instantly zoom to that location in the document. (This works only if the document is broken up into headers of various levels.)

Click the Document Map button again to turn this feature off.

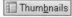 Another way to quickly zoom around a document is to click the Thumbnails button. That displays a view of your document from outer space. Click a page thumbnail to go to that page. That way you can find all the illustrations and just look at them instead of reading the text.

Click the Thumbnails button again to hide the document's thumbnail view.

 The Research button opens the Research task pane. You highlight a word, phrase, name, location, or whatever, and then click the Research button. In a few moments (longer if you're not already connected to the Internet), a list of referency material about the highlighted text is displayed: thesaurus entries, foreign language references, encyclopedic stuff, and the like.

 The Zoom buttons make text larger or smaller for easier or more difficult reading. This does not affect the text in the original document, just the appearance of the text on the screen.

 The Actual Page button is a waste of time, showing you how tiny and ugly the document looks in an unreadable, yet properly formatted state. Click the button again should you mistakenly click it once.

 The Multiple Pages button lets you see two screens of the document at once, which I'm not a big fan of.

✔ To close the task pane (should it open), press Ctrl+F1.

✔ Do not edit formatting in the Reading Layout view. That's not what it's for.

Getting out of Reading Layout view

 If you can see the Close button on the Reading Layout toolbar, click it to return to the previous view. Otherwise, you can choose View⇨Normal or View⇨Print Layout from the menu to return to a regular way of working with your document.

Chapter 26

Collaboration Tricks

. . . .

In This Chapter

▶ Slapping down comments in a document

▶ Highlighting your text

▶ Using revision marks

▶ Comparing two documents

▶ Tracking changes in any document you edit

. . . .

For the most part, writing is something you do by yourself. However, there are times when you need (or want) to share your work with others. For example, you want to make sure that your proposal is upbeat and inoffensive, so you run it by someone else. In these instances, you can use some of Word's collaboration tools to help you and your writing partners (or overlords or editors or whomever) communicate.

This chapter covers the Word tricks and techniques that let you happily work with others. This way, you and your comrades can cooperatively work on a new antigovernment manifesto, but when the state police come, they'll arrest just one guy.

✔ This book does not cover online collaboration, where you can meet on the Internet to mutually mangle a document.

Making Comments

Word's comments are like sticky notes for your text, though physically they look more like cartoon bubbles. This is the first of Word's various text-markup commands. You can use them to communicate with others (or yourself), offering suggestions, ideas, editing, or general advice.

Adding a comment

To shove a comment into your document, follow these steps:

1. **Switch to Print Layout view; choose View➪Print Layout.**

   It's best to use Print Layout view to see the comments.

2. **Select the chunk of text you want to comment on.**

   Be specific; though you may be tempted to select the entire document, just the first few words of a longer chunk are all that's necessary.

3. **Choose Insert➪Comment.**

   A cartoon bubble appears with the text Comment: in it (see Figure 26-1).

Figure 26-1:
Inserting a
comment
into your
text.

"Everyone, listen! Peter has just shot himself, but he's okay!"   Comment [DKG1]: Perhaps not state this right away. It would help to build suspense.

4. **Type your comment.**

   The cartoon bubble expands to contain all your comments — and they can be quite large, though short and to the point is best.

5. **When you're done, just click in your text and keep reading or reviewing.**

   The comments stay visible in your text unless you hide them, which is covered in the next section.

Repeat these steps to add more annotations to the text.

   ✔ The cartoon bubble comments can be made in both Print Layout and Reading Layout views.

   ✔ If you're using Normal view, the comment text is added in the reviewing pane at the bottom of the document window. This is a bit clumsy to deal with, which is why I recommend making comments in Print Layout view only.

   ✔ You can edit the comments as you edit any text in Word.

   ✔ Comment text has its own style: *Comment Text*.

▶ The comments also print, unless you direct Word not to print them. To do so, choose File➪Print. In the Print dialog box, use the Print What drop-down list to tell Word how to send the commented document to the printer. The Document choice prints the document without the comments.

▶ You can see how the comments will be printed by using the File➪Print Preview command. See Chapter 8 for the details.

Using the Reviewing toolbar

To best work with comments, summon the Reviewing toolbar, shown in Figure 26-2. Choose View➪Toolbars➪Reviewing from the menu.

Figure 26-2:
The
Reviewing
toolbar.

The Reviewing toolbar contains menus and options not only for creating comments, but also for highlighting text and reviewing changes made by others. Its functions are specifically covered in the remaining sections of this chapter.

Hiding comments

To dispense with the comments, and indeed all document markups, choose View➪Markup from the menu. This command hides the comments (and other document markups). This is the easiest way to show/hide the comments.

You can also hide the comments by using the Reviewing toolbar: Choose Comments from the Show drop-down list (see Figure 26-3). This action removes the check mark by the Comments item and hides the comments in your document.

Likewise, to show a document's comments, you can choose Comments from the Show drop-down list.

Reviewing all comments

 To see all a document's comments at once, click the Reviewing toolbar's Reviewing Pane button, which opens a frame below your document window. There, you see listed each comment, who made the comment, the comment's date and time, and the comment itself — a handy summary.

To locate a comment from the Reviewing Pane in the document text, just click it with the mouse; the document instantly scrolls to reveal the part of the text where the comment dwells. This is handy for reviewing comments strewn over a long document.

To close the reviewing pane, click the Reviewing Pane button again.

Deleting a comment

To delete a comment, point at it and click the right mouse button. Choose Delete Comment from the pop-up menu.

Whip Out the Yellow Highlighter

Word comes with a text highlighter that lets you mark up and colorize the text in your document without damaging your computer monitor.

 To highlight your text (onscreen, electronically, of course), click the Highlight button on the Formatting toolbar. Click!

Now you've entered Highlighting mode. The mouse pointer changes to something I can't describe verbally but can show in the left margin. When you drag the mouse over your text, that text becomes highlighted — just like you can do with a highlighter on regular paper. It's amazing what those whiz kids at Microsoft come up with. . . .

To stop highlighting text, click the Highlight button again or press the Esc key.

✔ To unhighlight your text, you can re-highlight it with the same color, which erases it. Or you can click the down arrow by the Highlight button and choose None as the highlight color. Then drag over any color highlighted text to unhighlight.

✔ You can also highlight a block of text by first marking the block and then clicking the Highlight button. See Chapter 6 for all the proper block-marking instructions.

 ✔ The highlighted text prints, so be careful with it. If you don't have a color printer, highlighted text prints black on gray on your hard copy.

✔ In addition to the None color for erasing highlight marks, you can choose any highlight colors available on the Highlight button's drop-down list. And to think that an office supply store would charge you an extra $1.20 for each color.

Sharing Work with Revision Marks

Every writer jealously guards his text. It's enough that someone must edit — some lowly editor who seethes with jealously over the fact that the noble writer is the one who gets all the fame and glory even though it's the editor who deserves the credit. Oh, editors can be nasty. *[Hey! — Ed.]* But other writers can be worse.

Revision marks are a way of tracking changes made to your document by evil people. Okay, maybe not evil, but people who change things without first making suggestions. To help protect yourself against such intrusion, you can use one of Word's many revision-tracking tools. The following sections outline two ways you can put them to use.

Tracking changes between two versions of the same document

Go ahead and put away the magnifying glass. When someone else returns your Word document to you, it's a cinch to have Word compare the "new" document with your pristine original. Word flags any changes, displaying them for you right on the screen. Here's how:

1. **Make sure that you have the edited (newer) document loaded and on the screen.**

   The original document should be saved to disk. That's okay for now; you don't need to open it. Just open the edited document and have it on the screen in front of you.

   Yup. The newer and original documents should have two different names. That's best.

2. **Choose Tools⇨Compare and Merge Documents.**

   An Open dialog box appears, though it's named Compare and Merge Documents and not Open.

3. **Find the original document on disk.**

   Use your finely honed Open dialog box skills to find and select the original document on disk.

4. **Click the Merge button.**

   Word thinks long and hard. What it's doing is comparing the document on the screen with the older copy on your hard disk.

5. **Peruse the changes.**

   Snoop over the changes made to your pristine prose by the barbarian interlopers!

What you're looking at is your original document, not the edited copy. (Check the name on the title bar.) Remember that!

New or added text appears underlined and in another color (red on my screen). Deleted text shows up as strikethrough (again red).

In Print Layout view, bubbles appear in the right margin describing what's been deleted or reformatted. In Normal view, this information can only be seen in the Reviewing Pane.

Yes, it is annoying to read. Oui, oui! That's why the next step is to review and accept or reject the changes, which is covered in the next section.

✔ Each "reviewer" is given his own color on your screen. For example, on my screen, I see the revision marks as red. Had a second reviewer gone over the text, those comments would appear in a second color, and so on for other reviewers.

> ✔ To see the changes as they appear according to the edited document, choose Original Showing Markup from the Display for Review drop-down list (the first item on the Reviewing toolbar).

> ✔ To hide the revision marks, choose Final from the Display for Review drop-down list.

Reviewing the changes

There is no sense in showing blind obedience to any editor or critic! If you're a budding writer, it's time for you to learn a new term: STET. It's Latin, and it means *to stand*. When you STET an edit, you're telling the editor that you reject the change that was made and wish the item to stand. Now, please keep in mind that the editor is there to guide you and, under most circumstances, wants to see your text read better than it probably did originally. Still, STET is a handy order to give.

To STET the changes in your text, you have several choices.

First, right-click on any revision. From the pop-up menu, you can choose either the Accept or Reject commands. Accept Insertion and Accept Deletion confirm that the change that was made is something you want. Reject Insertion and Reject Deletion are the STET commands; they tell Word to restore the text to its original, intended state.

Second, you can use the buttons on the Reviewing toolbar to find and then accept or reject changes:

 To quickly find the next markup, use the Next button on the Reviewing toolbar.

 The Previous button takes you back to the preceding markup.

 The Accept Change button can be used to grant your approval to any edit.

 The Reject Change button is used to, well, STET.

Third, if you're in a real hurry, you can use the drop-down menus beneath either the Accept Change or Reject Change buttons to choose either the Accept All Changes in Document or Reject All Changes in Document commands, respectively. It's kind of a global admission that either, yes, the editor is right or, no, STET STET STET.

> ✔ If you goof, you can choose Edit⇨Undo, just as you can undo any other boo-boo.

✔ Going through this process removes all the revision marks from your document. If you want to re-review the revisions, you have to repeat the steps in the preceding section for comparing two documents.

✔ Don't forget to save your revised text back to disk!

Tracking changes as you make them

Suppose that *you* are the editor! Ha! Crack an evil smile as you attempt to scissor and paste someone else's labors. Gads! That must be fun!

Please be gentle as you edit. Don't go nuts! To help, you can activate Word's revision-tracking feature, which lets you see your markups on the screen as you make them.

 Activate markup mode by clicking the Track Changes button on the Reviewing toolbar. Or, you can double-click the TRK acronym on the status bar. Or you can choose Tools➪Track Changes. Or you can press Ctrl+Shift+E on the keyboard.

(Ever get the idea that this command isn't trying to hide itself?)

Now edit!

Any text you add appears underlined. Deleted text is immediately banished to the right margin. Or, if you're using Normal view, deleted text is shown in ~~strikethrough~~.

Have fun.

Chapter 27

Working with Documents

. . . .

. . . .

*T*he more work you do in Word, the more documents you create — piles of files. And if you don't clean up or organize those piles, then just like manure in a barnyard, you're going to be hip-deep in files in a few weeks. Maybe sooner.

This chapter tackles the subject of files — using and organizing them. It's more of a Windows chapter, so I'll be brief on the file-management part. Still, you can do lots of file management right in Word, without ever having to mess with Windows, the Big Momma Operating System.

Also covered: importing and exporting files. No international license required or bribes to pay!

Creating a New Folder

To keep organized, you may need to create new folders for your new projects. For example, if you've just started your plan to corner the sheep market through genetically mutated fleas, you'll need a new folder to put all those memos and letters in. Here's how you do that:

1. **Summon the Save As dialog box with File⇨Save As.**

   Obviously, having something to save first helps, such as that first letter to New Zealand.

2. Click the Create New Folder button.

The New Folder dialog box appears.

3. Type a name for your new folder.

Be descriptive. Be creative. Be short and sweet. Be to the point. (Try really hard to achieve this goal if you're a lawyer.)

Have the folder name reflect its contents.

4. Click OK.

Through the magic of the computer, your new folder is created. Further magic: Word automatically opens the folder and displays its contents. It's empty.

5. Continue saving your document.

You don't really have to save a document every time you create a folder. You can click the Cancel button in the Save As dialog box to return to your work. The next time you go to save a document (or open one, for that matter), you're using the new folder you just created.

✔ You can create new folders in the Save As dialog box but not in the Open dialog box. I mean, like, duh. If you created a new folder in the Open dialog box, there wouldn't be anything in the folder for you to open. Some people. . . .

✔ You can get lots of mileage from a folder named Junk or Misc.

✔ Lawyer jokes are safe in this book because most lawyers use WordPerfect.

Using Another Folder

If you go into a folder-creating frenzy, you need to be able to access those folders whenever you want to see the documents they hold or save a new document in a specific folder. Here's how you go about it:

1. Summon the Open command with File⇨Open.

Or press Ctrl+O. Soon, the Open dialog box swings into full view.

2. First, see which folder you're using.

The folder's name appears in the Look In drop-down box at the top of the dialog box. Normally, it's the My Documents folder, which is where Word wants to save stuff.

If you're already in the folder you want to be in, skip to Step 6 (meaning that you're more or less done).

3. **Select the disk drive you want from the Look In drop-down list.**

   If you only have one hard drive, C, select it as well. Looking for your folder from the top down is best.

   Because most folders are kept in the My Documents folder, you can always click the big My Documents button on the left side of the Open dialog box. That zooms you to that folder, pronto.

4. **Select your folder from those listed in the dialog box.**

   You may have to scroll through the list to find the folder you want.

5. **Keep repeating Step 4 until you find the folder you're looking for.**

   For example, you may have to open My Documents, and then Projects, and then Memos to finally see the documents stored in the Memos folder.

6. **Open your document.**

   Click the Open button.

   ✔ Some folders contain other folders. To see their contents, double-click the folder's name in the Open dialog box.

   ✔ Try to avoid opening files on removable disks, floppies and Zip disks particularly. This can confuse Word when you remove the disk and it's not yet done with the file, often forcing you to re-insert the disk to regain control of the computer. A better solution is to copy the document(s) to the hard drive and work with them there. Then copy the files back to the removable disk when you're done.

   ✔ Also see Chapter 8 for more information on using the Open dialog box.

   ✔ Each disk in your system has its own set of folders. If you can't find the folder you want on one disk, try another. For example, scope out hard drive D if drive C turns out to be a dud.

Finding Files in Word

Finding files is really a Windows function. It's what Windows does best, but Word can also locate your wayward documents. Too bad finding socks or a clean shirt isn't this easy:

1. **Summon the Open dialog box.**

   When you think of this, it makes sense: You're searching for a file to open anyway, right? Choose File➪Open.

2. **Click the Tools button/menu in the upper-right corner of the Open dialog box.**

   Bet you didn't know that there was a menu up there. Few people do. That's why you're reading this book.

3. **Choose Tools⇨Search.**

   The File Search dialog box appears. It's too bizarre to show as an illustration here, so keep following these instructions carefully.

4. **Click the Basic tab in the File Search dialog box.**

5. **Type some text that's most likely to be in the document you're searching for.**

   This is the way most people think when they need to look for a document. They say, "That document about the peanut butter necklace. Where did I put it?" So, obviously, you would type **peanut butter necklace** into the Search text box to find all Word documents containing that text.

   There is no need to mess with anything else in the dialog box at this time.

6. **Click the Search button.**

   Everything sits still for a while as Word scours the hard drive.

   Scour. Scour. Scour.

   Eventually, you see a list of folders and documents that match the information you searched for. Or, if nothing was found, no files are displayed; try again using some other bit of text, or just give up now and cook yourself some yummy noodles.

7. **To choose a file, double-click it.**

   This throws you back to the Open dialog box.

8. **Click the Open button.**

   The file opens, and, well, there you are.

If the file isn't the one you're looking for, you'll have to try the search again. Alas, Word isn't clever enough (at least this version) to let you open up every file found to peruse their contents all at once.

✔ Honestly, the best way to locate a file is to use Windows and its Find or Search command for hunting down files. When Windows lists the files it finds, you can then select them all and open them all in Word (providing that your PC has enough memory).

✔ Refer to my book *PCs For Dummies* (Wiley Publishing, Inc.) for more information on finding files in Windows.

File management in Word

You can use the Save As or Open dialog boxes to perform some basic file management chores, all without leaving Word.

For example, to rename a file you see in the Open or Save As dialog box, click the file to select it, and then press the F2 key, which is the Rename command's keyboard shortcut. You can then enter a new name for the file, just as you would in Windows.

To delete a file in the Open or Save As dialog box, click to select the file and then press the Delete key on your keyboard. The file is "taken care of" by Windows.

Be careful with what you delete! Likewise, note that Word won't let you rename or delete any open files or documents in use by other programs.

(You can also move and copy files in the Open or Save As dialog boxes, though I don't recommend it; it's just too clumsy to do in a dialog box.)

Working with Groups of Files

For those of you with too much to do and not enough time to do it in, be thankful that Word has commands that let you open, save, or close all sorts of documents at once — without going crazy.

Opening a boatload of files at once

The Open dialog box allows you to open one file or a whole group. The secret to opening more than one file is to use the Ctrl key to select — just as you use the Ctrl key to select multiple files in Windows. The same trick works in the Open dialog box.

After using the Ctrl+Click trick to select multiple files, click the Open button. All the files then open into separate windows in Word.

✔ The secret to the Ctrl+Click is to hold down the Ctrl key as you use the mouse to click the files. Release the Ctrl key when you're done.

✔ There is a limit on the number of files Word can work with at once. No, I don't know what the maximum number is — but you will! You'll see some odd error message about not enough memory or "heap" space or something bizarre. Don't panic. Close a few windows — maybe even quit Word — and start over.

Saving a gang of documents simultaneously

To save a multitude of documents all at once, you can switch to each window and incant the File⇨Save command. Or, you can be sneaky and do the following:

1. **Press and hold the Shift key — either one.**

2. **Choose File⇨Save All.**

   Normally, you choose the Save item. But if you press the Shift key before choosing the File menu, it magically becomes the Save All menu item.

   There is no prompting and no wait-and-see. Everything is just saved to disk as fast as your PC can handle it.

✔ If a file has not yet been saved, you're prompted to give it a name. For more information, refer to the section in Chapter 8 about saving a document to disk the first time.

✔ I use the File⇨Save All command whenever I have to get up and leave my computer — even for a short moment, such as when the phone rings or when the Feds knock at the door and there are illegal laser beam parts lain all over the house.

Closing a gang of documents simultaneously

You can conjure up a Close All command just like the Save All command. The difference is that you choose the Close All item from the menu; just press the Shift key (either one) before you click the File menu with your mouse. Then choose the Close All option and — thwoop! — all your open documents are closed.

Word still asks whether you want to save any unsaved documents before it closes them. See the section in Chapter 8 about saving a document to disk the first time.

Working with Non-Word Document Formats

Believe it or not, Word isn't the only word processor in the world. It's not like Word is struggling for market dominance. Hey! It's there! Even so, other word processors exist as well as other document file formats. Occasionally, you may tangle with those file formats. When you do, you need to import their weird word-processing files into Word so that you can do something with them. Likewise, you can export your Word documents into weird word-processing formats. The following sections tell you how.

Loading an alien document

Prepare to welcome the intruder! Suppose that someone has sent you a text file, or a WordPerfect document, or a Web page, or some weirdo file that is in no way a Word document. No problem! Word can open and examine the document without so much as breaking an electronic sweat. Follow these steps:

1. **Do the Open command.**

2. **In the Files of Type drop-down box, select the file format.**

   If you know the format, choose it from the list. Here are some popular formats:

   - **Word Documents:** Any document created by Word.

   - **XML Files:** Documents saved in the common XML format (which could be other Office documents).

   - **All Web Pages:** HTML documents or Web pages that you've saved to disk.

   - **Rich Text Format (RTF):** A common file format for exchanging word processing documents between word processors.

   - **Text Files:** Plain, boring, text-only documents. No formatting. Blah, though this is a common file format. Also known as ASCII or MS-DOS Text.

   - **Recover Text from Any File:** A very handy option that lets Word extract text from any type of file. Use this one as a last resort.

   - **WordPerfect (various versions/platforms):** Used to read WordPerfect documents.

   - **Works (various versions/platforms):** Used to read in Microsoft Works documents.

   - **Word (various versions/platforms):** Reads in older Word documents and documents written on the Macintosh.

   - **Other formats:** Too weird to mention.

   When you choose a specific file format, Word displays in the Open dialog box only those files matching the format. Your next job is to find the file you want to open.

If you don't know the format, choose All Files from the drop-down list. Word then makes its best guess.

3. **Hunt down the text file you want to load.**

    Use the controls in the dialog box to find the file you want. See the section "Using Another Folder," earlier in this chapter, for more information.

4. **Click the text file's icon once with the mouse.**

5. **Click Open.**

    The alien file appears onscreen, ready for editing, just like any Word document.

    ✔ In some cases and with some file formats, you may need to fix the formatting.

    ✔ Word may display a File Conversion dialog box, allowing you to preview how the document appears. Generally speaking, clicking the OK button in this step is your best bet.

    ✔ If the Open dialog box doesn't display the file you're looking for — and you know that the file is there — try typing its name in the File Name box and clicking the Open button.

    ✔ Word *remembers* the file type! When you go to use the Open dialog box again, it has the same file type chosen from the Files of Type drop-down list. So, if you want to open a Word document after opening an HTML document, you *must* choose Word Documents from the list. Otherwise, Word may open documents in a manner that seems strange to you.

    ✔ Additional file types and conversion *filters* are available on the Word (or Office) CD. To install them, run the Setup program on the CD and choose to install only the new filters.

Saving a file in a horridly strange and unnatural format

Word is quite smart when it comes to saving files to disk. For example, when you open a WordPerfect document, Word automatically saves it back to disk in the WordPerfect format. Ditto for any other alien file format: Whichever format was used to open the document, Word chooses the same format for writing the document back to disk.

The secret, as with opening files of another type, is to check the Save as Type drop-down list in the Save As dialog box. In fact, choosing a new item from that drop-down list is the only way to save a document in another format.

For example, if you need to save a document as a text file, choose Text Only from the Save as Type drop-down list. Click the Save button, and your document is saved. Ditto for the HTML format, RTF, or any other alien document format.

Word (or the Assistant) may explain that saving the document in an alien format is, well, bad. Whatever. Click Yes to save the document.

✔ You can save a document to disk by using both the Word format as well as another format. First, save the file to disk as a Word document by selecting Word Document from the Save as Type box. Then save the file to disk using another format, such as Plain Text.

✔ To save in HTML format, choose Web Page from the drop-down list.

✔ Be aware that Word remembers the format! If you notice that your documents are not being saved to disk the way you want them, the Save as Type drop-down list is to blame! Always double-check it to ensure that you're saving documents to disk in the proper format.

Chapter 28

Modifying Word's Appearance

There are two ways to modify the way your computer looks. The first involves using a sledgehammer, axe, or shotgun. The second involves customizing the software. Both methods are very effective.

While the first method may be emotionally satisfying, studies have shown that the second method — using software — often is the best long-term solution to the changing-the-way-a-computer-looks problem. Take Word for example: All those toolbars you see are customizable. You can bend them, break them, twist them into tiny bits, and blow them off into the wind like a dandelion. This chapter shows you how to do that (well, sort of) as well as how to customize, rearrange, remove, mangle, spindle, fold, *and* mutilate Word's appearance to your heart's content.

Retooling the Toolbars

Messing with the toolbars is one of the first things I do when I start using Word on a new computer. Word has dozens of toolbars. In fact, if you display them all, you end up with only a tiny little pigeonhole of window in which to write!

Fortunately, all Word's toolbars are optional. You can show or hide them, you can rearrange them, you can turn them into floating palettes, and you can add or remove buttons. It's all up to you — and I encourage you to play with the toolbars and make them your own.

- ✔ The View menu is where you can control the items Word displays on the screen.

- ✔ The ruler is not a toolbar, yet it's controlled through the View menu. To see or hide the ruler, choose View➪Ruler.

- ✔ Word typically displays the Standard and Formatting toolbars. The Standard toolbar is the one with the New, Open, and Save buttons on the left; the Formatting toolbar contains the Style, Font, and Point drop-down lists on the left.

- ✔ You can remove *everything* from the screen by choosing the View➪Full Screen command. That gives you the entire screen on which to write. Click the Close Full Screen button (or press the Esc key) to switch back to non-Full Screen mode.

Looking at a toolbar

All toolbars are basically the same. They can sport buttons, some of which act like text fields, drop-down lists, menus, or some combination of each. Additionally, you should pay attention to three gizmos on a toolbar: the grabber, the toolbar menu, and the toolbar show-more arrows.

The grabber appears on the far-left side of the toolbar. You use the grabber to move the toolbar. (Even the menu bar has a grabber, which means that it can be moved as well.)

The menu button appears as a downward-pointing triangle on the far-right end of the toolbar. Clicking that triangle displays the toolbar's menu.

Toolbars also sport "show-more" arrows when needed. These appear above the toolbar's menu button, as shown in the margin. When these appear, you can click the toolbar's menu button to see a list of the currently hidden buttons along with the regular items on the toolbar menu, as shown in Figure 28-1.

- ✔ To get rid of the toolbar's show-more arrows, you need to rearrange (move) the toolbar so that its entire length can be displayed at once.

- ✔ Toolbars need not be on the same line; you may find that Word comes out of the box with both the Standard and Formatting toolbars on the same line. To fix the problem, choose Show Buttons on Two Rows from either the Formatting or Standard toolbar's menu.

- ✔ Refer to the "Moving and arranging toolbars" section, a little later in this chapter, for information on rearranging toolbars.

Figure 28-1:
A shortened
toolbar
displays the
rest of its
items.

Where are the toolbars?

Though most toolbars appear when they're needed (such as the Outlining toolbar when you enter Outlining mode), you can summon most any toolbar you want by choosing it from the View➪Toolbars submenu.

✔ A check mark appears by the toolbars that are already visible.

✔ To display a different toolbar, choose it from the submenu.

✔ To remove a toolbar, choose it from the submenu.

✔ A quick way to get at the toolbars submenu is to right-click on any toolbar in Word. That action displays a pop-up toolbars submenu, from which you can switch various toolbars on or off.

Moving and arranging toolbars

You move a toolbar in Word by dragging it with its grabber, located on the far-left side of the toolbar. When the mouse pointer changes into a four-way arrow thing (see margin), it means that you can drag the toolbar hither or thither to move the toolbar around.

Toolbars can also be dragged to floating palettes by using the grabber; just drag the toolbar into the document part of Word's window. There, it becomes a floating palette — a little mini-window that can hover over the top of all your other windows with its own Close button (the X in the upper-right corner), as shown in Figure 28-2.

To convert a floating palette into a toolbar, drag the palette away from the document part of Word's window. When you find the sweet spot, the palette changes to a toolbar.

✔ Toolbars can exist above, below, or to the left or right of the document window. Yes, toolbars can live to the left or right of the document window, though it's uncommon.

✔ Sometimes it takes a while to position a toolbar properly. Be patient.

Figure 28-2:
The
Standard
toolbar as
a floating
palette.

✔ The Standard and Formatting toolbars have a special menu item attached to them. You can choose the Show Buttons on Two Rows item to instantly arrange those two toolbars. Other toolbars do not have this menu, so you must arrange them solely by using the mouse.

✔ You can also resize a floating palette window, making it more square or even a vertical column of buttons. Resize the palette window as you would any window; drag by grabbing any edge or corner with the mouse.

✔ If you float and then accidentally close the Standard or Formatting toolbars, remember that you can resurrect them by using the View⇨ Toolbars submenu.

Zooming About

The Zoom command at the bottom of the View menu controls how big your document text looks. No, the command doesn't change the text size — that's done on the Font menu. Instead, the Zoom command controls how much of your text you see at once. Follow these steps for a quick demonstration:

1. Choose View⇨Zoom.

The Zoom dialog box appears, looking much like the one depicted in Figure 28-3.

2. Select a Zoom size.

For example, 200% makes your text look really big — ideal for Great Aunt Rebecca.

The Page Width option sets the zoom so that you see your entire document from left to right margins.

The Many Pages item zooms you out into the next room, where you can see several pages on a single screen, which is good for writing only if you have 5/5 vision.

You can set individual percent sizes by using the Percent box.

Figure 28-3:
The Zoom
dialog box.

3. **Click OK to view your document at a new size onscreen.**

✔ The Whole Page and Many Pages options in the Zoom dialog box are available only when you're in Print Layout view. Choose View➪Print Layout and select the Zoom command to play, er, experiment with those options.

✔ When zooming takes you too far out, your text changes to shaded blocks, called *greeking*. Although not keen for editing, zooming out that far gives you a good idea of how your document looks on the page before printing.

✔ Way over on the right side of the Standard toolbar lives the Zoom drop-down list. Click it to set a Zoom size for your document quickly. Or, you can type an amount. For example, on my screen the documents look best at 125% zoom. (Funny, but I didn't need that magnification before I turned 40. . . .)

✔ If you have a Microsoft IntelliMouse (or any other wheel mouse), you can zoom by pressing the Ctrl key on your keyboard and rolling the wheel up or down. Rolling up zooms in; rolling down zooms out.

✔ Alas, you can zoom only in Word. The FreeCell game lacks a Zoom command.

Tweak Central

Further tweaking in Word happens in a busy place called the Options dialog box, as shown in Figure 28-4. You visit that place by choosing the Tools⇨Options command.

Figure 28-4:
The Options
dialog box.

Alas, there are just way too many options to go through the Options dialog box in its entirely. Most of the settings are familiar to anyone who has used Word for a few months. You can turn items on or off, such as the task pane at startup (shown in the upper-left area in Figure 28-4), as well as sound, animation, and other options that may annoy you. Remember, it's *your* copy of Word. Set it up the way you want.

Click the OK button when you're done changing the options.

Chapter 29

Breaking Your Word

. . . .

In This Chapter

▶ Solving some common puzzles

▶ Understanding NORMAL.DOT

▶ Fixing a broken document

▶ Changing templates

▶ Finding lost things on the screen

▶ Recovering Word from utter disaster

. . . .

*O*h, come on! You trust your computer about as far as you could throw it. Although Word is an amazing program, deep with features and solid enough to write just about anything, there is still a dark corner of your soul that doesn't trust it. *And for good reason!* Computers can screw up! They go crazy! They wakka-wakka-bling-ping-doying!

It's for those insane times that I wrote this chapter — new for this edition of the book. Here I address Word's foibles from the mild flu-like symptoms to the raging tempest-like fury of a scrambled, eternally repaginating satanic document from the dank bowels of Hell! Generally, there is a solution for any Word burp or hiccup. Chances are it lies somewhere in the pages that follow.

General Things

There are an amazing number of things that can and do go wrong with Word. Because I include my e-mail address in this book (dgookin@wambooli.com), I get lots of messages about Word and have answered hundreds of questions over the years. The following questions (or actually "pleas for help") are perhaps the most common.

> # Using that Detect and Repair thing in the Help menu
>
> There is a handy menu item in the Help menu called Detect and Repair — a great thing to try when Word or any Microsoft Office program seems to be causing you headaches.
>
> To use this command, choose Help⇨Detect and Repair from the menu. A dialog box appears giving you some options to choose from. When you're ready, click the Start button.
>
> Detect and Repair can find missing files, fix broken shortcuts, and perform other minor touch-ups. It also checks the Windows Registry for anything there that may be afoul of Word. But, alas it doesn't do much to fix broken Word documents.

One first thing you should always try

Before getting into specifics, do keep in mind that the first weapon in your arsenal of Word-fixing tools is the Edit⇨Undo command, also the Ctrl+Z keyboard shortcut. This command undoes just about anything you've done, from radically changing formatting to deleting vast swaths of text. Do not forget the Undo command!

"I've just closed a document without saving it!"

Immediately: Turn off your computer. Just pull the plug. And pray.

Yes, this is a forbidden and wrong thing, not recommended by any computer book, manual, or manufacturer. But in this case, it *might* actually save your butt. The secret is Word's AutoRecover option (see Chapter 8). With that option set, Word keeps track of your document on disk — even if you haven't yet saved it.

Deliberately turning off the computer fools Word into thinking there was a system crash. After Windows restarts, run Word again. When Word starts, it displays document recovery information (shown in Figure 8-2). There, you can recover your document.

✔ This trick works only if you do not first quit Word. If you quit Word, the auto-recover information is *not* saved, and recovery is not possible. So keep Word open and then unplug the PC.

✔ AutoRecover is typically set at ten minute intervals, so you may lose anywhere from a few seconds to ten minutes of the last stuff you typed.

✔ You can also power-down most PCs by pressing and holding the power button.

✔ See Chapter 8 for more information on AutoRecover.

"I just saved the file, and now I can't find it!"

This is very common, and it's because you didn't follow my steps as outlined and recommended in Chapter 8: You most likely forgot which folder you placed the file into, and you did not use a clever name. For shame!

Word keeps a record of the four most recent files you opened down at the bottom of the File menu, as shown in Figure 29-1. Chances are that your file is down there.

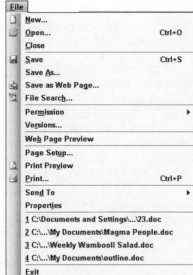

Figure 29-1: The four most recently opened documents at the bottom of the File menu.

And now a bunch of ifs:

- ✔ If the file isn't listed there, use the Find command as described in Chapter 27 of this book (or Chapter 11 of *PCs For Dummies*).

- ✔ If the file is listed, but when you choose the menu option, nothing comes up, then the file either had its named changed or has been deleted.

- ✔ Look into the Windows Recycle Bin to find deleted files.

- ✔ If the file was renamed on disk and you don't remember what you renamed it to, use the Find command to locate it by searching for a bit of text inside the file. See Chapter 27.

- ✔ If you were silly and saved the file to a floppy disk, you'll need to search through your floppy disk collection for the file. Pray that you labeled your floppy disks, and remember which one you saved the file on.

- ✔ Be sure that you're logged into the proper account for using Windows. Not all accounts are the same.

- ✔ If you do need to save a file and have more than one account access it, save it in the Shared Documents folder in Windows XP.

"I cannot delete this chunk of text"

Impossible-to-delete text comes in many flavors.

The first flavor is an inserted character. If you use the Insert➪Symbol command, you must Backspace *twice* over the symbol to fully delete it.

The second flavor is a field, which looks like text but cannot be deleted by pressing the Backspace or Delete keys once. Just as with an inserted symbol, press Backspace or Delete *twice* to kill off a field.

The final flavor is a text box or frame. Sometimes these are indivisible; they have no contents yet they affect how other text lays out on the screen. The key is to keep clicking on or around the text until you see the border, as shown in Figure 29-2. Then you can press the Delete key to remove the empty frame or box.

Figure 29-2:
An empty text box is revealed by clicking its border.

This text isn't to show on the screen because something is blocking it. That's probably a text box or frame hidden in the text.

The most annoying instance of nondeleting text happens in headers and footers. In fact, a rogue or empty text box in a header can affect a document's page layout. So if you can't find the stubborn chunk of text in your document, be sure to check the header and footer; choose View⇨Header and Footer.

"How can I get this extra page not to print?"

For some reason, everyone who uses a word processor ends up with extra spaces at the end of paragraphs and extra blank paragraphs at the end of a document. The extra spaces at the end of a paragraph are forgivable. But the extra blank paragraphs at the end of a document often cause a blank sheet of paper to print, which can be annoying.

To remove the extra blank page, follow these steps:

1. **Press Ctrl+End to move the toothpick cursor to the end of your document.**

2. **Press the Backspace key.**

3. **Repeat Step 2 until you've backspaced over all the extra paragraphs and spaces at the end of your document.**

Eventually, you'll back up into the last bit of text on the true last page. That's when you stop (obviously).

If you still find a blank page at the end of your document, then there is something invisible on that page that is refusing to go away. Most likely, it's a blank frame, text box, or drawing object. Switch to Print Layout view and start clicking the page or drag the mouse over the text to see if you can select the rogue object. Then delete it.

"What's up with the NORMAL.DOT file?"

NORMAL.DOT is the name of the global template file, the one that Word uses to store all its standard information.

Whenever you modify Word, change a toolbar, alter an option, or make some new setting permanent, you're generally given a choice in the dialog box of where to save the change, either in the document itself, the document's template, or in the global template, NORMAL.DOT.

When you save a change to NORMAL.DOT, the changes are available to all of Word's documents — which can be handy. However, when you quit Word, it asks if you want to save any changes to the global template file, NORMAL.DOT. The answer to that question is "Yes."

Working with a Busted Document

The first step in identifying a busted document is to determine whether it's really busted. You can do this several ways, as covered in the following sections.

- ✔ To determine if the problem is with a specific document or all of Word, try opening other documents in Word and see if the behavior is the same.
- ✔ The document's weirdness may be related to the template it's using, so try testing other documents that you know are using a different template or no template.
- ✔ Sometimes the behavior is a one-time thing; try to see if the document's weirdness can be repeated or is predictable.
- ✔ Try the document on another computer; it may be a wider problem specific to your computer system.

Opening a document in the proper format

The most common cause of a document looking weird is that you've chosen the wrong file type in the Open dialog box. So:

1. **Close the busted document; do not save it!**

2. **Choose File⇨Open to open the document again.**

3. **Use the Open dialog box to find and locate the document.**

4. **In the Files of Type drop-down list, ensure that Word Documents (*.doc) is the chosen type.**

5. **Click the Open button.**

That should open the document properly. If not, you can attempt to repair the document, as covered later in the section "Opening a document for repair."

Choosing another printer

Sometimes, formatting problems are related to a bad printer driver. In this case, you need to reassign a new printer driver to the program (which is where Word gets much of its page layout options). Here's how:

1. **Choose File⇨Print.**

2. **Select another printer from the Name drop-down list.**

3. **Click the Close button.**

   This tells Word to use the printer's information but not to print the document at this time.

Try not to choose the Fax printer or any other nonstandard printers. If you don't have any other printers connected or installed on the system, don't bother with this step — but do consider that your printer driver may be corrupted. If so, contact the manufacturer on the Web about getting an update.

Opening a document for repair

If a document exhibits odd behavior and the format isn't the problem, you'll need to open it for repair: In the Open dialog box, click the down arrow to the right of the Open button. Choose Open and Repair from the menu, as shown in Figure 29-3.

Figure 29-3:
Opening a
document
for repair.

This action attempts to fix a wacky document. If not, keep working through the next several sections to try and fix the problem.

Reassigning the document's template

The problem may be with the document's template, in which case you can reattach the NORMAL.DOT template to the document to see if that fixes things.

With the weird document on the screen, follow these steps:

1. **Choose Tools⇨Templates and Add-Ins.**

2. **Click the Templates tab in the Templates and Add-ins dialog box.**

3. **Check to see if** *Normal* **is listed in the Document template text box. If so, you're done. If not:**

4. **Click the Attach button.**

5. **Choose Normal or Normal.dot from the Attach Template dialog box.**

6. **Click the Open button.**

7. **Click OK.**

The weirdness may go away with this step. If so, fine: Save the document. Otherwise, keep working at it with the next several sections, which are more general Word cures.

- ✔ Some of the document's odd behavior may be due to macros in the template.

- ✔ Keyboard reassignments in the template may also cause things to behave oddly.

- ✔ Consider reediting the template, deleting it, or even creating it again from scratch. If someone else made the template, notify that person of the trouble.

Final, desperate acts

Sometimes I just give up: I select all the document's text and just paste it into a new document, and then save that document to disk. The original document gets deleted.

There are times, however, when copying the text into a new document also copies the problem. In that case, consider saving the document to disk in the plain text format, or the RTF format, or both. This may remove some of the trouble spots as Word-specific information is stripped out of both file formats. You can then open the plain text or RTF document in Word or in another Word processor to continue your work.

Fixing Word When It's Broken

The most visible sign that Word is broken is that it just looks damn peculiar on the screen. Things may be missing. Things may be added. Other things may appear or disappear. This could be due to someone's attempt to modify Word, or as these things sometimes go, "stuff" just happens. The following sections describe a few things you can try to get Word back into working order.

Are you in Full Screen or Print Preview mode?

Full Screen and Print Preview modes may fool you into thinking that Word is somehow broken or missing pieces. Don't fret! Instead, press the Esc key, and Word should pop back up on the screen.

✔ You can press Alt+C to exit from Full Screen mode.

✔ There is also a difference between Print Layout and Normal view. If you think Word's screen looks subtly different, consider choosing one command or the other from the View menu.

Has someone moved or hidden the toolbars?

The toolbars and the menu bar are moveable, and you can hide them, turn them into floating palettes, and get things all screwy.

Press the F10 to show the menu, should it be hidden.

Press Alt+V to show the View menu; then choose the Toolbars submenu to display the Standard and then the Formatting toolbars.

With the toolbars visible, quit Word. Then restart Word. This should retain these settings.

If the toolbars disappear again, it's probably due to a template you're using. To detach the template, refer to the section "Reassigning the document's template," earlier in this chapter.

Are macros messing with your brain?

Word may be configured to run with some startup macros, which can alter Word's appearance. This is a tricky thing, so follow these steps carefully:

1. **Locate the icon you use to start Word.**

   It may be an icon on the desktop, an icon in the All Programs menu, or an icon on the Quick Launch bar. Wherever and however you start Word, you most likely do so by clicking an icon or an icon on a menu. Locate that icon.

This must be a Word program icon, not a Word document icon.

2. **Right-click the icon.**

3. **Choose Properties from the pop-up menu.**

4. **If there is a Shortcut tab, click it; otherwise, click the General tab.**

   You will see a line of text that runs Word. It ends with the program name, WINWORD.EXE. If a startup macro is being used, it will follow WIN-WORD.EXE with a /m (or /M) and then the macro name.

5. **If you see the /m and the macro name, delete them.**

   Delete everything from the /m to the end of the line.

6. **Click OK.**

By deleting the /m followed by the macro name, you're removing that startup macro and whatever changes it's making to Word.

This is a rather rare thing, so don't be surprised if you don't find a startup macro.

Is NORMAL.DOT to blame?

Sometimes the evil lurks in what's supposed to be Word's main repository of sanity: the NORMAL.DOT template file. In that case, you may want to remove NORMAL.DOT and whatever filth is in it. Here's how:

1. **Quit Word.**

2. **Use the Windows Find Files command to locate NORMAL.DOT.**

3. **When Word finds NORMAL.DOT, right-click on the file.**

4. **Choose Rename from the pop-up menu.**

5. **Change the name to ABNORMAL.DOT.**

6. **Press Enter.**

This isn't the same thing as deleting the file, though by renaming it you are preventing Word from finding it. On startup, Word will rebuild a new NORMAL.DOT file and begin using that.

Starting Word naked (the final step)

When all hope is lost, and things are way, way too screwy, there is a way to start Word in what I call "naked mode." This mode drops all the fancy doo-dads from Word and, in most cases, restores Word back to sanity. Here's how:

1. **Choose the Run command from the Start menu.**

   Or you can use the keyboard shortcut Win+R.

2. **Type** WINWORD /A **into the box.**

   WINWORD is Word's program name.

3. **Click OK.**

Word should start normally at this point, and everything will be fine.

The /A is an optional switch that tells Word to start without modifying any of its default (natural) settings. In most cases, this fixes Word quirks lickety-split.

What to Do When You Abandon All Hope

The final act is to reinstall Word from the original CDs. Don't bother with uninstalling the current version; simply reinstall Word over what you already have. That just might fix things, though it may also set you back in other ways. But then again, remember that this is a final, desperate step.

If Word is beyond repair, then remember that Windows does come with a secondary, albeit feeble, word processor named WordPad. If all else fails, at least you can use WordPad to jot down your thoughts and hopefully fix those WordPad documents in Word later, when things are back up and running again.

Running Word in "safe mode"

Safe mode works similarly to the /A mode. The difference between the /A and safe mode is that you would type **WINWORD /SAFE** into the box in Step 2 of the "Starting Word naked (the final step)" section.

(You can also start Word in safe mode if you remember to press and hold the Ctrl key as Word starts.)

In safe mode, Word restricts certain operations and limits things Word can do. Like safe mode in Windows, it's basically a troubleshooting tool that allows Office to locate and fix things. Rarely will you be manually starting Word in safe mode, though Word may occasionally start itself in safe mode to fix something. When that happens, quit Word to exit safe mode and then restart Word again.

Part V
Creating Lotsa Stuff in Word

The 5th Wave   By Rich Tennant

"IT'S A SOFTWARE PROGRAM THAT MORE FULLY RE-FLECTS AN ACTUAL OFFICE ENVIRONMENT. IT MULTI-TASKS WITH OTHER USERS, INTEGRATES SHARED DATA, AND THEN USES THAT INFORMATION TO NETWORK VICIOUS RUMORS THROUGH AN INTER-OFFICE LINK-UP."

In this part . . .

Sometimes they make it look so easy. Just about any professional makes their talents seem natural and their abilities appear effortless. Athletes run effortlessly. Gymnasts twist and float into the air, defying gravity. Cooks toss in this and that and without burning so much as a toast point, and they have a fabulous dinner that you can almost smell through the TV's glass screen. I suppose part of being an expert is the ability to make it look easy. Even so, you know there are years of training and disappointing results paving that long road to success.

This part of the book is about getting that extra edge. It's a cookbook of sorts, showing you some interesting tricks and techniques for making your documents look really good without having to suffer through lots of learning. It's a fun, hands-on episode that, unlike the TV chef, will have you making great-tasting documents with a minimum of fuss. Go ahead. Salivate.

Chapter 30

Just Your Basic Letter and Envelope

Despite all its advanced technical features, Word is capable of creating the most minor of documents — from the to-do list to the basic letter. Granted, the letter is a wee bit more sophisticated than a to-do list. And there are times when you need to write a letter and have it look good — such as that convincing epistle to the IRS explaining how your dog really is like a child and therefore should qualify for an income tax deduction.

This chapter is about creating a basic letter and envelope. More than the simple how-to's, this chapter also gives you a few professional pointers and some not-so-obvious solutions to common missive problems.

Writing a Silly Old Letter

Letters are boringly simple. They have common elements, but the basic letter is really nothing more than a simple document on a page. In fact, the only way letters get more exciting is when you use stationery or fancy paper.

Despite their boring nature, letters do have common elements: There is the date, which always goes at the top. Then there is the recipient's address, which also goes at the top. And it just turns out that there are some interesting things you can do with those two items.

The date

To insert a date into any Word document, use the Insert⇨Date and Time command. Choose the format for the date from the list in the Date and Time dialog box; then click OK.

TIP

- ✔ If you want the date to be current, always showing the current date rather than the date on which you created the letter, put a check mark in the Update Automatically box. That inserts a date *field* into the document, which always reflects the current date. If you don't want a date field inserted, remove the check mark in the Date and Time dialog box.

- ✔ If you want the date shoved over to the right margin, press Ctrl+R after the date is inserted. Press the Enter key and then Ctrl+L to return to left-justify text in the next paragraph.

- ✔ You can also insert the date field code by pressing Alt+Shift+D.

An automatic date via AutoText

If you have AutoText working (and you probably do), then just start typing the date: **Wedn**. After that much text, Word suggests "Wednesday," and you can press the Enter key to have Word finish your typing.

Next, continue with the month, March. After you press the spacebar after the month, Word suggests the current date; press Enter to insert it into your document.

See Chapter 7 for more information about AutoText.

The address

Two lines below the date (press the Enter key twice), most letter-writing folks place the recipient's address. I have no idea why we do this; we just do. Type the address, press Enter a couple times, and then type the salutation — something like

```
David Neidermyer
Poor Ex-Husbands' Home
201 N. Second St.
Splitsville, GA 30401
```

You may notice that most salutations, such as "To Whom It May Concern," are stored in Word as AutoText entries; you need to type only the first part, and Word completes the rest if you press the Enter key. See Chapter 7 for more information.

The body of the letter

Typing the rest of the letter is up to you. Type away! La-la-la.

If the letter is longer than a page, consider adding page numbers. Use the Insert➪Page Numbers command for that. Or you can create page numbers in the footer, which is covered in Chapter 15.

Signing your letter

Finally, end the letter with a signoff and your own name. This is usually some type of parting word — Cordially, Warmly, Sincerely, Fondly, Love, Obesity — followed by enough space for your signature and then your name and address.

Note that it is not necessary to type your name and address if they also appear on the stationery. Or so the Mr. Manners people tell me.

The last step is to print the letter.

 ✔ Don't forget to save your letter! Even if it's a dumb letter, I recommend saving it.

 ✔ If you need to print the letter on fancy stationery, remember to load said fancy stationary into the printer before you start printing.

All about Envelopes

To add an envelope to any document, you use Word's Envelopes and Labels command. It allows you to print an envelope on-the-fly or to "attach" an envelope to a letter so that they print one after the other. The following sections tell you everything you need to know.

Telling your printer to love an envelope

Each printer eats envelopes in a different manner. Some printers even have fancy envelope feeders. Other printers have envelope slots. Still other printers have a pop-out, manual-feeding tray that somehow can be used to feed in an envelope. The following steps show you how to configure Word to properly print an envelope on your printer:

1. **Locate the envelope-feeder slot on your printer.**

   Notice exactly how the envelope is inserted: An icon is probably printed or molded on the printer that tells you to insert the envelope in the middle, to the left, to the right, longways, or whatever. Also check to see whether the envelope is fed face up or face down. (Check the printer's manual for an *envelopes* index entry.)

2. **Choose Tools➪Letters and Mailings➪Envelopes and Labels.**

   The Envelopes and Labels dialog box appears, as shown in Figure 30-1.

Figure 30-1: The Envelopes and Labels dialog box, please.

3. **Make sure that the Envelopes tab in the dialog box is up front.**

4. **Click the Feed button.**

   This step displays the Envelope Options/Printing Options dialog box.

5. **Select the envelope's proper position and orientation.**

   Choose one of the six orientations. Choose Face Up or Face Down. And, if necessary, click the Clockwise Rotation button. The object here is to match the way the envelope feeds into your printer. (So it's the printer that determines which options you select.)

6. **Click OK.**

   This step closes the Envelope Options dialog box.

Now you're ready to create or print an envelope, or you can click Cancel to return to your document. Word knows about your printer and can properly print an envelope the next time you demand one.

Adding an envelope to your letter

A quick way to print an envelope with every letter you create is to attach the envelope to the end of the letter. Here's how:

1. **Create your letter.**

   Refer to the sections at the beginning of this chapter for more information.

2. **Choose Tools⇨Letters and Mailings⇨Envelopes and Labels.**

   If your document has a proper address in it, Word magically locates it and places it in the Delivery Address box. Ta-da!

3. **If Word didn't automatically fill in the address, type it now.**

4. **Optionally, you can also type your return address in the Return Address area.**

5. **Click the Add to Document button.**

   The Envelopes and Labels dialog box goes away, and you're returned to your document.

It may not be obvious on the screen, but the first page of your letter is now the envelope. (Choose File⇨Print Preview to see this wondrous thing.) When you're ready to print the letter, the envelope prints first and then the letter. All you have to do is stuff the letter into the envelope, seal it, and apply the ever-increasing postage.

✔ The letter and envelope are printed when you use the File⇨Print command for your letter (or press Ctrl+P or use the Print tool).

✔ Most printers prompt you to manually enter an envelope if that's what it wants you to do. After doing so, you may have to press the Ready, On-line, or Select button for the printer to continue. (My LaserJet just says "Me Feed!" and, for some reason, it knows when I insert the envelope because it just starts going!)

✔ Check the envelope to make sure that you didn't address the backside or put the address on upside down — as so often happens to me. This last step is important because you can just repeat the preceding steps to reprint your envelope if you goof.

✔ If you have trouble remembering how the envelope feeds into your printer, draw a picture of the proper way and tape it to the top of your laser printer for reference.

Printing an envelope on-the-fly

Whenever you need an envelope, for any reason, you can have Word whip one up for you. Follow these steps:

1. **Choose Tools⇨Letters and Mailings⇨Envelopes and Labels.**

2. **In the Envelopes and Labels dialog box, type the address you want on the envelope.**

   If you want to format the address, type it in the document first. Format it, select it, and then choose Tools⇨Letters and Mailings⇨Envelopes and Labels. Beware, though! If you select too much text it may not all fit on the envelope.

3. **Click the Print button.**

   Your printer may beep or otherwise prompt you to insert the envelope, or it may just print it right then and there.

The Weird Concept of Envelopes as Documents

An envelope is basically a sheet of paper, albeit folded and layered with the foulest-tasting glue known to man. But, bottom line — an envelope is merely a specialized piece of paper. As such, it's possible to configure Word to print a custom envelope as you would print any document. Follow these steps:

1. **Start a new document.**

   Word splashes a new document on the screen. You're going to transform it from a mere sheet of paper to an envelope.

2. **Choose View⇨Print Layout to ensure that you're in Print Layout view.**

   You can see things better in Print Layout view.

3. **Choose File⇨Page Setup.**

4. **Click the Margins tab.**

5. **Set the margins to .5 all around.**

   Envelopes are small, and just about any printer can handle a half-inch margin all the way around: Enter **.5** in each of the Top, Bottom, Left, and Right boxes.

6. **Choose Landscape orientation.**

   Envelopes are wider than they are tall, but this move is made so that the printing on the envelope goes longways rather than on its side (which I hear bugs the post office).

7. **Click the Paper tab.**

8. **Choose the option** Envelope #10 4¹/₈ x 9¹/₂ in. **from the Paper Size drop-down list.**

   Note the preview in the lower-right part of the dialog box. There's your envelope.

9. **Click OK.**

   The Page Setup dialog box goes bye-bye.

   In Print Layout view, you see the envelope floating in the document part of the window, as shown in Figure 30-2, though that envelope has text on it.

10. **Type the return address.**

    Unlike using the Envelopes and Labels dialog box, you can apply styles here, even add a graphic (as long as it's small enough not to offend the post office).

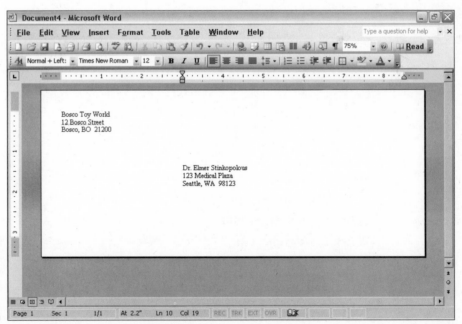

Figure 30-2:
Manually
creating an
envelope.

11. **Space down for the address.**

    Press the Enter key a few times until it's about even with the 1-inch marker on the left ruler. Or, just use your eyeball; you want the address to be roughly above center in the middle of the envelope.

12. **Indent the left margin 3 inches.**

    To indent the address, drag the Left Indent gizmo on the ruler to the 3-inch position (see Figure 30-2).

13. **Type and format the address.**

    And there is your envelope, reading for saving and printing.

If you need to add a memo to the envelope, press Enter a few times after typing the address and then restore the left margin back to 0. There, in the lower-left corner of the envelope "page," you can type `Attention: Mary in Marketing` or whatever memo you like.

This method of creating an envelope as a document is far more versatile than using the Envelopes and Labels dialog box. Consider saving this document to disk and reusing it or saving it as a template for use over and over again. Refer to Chapter 17 for more information on creating templates.

Chapter 31

Brochures and Greeting Cards

. . . .

In This Chapter

▶ Planning a three-part brochure

▶ Designing various document titles

▶ Using the Drop Cap command

▶ Adding a floating text box

▶ Printing a three-part brochure

▶ Printing a greeting card

. . . .

If you want to create something in Word that will just *dazzle* someone, you've come to the right chapter. The information here isn't secret, and it definitely isn't advanced. It's just a collection of information already offered in this book, but with a *purpose:* to create a threefold pamphlet or a greeting card. Go ahead. Amaze yourself!

Your Basic Three-Part Pamphlet

Some chores that you would think Word may utterly choke on, it can handle with ease. Take the typical threefold brochure, as shown in Figure 31-1.

Although Thomas Jefferson toiled away for days to pen the Declaration of Independence, Word and I whipped out a threefold brochure in about three minutes. In another few moments, the brochure could be flying out of my printer — provided the British don't storm my office before then.

Figure 31-1:
A typical threefold brochure is a cinch for Word to make.

Building the pamphlet

A *threefold* brochure is essentially a regular sheet of paper turned longways (landscape) and folded twice. In Word, you do this in two simple steps — *after* you write your text.

It's always best to work on the writing first and create the document later. Also, Word works faster when it's in normal (non-column) mode. If you need to edit later, fine.

To turn a document longways, follow these steps:

1. **Choose File⇨Page Setup.**

   The Page Setup dialog box appears.

2. **Click the Margins tab.**

3. **Select the Landscape option from the Orientation area.**

   Behold, your world is 90 degrees out of sync.

4. **Ensure that the Whole Document menu option is selected on the Apply To drop-down list.**

5. **Click OK.**

To make the three columns for the brochure, follow these steps:

1. **Choose Format⇨Columns.**

2. **Select Three from the Presets list.**

   It's at the top of the dialog box.

3. **Ensure that the Whole Document menu option is selected on the Apply To drop-down list.**

4. **Click OK.**

You don't see any real changes on the screen, but still your document is formatted for three panels that fold over on a single page. To get your text to print on both sides of the page requires a few more tricks, all of which are covered in the section "Printing the brochure," later in this chapter.

Giving your brochure a title

The best way to create a title for a brochure is to draw a table. A table not only has built-in borders but also allows you to put bits of text to the right or left of the title without having to overly mess with Word's paragraph or tab formatting.

Use the table-drawing instructions from Chapter 20 to draw in the title part of the document, which is what I did in Figure 31-1. I then used the Format⇨ Borders and Shading command to add the top and bottom borders. I could have used the Shading part of the Borders and Shading dialog box to add shading or color to the document title.

If you want to get fancier, draw in additional rows or columns of text. For example, create a three-column title with the information in the left and right columns and the document title in the center. And don't forget that you can add graphics to a table easily.

Starting a paragraph with a big letter (a drop cap)

A *drop cap* is the first letter of a report, article, chapter, or story that appears in a larger and more interesting font than the other characters. Figure 31-1 shows an example. Here's how to add a drop cap to your brochure (or just any old document):

1. **Select the first character of the first word at the start of your text.**

   For example, select the *O* in "Once upon a time."

   It also helps if this paragraph is left justified and not indented with a tab or any of the tricky formatting discussed in Part II.

2. Choose Format➪Drop Cap.

The Drop Cap dialog box appears, as depicted in Figure 31-2.

Figure 31-2:
The Drop
Cap dialog
box.

3. Select a drop cap style.

The first option, None, isn't a drop cap at all. The Dropped style is second, and the In Margin style is third. I prefer the Dropped style myself. Click in the box you prefer to select that style.

Select a font if you wish. Olde English, for example, if you want a really decorative drop cap, or some other fancy font (you may not have the Olde English font).

Oh, and you can mess around with the other options if you like — especially if you're just starting a new novel. Writer's block is a terrible thing. . . .

4. Click OK.

If you're not in Print Layout view, Word switches your document there so that you can see the drop cap in action.

The drop cap is highlighted and shown inside a hatched box with eight black handles — yes, astute reader, just like a pasted-in graphic image. (See Chapter 23.)

You may have to drag the drop cap/picture around, especially if you're using a table for the document title, as shown in Figure 31-1. Just point the mouse at the drop cap and drag when the mouse pointer changes to the four-pointed arrow thing.

5. Click the mouse in your text (not on the drop cap) and continue editing.

You're free to go on with your work. Switch back to Normal view, if you prefer.

TIP

You can undo a drop cap by clicking its box and then choosing Format➪Drop Cap. In the Drop Cap dialog box, double-click the None position, and the drop cap vanishes. (You must be in Print Layout view for this to work.)

Floating a box of text

Another fun element to add to the brochure is the floating text box. Basically, it works like a graphic image, floating in front of your text. The difference is that the "image" is really a chunk of text you can format and write. Here's how to add one to any document:

1. **Position the toothpick cursor to approximately the location where you want the text box.**

   You can move the position later, but you need to start somewhere.

2. **Choose Insert➪Text Box.**

   If you're in Normal view, you're instantly switched to Print Layout view.

   A placeholder for the text box is inserted into your text. You don't need it, so:

3. **Press the Delete key.**

4. **Drag the mouse to create the text box.**

   Drag from the upper-left corner down to the lower-right to create the box. When you release the mouse button, you see the text box floating over your text, as shown in Figure 31-3.

Figure 31-3: Drawing the text box in your document.

5. **Type and format the text inside the box.**

   You can use all your basic text writing and formatting skills inside the box, just as you would type text outside the box. You can choose fonts, styles, bold, center, and indent. You can even turn the text sideways.

   You can resize the box by dragging its edges or corners in or out.

   Move the text box by pointing the mouse at it until the mouse pointer changes to the four-pointed arrow thing. Then drag the box hither, thither, or yon.

   Use the Line Style button on the Drawing toolbar to set the border style for the box. Other buttons on the toolbar affect the box as well; experiment with them in your free time.

6. **Click the mouse back in your document when you're done.**

   This step leaves text box mode and returns you to the document's regular text for editing and whatnot. (You may need to manually close the Drawing toolbar; click its X, or Close, button.)

You can return to the text box for editing by simply clicking the mouse inside.

Note that to work with the text box it's best to be in Print Layout view, but you can still use Normal view if you prefer it for editing.

Printing the brochure

Printing brochures is something best done by Kinko's or Insty-Prints or some other printing professional. But, if you're on a budget, you can do it yourself.

First, print a sample brochure just to get the process down. Then you can print a bunch of brochures in batches.

To print a sample brochure, follow these steps:

1. **Get the printer ready to print.**

2. **Choose File⇨Print from the menu.**

3. **Select the Odd Pages option from the Print drop-down list.**

   The Print drop-down list is located in the lower-left corner of the Print dialog box. What you're doing is printing the front side of the brochure first — the odd pages.

4. **Click OK.**

The odd pages of your brochure print. If you have a one-page brochure, only one page spews forth from the printer. Otherwise, you get only pages 1, 3, 5, and so on.

Now, the tricky part:

Gather those pages and put them back in your printer's feed tray *upside down*. You want to print on their backside. This may take a few steps. You need to ensure that the odd-numbered printed pages are oriented in the paper tray so that the even-numbered pages are printed properly. Don't be discouraged if this takes you a few tries. (And don't feel reluctant to use a permanent marker and write *UP* on one side of the paper tray.)

After you reload the paper, follow these steps to print the even pages:

1. **Choose File⇨Print from the menu.**
2. **Select the Even Pages menu option from the Print drop-down list.**
3. **Click OK.**

Check your results. If you have to try again, do so.

Another conundrum you may notice: The brochure may not fold the way you want it to. Don't worry! Use the Columns dialog box to adjust the width and spacing of the columns. Or, use the Page Setup/Margins dialog box to move the margins in or out.

When you're ready to mass-produce, simply repeat the preceding steps, but in the Print dialog box enter **50** in the Number of Copies box. That way, you're printing 50 copies of the brochure, front and back, each time. (Any more than 50, and you may run out of paper.)

Do-It-Yourself Greeting Cards

Greeting cards are simply a variation of the brochure example shown earlier in this chapter — with one special exception.

To set up Word to create a greeting card from a single sheet of standard letter-size paper, follow these steps:

1. **Choose File⇨Page Setup.**
2. **Click the Margins tab.**
3. **Select the Landscape option in the Orientation area.**
4. **Choose the 2 Pages per Sheet option from the Multiple Pages drop-down list.**

   This option tells Word to vertically split each page down the middle, creating (aha! — you guessed it) a greeting card.

5. **Click OK.**

Now your document is properly formatted. All that remains is for you to fill in the greeting card with text and maybe a few graphics. But there's a special way you need to do it!

The greeting card must be four pages long: two pages on the inside and two pages on the outside. (Only one sheet of paper is used, two "pages" per sheet.) Here's how the various pages shape up:

✔ **Page 1** is the inside left-hand page. Usually, this page is left blank. So, in your document, you can press Ctrl+Enter to create a hard page break and leave that page blank.

✔ **Page 2** is the inside right-hand page. This page is where you put your sappy message — maybe a graphic.

✔ **Page 3** is the outside "back" cover. This page can be blank, or you can put at the bottom some tiny text boasting of your word-processing prowess or that the card would have cost $3.95 ($5.95 Canadian) had you bought it at Hallmark.

✔ **Page 4** ends up being the *cover* for the greeting card. Put a graphic or flowery text here.

Got it? If not, trust me — it all works out.

Fill in your greeting card accordingly.

To print the greeting card, you need to be tricky. Follow these steps:

1. **Choose File➪Print.**

2. **Type** 1-2 **in the Pages box.**

   You want to print only pages 1 and 2 the first time.

3. **Click OK.**

   Take the page out of the printer and put it back into the printer tray. Ensure that the page is in the printer tray *upside down* so that the next page prints on the backside. (This may take a few tries, so be patient.)

Now, print the backside:

1. **Choose File➪Print.**

2. **Type** 3-4 **in the Pages box.**

   You want to print only pages 3 and 4 this time.

3. **Click OK.**

   If everything goes well, you should be able to fold the paper down the middle and — voilà! — you have a greeting card.

✓ If you're into elaborate greeting-card formatting, consider using section breaks to divide the greeting card and not just the hard page breaks you get by pressing Ctrl+Enter.

✓ Watch out for fancy, thick paper. It tends to jam most laser printers. (If your laser printer has a single-sheet feed and a pass-through slot out the back, printing on thick paper may work.) Greeting-card stock is difficult as all heck to get through an inkjet printer, too!

Chapter 32

Making Some Labels

*O*ne of Word's most esoteric duties is printing labels. Now, this task isn't too far out of the realm of word processing. The first time I printed up my own return labels was with WordPerfect 4.0, back in the dark ages of DOS. Unlike WordPerfect 4.0, however, Word has its own Label command and many exciting label options. This chapter discusses how to put them to use.

All about Labels

Because my handwriting is so darn lousy, I print labels with my return address on them and stick those on my bills and whatnot. I do it as a favor to the overworked men and women of the U.S. Postal Service. Of course, labels can be used for more than addressing envelopes.

If you're curious about what types of labels are available, visit your local office-supply store (or megawarehouse). You can find all sorts of ingenious labels there, from the mundane "Hello, my name is" to labels you can use in creating your own CDs.

Ensure that you buy labels compatible with your printer. Laser printers need special laser printer labels. Some inkjet printers require special, high-quality paper to soak up the ink.

Of all the label brands available, I recommend Avery. Its stock numbers are standard for almost all computer programs. So, if you buy Avery stock number 5160 or something similar, your software and printer know which type of label you have and in which format it is.

Printing a Sheet of Identical Labels

Here are the instructions for printing an entire sheet of labels in Word, such as your name and address for return mailing labels:

1. **Choose Tools⇨Letters and Mailings⇨Envelopes and Labels.**

2. **Click the Labels tab.**

   What you see on your screen should look like Figure 32-1.

Figure 32-1:
The Labels
side of the
Envelopes
and Labels
dialog box.

3. **Choose the type of label you're printing on.**

   Confirm that the stock number in the lower-right corner of the dialog box matches the labels on which you're printing.

   If the numbers don't match up, click the Options button to display the Label Options dialog box. Locate the correct Avery stock number in the Label Options dialog box's scrolling list. Select it; then click OK.

4. **Type in the Address box what you want printed on the label.**

   Keep in mind that you have only so many lines for each label and that each label is only so wide.

   Press the Enter key at the end of each line.

   You can apply some simple formatting at this stage: Bold, Italics, Underline. If you right-click in the address box you can choose Font or Paragraph from the pop-up menu to further format the label.

5. **Click the New Document button.**

   Ha! I bet that you thought you'd click the Print button. No way! The labels are typically more ugly than you'd think, and you may want the chance to spiff them up a bit before you print.

The labels appear as a table in your Word document. From this point on, you can work with the labels in your document just as you work with a table. (Refer to Chapter 20 for more information on working with tables.)

Be careful not to adjust the table's columns and rows! Everything is formatted just so. If you change something, the labels may not print properly.

6. Format the labels (if you like).

Press Ctrl+A to select the entire document (it's only a page long), and then change the font to something more pleasing. Refer to Chapter 11 for more information.

Don't mess with the margins or paragraph formatting. This is all carefully tuned to print on the labels you specified.

You can edit the labels. Sure, they all look the same, but if you like, you can type a few new names or other information in several of the little boxes.

7. Print the document.

Make sure that your printer is on and ready to print and that you have the proper type of label-printing material in the printer, right side up and all that. Then print your document as you normally would. Click the li'1 Print button, and the labels soon unfurl from your printer, ready for lickin' and stickin.'

✔ You don't have to save this document to disk, unless you just like the labels and want to keep them around. Press Ctrl+W to close the document and press N for _no_ save.

✔ Avery, the Label People, make a software program called Label Pro, which I use instead of Word to manage and print labels. Recommended.

✔ It's also possible to print labels from a database of labels using Word's Mail Merge feature. Alas, this complex and detailed process lies in the realm of Advanced Word Tricks. It works best if you use Microsoft Outlook to maintain a contacts list. Even with all that work done, there is still a massive amount of formatting and other hoops to jump through, making the operation more toil than trick.

Printing a Sheet of Identical Labels with Graphics

It's possible to add a graphic image to the mailing label, but to do so, you must twist Word's arm and fool it into thinking you're doing a mail merge. Follow these naughty steps:

1. **Start a new, blank document in Word.**

2. **Choose View➪Toolbars➪Mail Merge.**

   The Mail Merge toolbar appears, though most of it isn't used for this operation.

3. **Click the Main Document Setup button.**

4. **Choose Labels from the Main Document Type dialog box.**

5. **Click OK.**

   The Label Options dialog box appears.

6. **Select the type of label you'll be printing on from the Product Number scrolling list.**

   For example, select the standard 5160 Avery Address label. Though it can be any label, from a CD-ROM label to a HELLO label — whatever you're printing on.

7. **Click OK.**

   The document is now divided into cells — essentially a great big table. This is what you'd also get with the Label command as described in the previous section. But by abusing the Mail Merge function, it's easier to replicate non-text stuff in the labels.

8. **Choose Insert➪Picture➪From File.**

9. **Use the Insert Picture dialog box to search out the picture you want on the label.**

10. **Click the Insert button after you've found and selected the picture file.**

    Fortunately Word is smart here and will resize your picture to fit into the label box. Even so, you may want to shrink it down even more:

11. **Click the picture once to select it.**

    The picture grows eight *handles* that you can grab with the mouse for resizing.

12. **Grab the picture's lower-right-corner handle and drag up and left to reduce the image's size a tad.**

    Now you need to do some additional image formatting:

13. **Double-click the image.**

    The Format Picture dialog box appears.

14. **Click the Layout tab.**

15. **Choose the Square option.**

16. **Click OK.**

17. **Use your mouse to position the picture inside the label.**

    Again, you can use one of the eight handles to resize the image, or use the green handle to rotate the image.

    Time to create the text:

18. **Click the mouse outside of the image, elsewhere in the same cell.**

19. **Type the text you want to appear in every label.**

    That purple dotted underline you see is Word's Smart Tags feature in action. I don't cover smart tags in this book because they don't work.

 20. **Click the Propagate button on the Mail Merge toolbar.**

    And your single label is replicated throughout the entire sheet, graphics and all, as shown in Figure 32-2. The only problem remaining is to get rid of the "Next Record" text that the Mail Merge procedure added (but which you don't need).

21. **Carefully select the text <<Next Record>>, including the angle brackets on either side.**

22. **Press Ctrl+C to copy that text.**

23. **Press Ctrl+H to conjure up the Find Replace dialog box.**

24. **Click the mouse into the Find What box and then press Ctrl+V to paste.**

    This pastes the text <<Next Record>> into the box.

    Leave the Replace With box blank.

25. **Click the Replace All button.**

    And all of those annoying <<Next Record>> things are gone from the labels.

Now your labels are ready to save and print.

✔ If you only mean to print a sheet of identical labels, follow the steps from the previous section, "Printing a Sheet of Identical Labels," instead of this. This section's rather long list of steps is only necessary should you want a graphic image on each label.

✔ Don't forget to save! It's easier to redo the sheet if it's saved to disk.

✔ This book does not cover Mail Merge. For more information, refer to my Web page where I have specific support for this book:

    www.wambooli.com/help/word/

✔ For more information on inserting pictures into Word, see Chapter 23.

Figure 32-2:
Creating
duplicate
labels with
a graphic
image.

Part VI
The Part of Tens

The 5th Wave   By Rich Tennant

In this part . . .

1 love lists. I was a big fan of *The Book of Lists,* first published some 25 years ago. Based on that, I thought I'd come up with my own lists. Not necessary top ten lists, but lists of ten items relating to various and interesting topics, such as: "Ten cruel things to say to the grocery store clerk who asks, 'Paper or plastic?'" or "Ten things I've found in my 6-year-old's ear" or even "Ten things not to throw on a burning lemur."

In keeping with my love of lists, especially lists of 10 things, the remaining chapters in this book contain tips, warnings, treasures, and secrets all about Word. Sometimes it's stuff that just couldn't fit in any other chapter, such as the 10 items you'll find in the chapter, "Ten Truly Bizarre Things," but mostly it's just good advice.

Be advised that not every chapter has exactly ten items. Some have more, some less. After all, if an eleventh thing comes out of the kid's ear, why leave it off the list?

Chapter 33

The Ten Commandments of Word

Moses was probably the first guy to come up with a well-known list of ten. In fact, it's odd that there weren't 12 commandments. At the time, there were 12 Egyptian deities, 12 months in the year, 12 crocodile eggs in a dozen. 12 this, 12 that, 12 everything! Why not 12 commandments? Or perhaps Moses did a little editing. . . . ?

This chapter contains the ten commandments of word processing, specific to Word, but you can apply these tips to other word processors as well (just don't tell). These are the rules and suggestions I make throughout this book, condensed into one handy little chapter — much lighter than two of those tablet things Charlton Heston had to lug down that papier-mâché mountain.

Thou Shalt Not Use Spaces Unnecessarily

Generally speaking, you should never find more than one space anywhere in a Word document. Whenever you have more than one space in a row in your document, you should probably be using the Tab key instead. Use the

Spacebar to separate words and to end a sentence. If you align lists of information, use the Tab key. If you want to organize information into rows and columns, use the Table command (see Chapter 20).

A special note to all high school typing teachers: Please do not insist that your students continue the arcane habit of typing two spaces at the end of a sentence. With a word processor, that's unnecessary. And I doubt that any of your students will be employed using a typewriter in the near future, so continuing this practice is a waste of time.

Thou Shalt Not Press Enter at the End of Each Line

Word automatically wraps your text down to the next line as you approach the right margin. You have no need to press Enter, except when you want to start a new paragraph. (Of course, if your paragraph is only a line long, that's okay.)

If you don't want to start a new paragraph but need to start a new line, use Shift+Enter, the *soft* return command.

Thou Shalt Not Neglect Thy Keyboard

Word is Windows, and Windows is mousy. You can get lots done with the mouse, but some things are faster with the keyboard. For example, when I'm working on several documents at once, I switch between them with Alt+Tab. And stabbing the Ctrl+S key combo to quickly save a document or Ctrl+P to print works better than fumbling for the mouse. You don't have to learn all the keyboard commands, but knowing those few outlined in this book helps.

Thou Shalt Not Reset or Turn Off Thy PC until Thou Quittest Word and Windows

Always exit properly from Word and especially from Windows. Shut off or reset your computer only when you see the "It's now okey-dokey to turn off this PC" type of onscreen prompt — never when you're running Word or have Windows active. Believeth me, if ye do, ye are asking for mucho trouble, yea, verily, woe.

Thou Shalt Not Manually Number Thy Pages

Word has an automatic page-numbering command. Refer to the section in Chapter 14 that talks about where to stick the page number.

Thou Shalt Not Use the Enter Key to Start a New Page

Sure, it works: Brazenly press the Enter key a couple of dozen times, and you're on a new page. But that's not the proper way, and you mess up your new page if you go back and re-edit text. Besides, pressing Ctrl+Enter is quicker. Doing so inserts a *hard page break* into your document.

For the details, refer to the section in Chapter 14 about starting a new page.

Thou Shalt Not Quit without Saving First

Save your document to disk before you quit. Shift+F12 is the key combo to remember. Or, Ctrl+S is the one you don't even have to remember because it's so sensible. If only all of life — no, forget life — if only all of Word were so sensible.

Thou Shalt Not Click OK Too Quickly

Word has many Yes/No/OK-type questions. If you click OK without thinking about it (or press Enter accidentally), you can delete text, delete files, or perform a bad replace operation without meaning to. Always read your screen before you click OK.

Some dialog boxes have a Close button rather than an OK button. These buttons are typically used when you make some choice or reset some option and you don't want to continue with the command. For example, you can change printers in the Print dialog box and then click the Close button to continue without printing.

And don't forget your handy undo key, Ctrl+Z!

Thou Shalt Not Forget to Turn On Thy Printer

The biggest printing problem anyone has is telling Word to print something when the printer isn't on. Verify that your printer is on, healthy, and ready to print before you tell Word to print something.

Never (or at least try not to) keep using the Print command over and over when a document doesn't print. Word tries to print once every time you use the Print command. Somewhere and sometime, those documents will print, unless you do something about it.

Thou Shalt Remember to Save Thy Work

Save! Save! Save! Always save your stuff. Whenever your mind wanders, have your fingers wander to the Ctrl+S keyboard shortcut. Honor thy documents. Savest thy work.

Chapter 34

Ten Truly Bizarre Things

Everything in Word is bizarre, but some things are more bizarre than others. In this chapter, I've listed what I feel are the ten *most* bizarre things, in no particular order. Read on. If you dare.

The Unbreakables

The two weird keys on your keyboard are the spacebar and the hyphen (-). They're weird because Word uses both to split a line of text: The space splits a line between two words, and the hyphen splits a line between two word chunks.

There are times, however, when you don't want a line to be split by a space or a hyphen. For example, splitting a phone number is bad — you want the phone number to stay together. And spaces can be annoying as well. Suppose that you work for the firm of Bandini, Lambert, and Locke, and by golly, Mr. Locke doesn't like to be left on a line by himself. If so, insert a nonbreaking (hard) space between each name to make sure that they're always together.

To prevent the space character from breaking a line, press Ctrl+Shift+spacebar rather than the spacebar by itself. That inserts a nonbreaking space between two words.

To prevent the hyphen character from breaking a line, press Ctrl+Shift+- (hyphen) rather than the hyphen by itself. If you type the first three digits of the number and then press Ctrl+Shift+-, the phone number doesn't split between two lines. (Use the hyphen key, not the minus key on the numeric keypad.)

The Document Map

I suppose that the Document Map feature is there to help you see the big picture, especially if you use Word's Heading styles. Choose View⇨Document Map, and a pane opens to one side of your document, listing a quick summary.

This feature can be useful. In fact, because I use the Heading styles, the document map gives me a quick overview of how my document is laid out — like a mini-outline view. It's just a *bizarre* feature, which is why it's in this chapter.

Choose View⇨Document Map a second time to close it.

Hyphenation

Hyphenation is an automatic feature that splits long words at the end of a line to make the text fit better on the page. Most people leave it turned off because hyphenated words tend to slow down the pace at which people read. However, if you want to hyphenate a document, choose Tools⇨Language⇨Hyphenation. Continuously jab the F1 key when you need Help.

Math

Did it ever dawn upon the Word people that math and English are two separate subjects for a reason? The math and English parts of the SAT scores are separate. Math and English are always taught as separate courses. And math comes from Greece and Arabia, whereas English comes from England (or so I've heard). So who needs a math function in a word processor? I don't know. Even if you do, it's still easier to calculate the numbers by using your desk calculator and typing them manually.

A scary, weird thing you should avoid at all costs

Over many years of using Word, I've discovered one of the most annoying commands in the history of word processing. It's the terrifying menu item remover, something you may stumble over accidentally someday. (I hope you don't.)

If you press Ctrl+Alt+- (hyphen) in Word, the mouse pointer changes to a thick, horizontal line. That line is the *menu item removal cursor*. Just choose any menu item and — thwoop! — it's gone, deleted, zapped, dead. And there's no

way to get that menu item back, either. Deadly! Scary! Not even Rod Serling could dream up something that bizarre.

If you do accidentally press Ctrl+Alt+-, quickly press the Esc key to cancel that mode. Yikes! What kind of sick mind thought up that trick, huh? Also visit the following Web page for more information: www.wambooli.com/help/Word/menu_deletor/

To use the Math command, you must first place your data in a table. Then highlight the row or column you want computed. Choose Table⇨Formula. Word suggests a formula type, or you can tell Word what you want done with the numbers. On second thought, I guess that this woulda been kinda handy during algebra class. Anyway, Word puts the answer wherever you left the blinking toothpick cursor.

Macros

Macros are beyond the scope of this book.

Making a Cross-Reference

The Insert⇨Reference⇨Cross-Reference command allows you to insert a "Refer to Chapter 99, Section Z" type of thing into your document. This feature works because you've taken the Krell brain-booster and now have an IQ that can be expressed only in scientific notation. Fortunately, you may have also used the Heading style to mark in your document some text you want to cross-reference. Using the Heading style means that the Insert⇨Reference⇨ Cross-Reference command works and sticks a "Refer to Chapter 99, Section Z" type of thing in your document — complete with an updated reference to that page in case you overhaul your document.

The Joys of Research

Beyond spell checking, beyond the Thesaurus, and even beyond Word's ability to translate text into a foreign tongue (see Chapter 7) is the Research task pane. What it does is to instantly (or longer with a dial-up connection) connect you to the Internet to peruse several online references regarding whatever it was you recently Alt+clicked with the mouse.

For example, say you write the word Mesopotamia in your document. With the finger of your left hand, press and hold the Alt key. With the finger of your right hand, point the mouse and click the word "Mesopotamia." Instantly (or longer if you have a dial-up connection), you're connected to the Internet and see a whole slew of interesting references about Mesopotamia, or whatever word you Alt+clicked. That's Research.

Teaching Word to Read Your Lips

All Microsoft Office applications have the ability to take dictation, that is to hear you speak and actually type the words you speak. Word is the home base for this speech recognition ability, but sadly, it's not all it's cracked up to be.

To get speech recognition to work in Word, your PC needs a microphone, preferably a microphone-headset (because you still need to type despite all the blah-blah). Then you need several *hours* to train Word how to understand you. For several hours, longer in some parts of the country, you must read text into Word so that it gets a feel for how you talk. The more you practice, the better Word can take dictation. From what I hear, those who are really into this feature practice with Word for at least 15 hours, sometimes longer.

The results of Word's speech recognition are less-than-stellar, which is why the feature was touted as a major improvement to Word for the previous version but yet is hardly mentioned now.

For more information on speech recognition, please refer to my Web site:

    www.wambooli.com/help/word/

Understanding Smart Tags

Word guesses at who's who in your document. When Word believes that it has found someone, it wiggles a dotted purple underline beneath that person's name. To Word, that person is a contact. And the purple underline is a sign that Word has attached a *smart tag* to the name.

If you point the mouse at the smart tag, the Smart Tag icon appears, as shown in the margin. Click that icon to display the Smart Tag menu, which works only if you have Microsoft Outlook (not Outlook Express) on your computer and it's all set up and ready to use as your contacts database.

To disable smart tags, choose Tools➪AutoCorrect Options and click the Smart Tag tab. Remove the check mark by the Label Text with Smart Tags option. Click OK.

What the Heck Is a "Digital Signature"?

A *digital signature* is a widely accepted method of guaranteeing that something has not been modified since the original creator "signed" that something. It's used mostly for creating Word macros (which this book does not cover); by digitally signing the macro, you can guarantee to others that it is your original work and has not been modified or hacked without your permission. Weird stuff.

Chapter 35

Ten Cool Tricks

• •

In This Chapter

▶ Inserting weird characters

▶ Making fractions

▶ Inserting super- and subscript text

▶ Making those weird, foreign language characters

▶ Playing leapfrog with paragraphs

▶ AutoSummarizing

▶ Blocking it all

▶ Timing and dating

▶ Sorting stuff

▶ Saving automatically

• •

Determining what's a cool trick (and what's not) is purely subjective. I'm sure that people who formerly numbered their pages manually think that Word's Page Numbers command is a cool trick. I think AutoCorrect is a great trick. Then again, it's simply amazing that I can save something on the computer, turn it off, and be able to find that same thing again the next day — now, *that's* a cool trick.

This chapter explains some of the neater Word tricks — mostly obscure stuff I may not have mentioned elsewhere in this book. Some are simple and straightforward; some take a little longer for the human mind to grasp.

Typing Strange Characters

You can use the Insert⇨Symbol command to stick odd and wonderful characters into your document. Quite a few Windows fonts have a few weird and wonderful characters in them. The Symbol font is full of neat stuff; the Wingdings font has all sorts of fun doodads; even the normal font, Times New Roman, has several cool characters in it.

To insert any of a number of weird and wonderful characters, follow these steps:

1. **Choose Insert⇨Symbol.**

   The exciting Symbol dialog box appears, as shown in Figure 35-1.

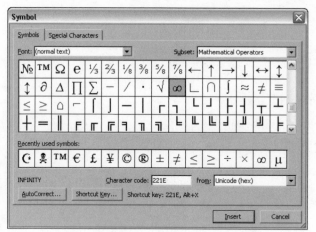

Figure 35-1:
The Symbol
dialog box.

2. **Choose a font.**

   Some fonts are designed for fun, such as the Symbol, Webdings, and Wingdings fonts. Choose them from the Font drop-down list, and you'll see their various characters displayed.

   To see a smattering of all sorts of cool characters, choose (normal text) from the top of the Font drop-down list. Unlike in some fonts, those characters are available to anyone who uses Windows. (They're not specific fonts tied to specific computers.) Furthermore, you can choose which type of "normal" symbol you want by using the Subset drop-down list. In Figure 35-1, the Mathematical Operators subset is chosen. That merely scrolls the list of cool characters down to the math-like ones, such as the fractions you see in the figure.

3. **Choose the character you want to insert.**

   The character is highlighted.

4. **Click the Insert button.**

   This step inserts the character in your document.

5. **Click the Cancel button when you're done.**

Some interesting symbols to consider inserting: the multiplication symbol ×
rather than X, and the division symbol ÷ rather than /. I typically use this
command to insert the left, right, up, and down arrows for use when I write
about, oh, word processing!

✔ You have to click the Insert button once for each symbol you want
  inserted. If you're putting three Σ (sigma) symbols into your document,
  you must locate that symbol in the grid and then click the Insert button
  three times.

✔ Note that some symbols have shortcut keys. These appear at the bottom
  of the Symbol dialog box. For example, the shortcut for the degree symbol
  (°) is Ctrl+@, Space, which means to type Ctrl+@ (actually, Ctrl+Shift+2)
  and then type a space. Doing so gives you the degree symbol.

✔ In addition to choosing them from the Symbol dialog box, many foreign
  language characters can be produced by using special key combinations. See the section "Typing Characters Such as Ü, Ç, and Ñ," later in
  this chapter.

✔ Some characters, such as ☺ or © or ™, can be inserted by using
  AutoText. See Chapter 7.

✔ It's possible to insert symbols by typing the symbol's code and then
  pressing the Alt+X key combination. For example, the code for Σ (sigma)
  is 2211: Type **2211** in your document and then press Alt+X. The 2211 is
  magically transformed into the Σ character.

✔ Also note the Recently Used Symbols list near the bottom of the dialog
  box. Very handy.

Creating Fractions

The Symbol dialog box contains many handy fractions you can insert into
your document (see the preceding section). And, if you have Format on,
Word automatically converts the fractions 1/2 and 1/4 for you. Otherwise,
you need to build your own fractions by using the superscript command.
Here's how:

1. **Press Ctrl+Shift+= (the equal sign).**

   This is the keyboard shortcut for the superscript command.

2. **Type the numerator — the top part of the fraction.**

   For example, 4 for ⅘.

3. **Press Ctrl+Shift+= again to turn off superscript.**

4. **Type the slash.**

5. **Press Ctrl+= to turn on subscript.**

6. **Type the denominator — the bottom part of the fraction.**

7. **Press Ctrl+= to turn off subscript.**

There's your fraction.

Super- and Subscript Buttons on the Toolbar

If you plan on typing lots of fractions or the idea of super- and subscript text appeals to you, why not add those buttons to the Formatting toolbar?

Click the downward-pointing triangle at the toolbar's far-right end. Choose Add or Remove Buttons➪Formatting, and a huge menu appears. Near the bottom are commands for Superscript and Subscript. Choose each one and then press the Esc key.

The superscript (x^2) and subscript (x_2) buttons are added to the toolbar for you.

Typing Characters Such as Ü, ç, and Ñ

Word has all sorts of nifty tricks for typing foreign language characters with *diacriticals.* Those are the tiny commas, apostrophes, and various accent marks that appear over vowels and other characters in various and sundry tongues. For example, you could be dull and type *resume* or be spiffy and type *résumé.* It's cinchy, after you figure out how Word thinks.

Most diacriticals are created by using special prefix keys. You type the prefix key and then the corresponding letter to create a diacritical. And, lucky for you, the prefix keys sort of make sense. They're shown in Table 35-1.

Table 35-1	Typing Those Pesky Foreign Language Characters
Column 1	*Column 2*
Ctrl+'	á é í ó ú
Ctrl+´	à è ì ò ù
Ctrl+,	ç

Column 1	Column 2
Ctrl+@	å
Ctrl+:	ä ë ï ö ü
Ctrl+^	â ê î ô û
Ctrl+~	ã õ ñ
Ctrl+/	ø

Just follow the prefix key with the vowel (or *N* or *C*) to get the accent mark. For example, to get an é into your document, type Ctrl+' and then the letter *E*. Uppercase *E* gives you É, and lowercase *e* gives you é. And that makes sense because the ' (apostrophe) is essentially the character you're adding to the vowel.

Ctrl+' followed by a D equals þ (or Þ).

Be sure to note the difference between the apostrophe (or *tick*) and back tick, or *accent grave*. The apostrophe (') is by your keyboard's Enter key. The back tick (`) is below the Esc key.

For the Ctrl+@, Ctrl+:, Ctrl+^, and Ctrl+~ key combinations, you also need to press the Shift key, which is required anyway to get the @, :, ^, or ~ symbols on your keyboard. Therefore, Ctrl+~ is really Ctrl+Shift+`. Keep that in mind.

If this trick doesn't work, then it doesn't work. For example, if you type Ctrl+' and then a D to put a back tick over a D and nothing happens, well, then, it doesn't work! You have to use the Symbol dialog box (discussed earlier in this chapter) to see whether you can find that particular symbol.

Lugging Blocks Around

Here's a weird trick: Select a paragraph of text, or any old chunk of text. To move that text up one paragraph at a time, use Alt+Shift+↑. Every time you press Alt+Shift+↑, the block moves up one paragraph.

The Alt+Shift+↓ shortcut moves the selected block down one paragraph. Interesting, no?

I believe that you may find these keyboard shortcuts handy for moving chunks of text that would take the mouse a while to master.

AutoSummarize

In the category of "How the heck did they do that?" comes the Auto-Summarize tool. Just like those prehighlighted, used college textbooks, this tool takes any document and immediately fishes out all the relevant points, highlighting them on the screen. I have no idea how this tool works, but it's pretty keen — for Word, that is.

To AutoSummarize your document, choose the Tools⇨AutoSummarize command. Heed the steps on the screen. In a few minutes (longer if the computer is unplugged), the AutoSummarize dialog box appears. Click OK. (You can peruse the options in the AutoSummarize dialog box on your own, if you like; clicking the OK button generally does what you want it to do.)

Splat! Your document then appears on the screen with relevant parts highlighted in yellow. Also visible is an AutoSummarize floating palette, which I have yet to figure out.

To return to normal editing mode, click the Close button on the Auto-Summarize palette.

No, it's not the AutoSummerize tool that makes it bright and sunny outside.

Select All

There are times when you want to block the whole shooting match; highlight everything from top to bottom and from beginning to end; select the entire document. When you want to do so, click the mouse three times in your document's left margin. Click, click, zowie! There it is.

Oh, and you can hold down the Ctrl key and press the 5 key on the number keypad. Zap, zowie! There you go.

Oh, and you also can press F8 (the Extended Text key) five times. Zap, zap, zap, zap, zowie! There you go again.

Oh, and the Edit⇨Select All command does the same thing. Press Ctrl+A. Zowie!

Inserting the Date

Word's date command is named Date and Time and hangs under the Insert menu. Selecting this option displays a dialog box full of date and time formats, one of which you're bound to favor. Click OK to insert the current date or time or both.

You can quickly insert the date field by pressing Alt+Shift+D. Remember to right-click the field and choose Toggle Field Codes to switch between the ugly field and the actual date.

Sorting

Sorting is one of Word's better tricks. After you understand it, you go looking for places to use it. You can use the Sort command to arrange text alphabetically or numerically. You can sort paragraphs, table rows, and columns in cell tables and tables created by using tabs.

Always save your document before sorting.

Sorting is not that difficult. First arrange what needs to be sorted into several rows of text, such as

```
Dopey
Sneezy
Sleepy
Doc
Happy
Grumpy
Bashful
```

Word sorts by the first item in each line, so just select all the lines as a block and then choose Table➪Sort. The Sort Text dialog box appears. (Yes, the Sort command is on the Table menu, though your text need not be in a table.)

Mess around in the dialog box if you need to, but as Word tosses it up on the screen, the dialog box is set to sort your text alphabetically. Just click OK to do so.

Automatic Save

When the AutoSave feature is active, your document is periodically saved to disk. This isn't the same as pressing Ctrl+S to save your document. Instead, Word makes a secret backup copy every so often. In the event of a crash, you can recover your work from the backup copy — even if you never saved the document to disk.

To turn on AutoSave, choose Tools⇨Options. Click the Save tab. Put a check mark by the Save AutoRecover Info Every option. Then enter the backup interval in the Minutes text box. For example, I type **10** to have Word back up my documents every ten minutes. If the power is unstable at your home or office, enter **5**, **3**, **2**, or even **1** minute as the backup interval. Press Enter to return to your document.

With Automatic Save, you don't recover your document in case of a mishap, but you get most of it back.

Chapter 36

Ten Things Worth Remembering

*T*here's nothing like finishing a book with a few hearty words of good advice. As a Word user, you need this kind of encouragement and motivation. Word can be an unforgiving, but not necessarily evil, place to work. This book shows you that having lots of fun with Word and still getting your work done is possible. To help send you on your way, here are a few things worth remembering.

Let Word Do the Work

There's so much Word can do. Even so, some stubborn people still insist on doing things their way because, well, that's just the way things get done around here. Wrong! You can use a handy Word command to do just about anything, and you'll never remember the commands if you're afraid to try them.

Keep Printer Paper, Toner, and Supplies Handy

When you buy paper, buy a box. When you buy a toner cartridge or printer ribbon, buy two or three. Also keep a good stock of pens, paper, staples, paper clips, and all the other office supplies handy.

If you want to back up your work, use floppy disks, Zip disks, or a CD-R/RW. These removable disks can be used to hold a copy of your data, which you can store in a safe place. (I put my Zip disk backups into a fire safe.) Use Windows to copy your Word document files to the removable disk; see *PCs For Dummies* (Wiley Publishing, Inc.) for more information on copying files to a removable disk.

Keep References Handy

Word is a writing tool. As such, you need to be familiar with and obey the grammatical rules of your language. If that language just happens to be English, you have a big job ahead of you. Even though a dictionary and a thesaurus are an electronic part of Word, I recommend that you keep these books handy. Strunk and White's *Elements of Style* (Allyn & Bacon) is also a great book for finding out where apostrophes and commas go. If you lack these books, visit the reference section of your local bookstore and plan on paying about $50 to stock up on quality references.

Keep Your Files Organized

Use folders on your hard drive for storing your document files. Keep related documents together in the same subdirectory.

Remember the Ctrl+Z Key!

The Ctrl+Z key is your undo key. If you're typing away in Word, press it to undelete any text you mistakenly deleted. This command works for individual letters, sentences, paragraphs, pages, and large chunks of text.

Save Your Document Often!

Save your document to disk as soon as you get a few meaningful words down on the screen. Then save every so often after that. Even if you're using the AutoSave feature (discussed in Chapter 35), continue to manually save your document to disk: Ctrl+S.

Take Advantage of Multiple Windows

Each document in Word appears as its own window on the screen. It's possible to have dozens of them open at once. Typically, when I write a book, I have an outline open in one window, the current chapter in another, and maybe some other chapters, references, or appendixes open in other windows. I use the buttons on the taskbar, or the Alt+Tab key combination, to switch between these windows.

Use AutoText for Often-Typed Stuff

To quickly insert things you type over and over, like your name and address, use an AutoText entry. Type your entry once, and then define it as a glossary entry under the Edit menu. Then use the shortcut key to zap it in whenever you need it. See Chapter 7 for more about AutoText.

Use Clever, Memorable Filenames

A file named LETTER is certainly descriptive, but what does it tell you? A file named LETTER TO MOM is even more descriptive but still lacking some information. A file LETTER TO MOM, APRIL 23 is even better. If you want to be brief, try 4-23 MOM LETTER. (Or just throw them all into a MOM folder.) You get the idea here: Use creative and informative filenames.

Don't Take It All Too Seriously

Computers are really about having fun. Too many people panic too quickly when they use a computer. Don't let it get to you! And please, please, don't reinstall Word to fix a minor problem. Anything that goes wrong has a solution. If the solution is not in this book, consult with your guru. Someone is bound to be able to help you out.

Index

• C •

• N •

"naked" mode, starting Word in, 332–333
naming
  documents, 37, 108–110
  folders, 308
  renaming files, 311
  templates, 217
navigating in documents
  arrow keys, 42–43
  Bookmark command, 47–49
  collaborative revised, 305
  End and Home keys, 44–45
  Find command, 50
  Go Back keyboard shortcut (Shift+F5),
    45, 47, 128
  Go To command, 46–47
  going back to previous spot, 47
  mouse, 45–46
  PgUp/Page Up and PgDn/Page Down keys,
    43–44
  in Reading Layout View, 297
  scroll buttons, 49–50
network printers, 118, 125
New button, 27
New Document button, 24
New Document task pane, 235
New Style dialog box, 203–205
newsletters. *See* columns
nonbreaking (hard) spaces
    (Ctrl+Shift+spacebar), 367–368
nonbreaking hyphens (Ctrl+Shift+hyphen),
    367–368
nonprinting characters, 33
Normal (default) style, 198
Normal view, 17, 32
NORMAL.dot document template
  caution on extensive changes, 221
  deleting corrupted, 332
  editing, 221, 327–328
  for global, Normal style (default) storage,
    199, 214, 327
  need to edit, 207
  overriding with different template, 219–220
  use with new documents, 215, 219, 220

Num Lock key, 28, 42
numbered lists with AutoFormat As You
    Type option, 233–234
numbering
  pages, 182–185, 365
  paragraphs, 264–265
Numbering button, 265
numbers/digits, searching for, 65
numeric keypad, 20, 28, 42

• O •

O (Oh) key, caution on use for number
    zero, 28
Odd/Even Page section breaks, 191
Office Assistant ("Clippit" or animated
    paper clip), 18–19, 34, 35–36, 127–128
OK buttons, caution on clicking, 365
Open button, 114
Open dialog box, 114, 115
  Open and Repair, 329
opening documents
  existing documents, 24, 113–114
  from floppy or removable disk, 114
  one inside another, 115–116
  previewing prior to, 129–131
  recently worked on, 115, 325
  of specific kinds, 115
Options dialog box, 322
organization charts, 286
Organizer dialog box, 211
organizing
  AutoText items for reuse in other
    documents, 212
  documents in folders, 110,
    307–309, 382
  styles for reuse in other documents,
    210–212
orientation settings for pages (portrait or
    landscape), 179–181
Outline View, 289
Outline View button, 290
outlines
  adding subtopics, 292–293
  adding text topics, 293

• *T* •

Notes

Notes

FOR DUMMIES®

A world of resources to help you grow

TRAVEL

0-7645-5453-0

0-7645-5438-7

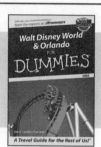

0-7645-5444-1

Also available:

America's National Parks For Dummies
(0-7645-6204-5)

Caribbean For Dummies
(0-7645-5445-X)

Cruise Vacations For
Dummies 2003
(0-7645-5459-X)

Europe For Dummies
(0-7645-5456-5)

Ireland For Dummies
(0-7645-6199-5)

France For Dummies
(0-7645-6292-4)

Las Vegas For Dummies
(0-7645-5448-4)

London For Dummies
(0-7645-5416-6)

Mexico's Beach Resorts
For Dummies
(0-7645-6262-2)

Paris For Dummies
(0-7645-5494-8)

RV Vacations For Dummies
(0-7645-5443-3)

EDUCATION & TEST PREPARATION

0-7645-5194-9

0-7645-5325-9

0-7645-5249-X

Also available:

The ACT For Dummies
(0-7645-5210-4)

Chemistry For Dummies
(0-7645-5430-1)

English Grammar For
Dummies
(0-7645-5322-4)

French For Dummies
(0-7645-5193-0)

GMAT For Dummies
(0-7645-5251-1)

Inglés Para Dummies
(0-7645-5427-1)

Italian For Dummies
(0-7645-5196-5)

Research Papers For Dummies
(0-7645-5426-3)

SAT I For Dummies
(0-7645-5472-7)

U.S. History For Dummies
(0-7645-5249-X)

World History For Dummies
(0-7645-5242-2)

HEALTH, SELF-HELP & SPIRITUALITY

0-7645-5154-X

0-7645-5302-X

0-7645-5418-2

Also available:

The Bible For Dummies
(0-7645-5296-1)

Controlling Cholesterol
For Dummies
(0-7645-5440-9)

Dating For Dummies
(0-7645-5072-1)

Dieting For Dummies
(0-7645-5126-4)

High Blood Pressure For
Dummies
(0-7645-5424-7)

Judaism For Dummies
(0-7645-5299-6)

Menopause For Dummies
(0-7645-5458-1)

Nutrition For Dummies
(0-7645-5180-9)

Potty Training For Dummies
(0-7645-5417-4)

Pregnancy For Dummies
(0-7645-5074-8)

Rekindling Romance For
Dummies
(0-7645-5303-8)

Religion For Dummies
(0-7645-5264-3)

Available wherever books are sold. Go to www.dummies.com or call 1-877-762-2974 to order direct

FOR DUMMIES®

Helping you expand your horizons and realize your potential

GRAPHICS & WEB SITE DEVELOPMENT

0-7645-1651-5

0-7645-1643-4

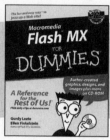

0-7645-0895-4

Also available:

Adobe Acrobat 5 PDF
For Dummies
(0-7645-1652-3)
ASP.NET For Dummies
(0-7645-0866-0)
ColdFusion MX For Dummies
(0-7645-1672-8)
Dreamweaver MX For
Dummies
(0-7645-1630-2)
FrontPage 2002 For Dummies
(0-7645-0821-0)

HTML 4 For Dummies
(0-7645-0723-0)
Illustrator 10 For Dummi
(0-7645-3636-2)
PowerPoint 2002 For
Dummies
(0-7645-0817-2)
Web Design For Dummies
(0-7645-0823-7)

PROGRAMMING & DATABASES

0-7645-0746-X

0-7645-1626-4

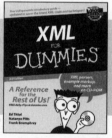

0-7645-1657-4

Also available:

Access 2002 For Dummies
(0-7645-0818-0)
Beginning Programming
For Dummies
(0-7645-0835-0)
Crystal Reports 9 For
Dummies
(0-7645-1641-8)
Java & XML For Dummies
(0-7645-1658-2)
Java 2 For Dummies
(0-7645-0765-6)

JavaScript For Dummies
(0-7645-0633-1
Oracle9*i* For Dummies
(0-7645-0880-6)
Perl For Dummies
(0-7645-0776-1)
PHP and MySQL For
Dummies
(0-7645-1650-7)
SQL For Dummies
(0-7645-0737-0)
Visual Basic .NET For
Dummies
(0-7645-0867-9)

LINUX, NETWORKING & CERTIFICATION

0-7645-1545-4

0-7645-1760-0

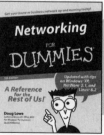

0-7645-0772-9

Also available:

A+ Certification For Dummies
(0-7645-0812-1)
CCNP All-in-One Certification
For Dummies
(0-7645-1648-5)
Cisco Networking For
Dummies
(0-7645-1668-X)
CISSP For Dummies
(0-7645-1670-1)
CIW Foundations For
Dummies
(0-7645-1635-3)

Firewalls For Dummies
(0-7645-0884-9)
Home Networking For
Dummies
(0-7645-0857-1)
Red Hat Linux All-in-One
Desk Reference For Dum
(0-7645-2442-9)
UNIX For Dummies
(0-7645-0419-3)

Available wherever books are sold.
Go to www.dummies.com or call 1-877-762-2974 to order direct

WILE